Company's Coming

E a s y
Entertaining

Front Cover Photo:
1. Devil's Food Cake, page 75, with   3. Italian Vegetable Bowl, page 162
   Seven-Minute Icing, page 82   4. Mixed Green Salad, page 146
2. Crab Extraordinaire, page 107

Easy Entertaining
Copyright © Company's Coming Publishing Limited

All rights reserved worldwide. No part of this book may be
reproduced in any form by any means without written
permission in advance from the publisher. Brief portions of this
book may be reproduced for review purposes, provided credit
is given to the source. Reviewers are invited to contact the
publisher for additional information.

Seventh Printing March 2003

Canadian Cataloguing in Publication Data

Paré, Jean
    Easy entertaining: flair without fuss

    Includes index.
    ISBN 1-896891-48-9

         1. Cookery.   2. Entertaining.   3. Menus.
I. Title
TX731.P7372 1998   642   C98-900390-6

Published also in French under title: Jean Paré reçoit avec simplicité
ISBN I-896891-42-X

Published by
COMPANY'S COMING PUBLISHING LIMITED
2311 - 96 Street
Edmonton, Alberta, Canada T6N 1G3
Tel: (780) 450-6223   Fax: (780) 450-1857
www.companyscoming.com

Company's Coming is a registered trademark owned by
Company's Coming Publishing Limited

Color separations by Friesens, Altona, Manitoba, Canada
Printed in China

This book will help you enjoy time spent with family and friends—and when everyone has left you'll say to yourself, "That was easy!"

Jean Paré

Easy Entertaining was created thanks to the dedicated efforts of the people and organizations listed below.

COMPANY'S COMING PUBLISHING LIMITED

Author	Jean Paré
President	Grant Lovig
Research Assistant	Helen Urwin
Vice President, Product Development	Kathy Knowles
Design Manager	Derrick Sorochan
Designer	Nora Cserny
Illustrator	Jaclyn Draker
Typesetter	Marlene Crosbie
Copywriter	Debbie Dixon

THE RECIPE FACTORY INC.

Research & Development Manager	Nora Prokop
Editor	Stephanie Amodio
Assistant Editor	Michelle White
Proofreader	Mimi Tindall
Test Kitchen Supervisor	Lynda Elsenheimer
Test Kitchen Staff	Ellen Bunjevac
	Allison Dosman
	Jacquie Elton
	Sharon Frietag
	Marg Steeden
	Audrey Thomas
	Pat Yukes
Photographer	Stephe Tate Photo
Food Stylist	Cora Lewyk
Prop Stylist	Gabriele McEleney
Nutrition Analyst	Margaret Ng, B.Sc. (Hon.), M.A., Registered Dietician

Our special thanks to the following businesses for providing extensive props for photography.

Chintz & Company	Mystique Pottery & Gifts
Creations by Design	Scona Clayworks
Dansk Gifts	Stokes
Eaton's	The Basket House
Enchanted Kitchen	The Bay
Exquisite Sewing Centre	The Glasshouse
La Cache	The Royal Doulton Store
Le Gnome	Wicker World
Mugsie's Coffee House	

Table of Contents

Fondue
Left: Cheesy Artichoke Fondue, page 20
Right: Casual Beer Fondue, page 20

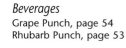

Beverages
Grape Punch, page 54
Rhubarb Punch, page 53

Appetizers
Ripe Olive Snacks, page 43
Forest Mushrooms, page 42

Pies
Left: Banana Cream Pie, page 144
Center: Fresh Strawberry Pie, page 143
Right: Frosty Peanut Butter Pie, page 144

Meat & Poultry
Company Meatloaf, page 120
Beef Burgundy, page 122
Beef With Ginger, page 116
Lasagne, page 124

Foreword

Have you ever wondered how some people seem to entertain with little or no effort?

✿

Without hesitation they open their door to unexpected company, wave neighbors to come over for the evening, and relax among a house full of guests—all seemingly without fuss. These individuals recognize that friendship, not elaborate food or decorations, is the key to what makes these events successful. After all, we are social creatures at heart, always ready to relax and enjoy the company of friends and family.

✿

We best remember the times spent together when there was laughter, good food and a comfortable atmosphere, where the host or hosts were part of the conversation.

✿

This is the role of EASY ENTERTAINING—to give you ideas and guidance on how to entertain at home with little effort and lots of success. Before your next party approaches, take a moment to glance through each section; you will be inspired to start planning your next gathering as soon as you find a pencil and a piece of paper.

✿

There are lots of reasons for hosting a party or event. It could begin with a simple telephone call urging a neighbor who lives alone to come over for dinner. Or it may be a larger family celebration such as a baptism, graduation, or golden wedding anniversary. You may feel a sit-down dinner would work best, or perhaps a buffet arrangement would be more suitable. If you would like to offer something simple yet different, take a look at the section on fondue. This style of meal preparation is perfect for when close friends or family are visiting—it offers an intimate, relaxed atmosphere made casually elegant by the unique menu and table layout.

✿

Included in these pages is a collection of menu suggestions for all sorts of gatherings. With over 250 great recipes to choose from, you may find it helpful to consider some of the combinations suggested for certain occasions. And when you look through the recipes themselves, you will see that each one is accompanied by a tip for preparing all or part of the dish in advance. Also, glance through the section on garnishes and presentation. Simple food can be transformed into a visual delight just by adding a mint leaf, a strawberry fan or a sugared rose petal.

✿

Don't feel obliged to serve a multi-course
gourmet dinner unless you want to. A simple
meatloaf or pasta dish, accompanied by salad, fresh
bread and a nice wine, is just as likely to satisfy your
guests as any elaborate fare you might prepare.

❖

Some occasions may inspire you to add
decoration to your home—or at least to your table.
Again in the theme of simplicity, the calm beauty of candles
and flowers is all you need to introduce a sense of flair
without fuss. The chapter on "Creating a Mood" includes
a wonderful collection of decorating tips using flowers and
candles. What flowers work best for easy handling and
long-lasting effect? Would votive candles or tapers
look better on your buffet table?

Take a moment to glance through the chapters
on decorating ideas and how to set a visually-pleasing
table. There are inspiring tips on simple centerpieces,
colorful floral eye-catchers and decorative table settings.
And don't forget the aromatic touches of
scented oils and potpourri.

❖

So how do you pull all this off without worry
or fuss? The chapter on stress-free entertaining will give
you a wealth of tips and hints on what to plan ahead and
how to enjoy your own party once it's underway.

❖

Entertaining has always been a large part
of my life, and I have found it to be an inspirational
and rewarding experience to open my home and welcome
guests across my doorstep. Today our lives have become
much busier, and we find ourselves greeting friends
and neighbors with little more than a wave hello and
a promise to get together "soon." EASY ENTERTAINING
is designed to help you entertain without fuss, but it
has also been created with the hope that you will be
inspired to visit with family and friends more often.
Open your home, as you would your heart, and
celebrate the simple joy of easy entertaining.

❖

Jean Paré

Creating a Mood

When interior designers plan office layouts, they include features to inspire an energetic work environment. By the same token, when we entertain at home we want to establish a comfortable, relaxed environment suitable to the occasion. Creating "atmosphere" is like invisible decorating—it appeals to all of the senses.

This chapter is filled with wonderfully inspiring ideas on how to set the mood for your event. It includes helpful information on flower-arranging, tips on how to turn simple kitchen items into unique vases, and suggestions on how to make the most of aromatic and odor-absorbing candles.

Take a moment to consider what kind of get-together you have planned, assess your needs, then glance through this section. These fun and simple suggestions are certain to bring just the right mood to your gathering!

Floral Fun

Fresh flowers, whether placed on the breakfast table, gracing the dinner table or adorning the mantel, add creative color, subtle scents and visual vitality to your entertaining. Many North American climates support flower-gardens year-round. Even in areas with shorter growing seasons, most florists and grocery stores carry a wide range of cut flowers at reasonable prices.

When your living room, family room, rumpus room or even bathroom needs a spot or splash of color, flowers provide an endless choice of shade, texture, height and aroma. In the language of flowers, red shades speak of love, white of truth and yellow of cheerfulness and optimism.

The following flowers are commonly used in floral bouquets:

A. Choose from these flowers for overall color or mixture of color:

Alstroemeria (lasts 7+ days)

Also called a Peruvian Lily, this small, trumpet-shaped flower holds several buds per stem and is available in a variety of colors. Attractive seed pods are an additional bonus in an arrangement.

Carnation (lasts 7+ days)

A symbol of passion, these popular and economical feathered flowers come in a variety of sizes and vibrant colors.

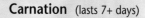

Chrysanthemum (lasts 7+ days)

This noble flower can be found in a wide variety of sizes, but flowers with a smaller, 2 to 3 inch head work best in a formal arrangement. Crush cut end of woody stems and soak for several hours before arranging.

Daffodil (lasts 3 to 5 days)

This popular spring bulb with trumpet-shaped flowers is most often bright yellow but also appears in white, orange and pink.

Daisy (lasts 7+ days)

This morning bloom is symbolic of innocence and fond memories. Daisies are commonly recognized as a white flower, but they can also be found in striking shades of yellow, pink and mauve.

Freesia (lasts 3 to 5 days)

One of the most scented of the cut flowers with 4 or 5 blooms on a gentle arched stem. This symbolic flower of innocence lends a vibrancy to any arrangement and is available in a wide range of colors.

Iris (lasts 3 to 5 days)

This tall, regal flower features darker outer petals with lighter center ones, and can bring vibrant shades of blues, purples and yellows to your arrangement. Remove flower heads as they die so that other buds can blossom.

Lily (lasts 7+ days)

One of the longest lasting cut flowers, lilies adds a dramatic look to any arrangement. There are generally 4 to 6 blooms on a single sturdy stem, and different varieties offer many choices of sizes and colors.

Rose (lasts 3 to 5 days)

Appreciated for their beauty and fragrance, roses bring a classic touch to any decor. Available in many varieties of shapes, sizes and colors. The stark beauty of this flower makes a striking arrangement, whether singly as a lone blossom or as part of a bouquet.

Snapdragon (lasts 3 to 5 days)

This haughty flower features several blooms on a tall, sturdy straight stem, and comes in many colors and heights.

Tulip (lasts 4 to 6 days)

This popular spring flower can be found in both bright and pastel colors, and offers a beautiful fragrance. Tulips are unusual in that they continue to grow after being cut from the bulb. Because they are heavy water drinkers, avoid placing them in a florist's oasis. Instead, place in approximately 2 inches of water and check water level daily.

B. Choose from these flowers if you would like a focal point in your bouquet:

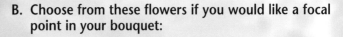

Bird of Paradise
(lasts 4 to 6 days)

Brightly colored on a thick stem, this tall flower resembles the head of one of the most beautiful birds in the world. Its striking features lend an exotic, modern look to any arrangement.

Calla Lily (lasts 4 to 6 days)

This stylish lily features a folded trumpet-shaped outer single petal and an inner central spike on a tall thick stem. Available in pure white with large glossy leaves. A simple, elegant container will bring out the classic beauty of this tranquil flower.

Gerbera Daisy (lasts 7+ days)

Named after German botanist Truagott Gerber, this larger daisy-like flower is available in a variety of bright solid colors, and is perfect as part of a simple, modern arrangement.

Gladiolus (lasts 4 to 6 days)

Gladiolus feature multiple blooms on a tall, slightly arcing stem with large sword-like leaves, and come in a variety of bright and pastel colors. To help flowers last longer, cut stems again after a few days.

Orchid (lasts 7+ days)

The dainty orchid is a wax-like, fairly large flower, available in a variety of sizes and colors, often with a shaded center. This classic flower brings a touch of elegance to any arrangement.

C. These provide the filler for your bouquet:

Baby's Breath (lasts 7+ days) Airy plant with fine wiry branched stems and little puffs of dainty white or pink flowers. Appropriately named for its delicate, softly-scented blooms.

Ferns (lasts 7+ days) Wide range of shapes and textures; fronds are long and branched and can be feathery or quite solid. Available in many shades of green.

Statice (lasts 7+ days) Also called sea lavender. Tiny, brightly colored flowers on branched stems. Greek word meaning "causing to stand." These spikes stay fresh for months.

Stock (lasts 7+ days) Very popular with a small spired, soft-colored scented flower. Available in ranges of pink, purple, white, yellow and cream.

Choosing Containers

The container you choose, whether a crystal vase or a hollowed-out orange bell pepper or cantaloupe, (page 25) needs to be given as much consideration as the flowers you place in it.

The shape of the container should shadow the shape of the arrangement. In a way, this begs the question—do I choose my container first or decide on the shape of the arrangement? It can work either way.

First, decide where the arrangement will be placed. Next, determine the kind of arrangement. Will this location (and the purpose of the event) warrant an informal or more formal look? Now look at the space where the flowers will be placed. Is it a nook or an open area? Will people see the arrangement from all sides or just the front? Will people be reaching or talking over the flowers? The answers to these questions will determine the maximum height of the arrangement. Keep in mind that you don't want your guests knocking the flowers over.

Now it's time to search your cupboards and shelves for unique, eye-catching containers. Our yellow teapot and accompanying "swarm of bees" is ideal for the breakfast table. Tulips and gladiolus have been cut low and placed in a shape (without additional greenery) to enhance the teapot. Because they are contrasting colors (dark and light) but also complementary colors (purple and yellow), both the flowers and the teapot carry the same visual emphasis.

This pedestal mug is perfect for a brunch or lunch buffet. It serves as a striking visual centerpiece without overwhelming the myriad of items that are to accompany it on the table. The sunflower pops out over the pink sunrise of snapdragons, freesia, carnations and gerbera daisies. Even the green color of the mug lends a complementary flair without detracting from the main focal point—the flowers. The shape of the arrangement flows with the handle and continues to "spill" over the other side, as if being poured.

A tin pail makes an ideal receptacle for bright daffodils, giving the appearance that they have just been picked. Diasmo is used as a filler and provides a delicate pink accent. The pail also has an angular shape that matches the sharp angles of the pointed daffodil petals. Great at an afternoon gathering or patio party.

The large colored glass pitcher with its wide mouth is well balanced to handle this large assortment of spring flowers—irises, lilies, freesia and stock. The portly shape of the pitcher has been carried through in the bulbous shape of the arrangement. The greenery offers an important contribution to the overall shape.

There are even containers around your home that can be used for single blooms. Here we have used empty film roll canisters for these tulip heads. Just fill the canisters about ⅔ with water and leave about 1 inch (2.5 cm) of stem on the flowers. Or, find a brandy snifter, fill it about halfway with water, add 1 or 2 drops of desired food coloring and float a carnation on top.

Arranging Bouquets

The colors you choose for your arrangement can be in shades of a single hue, a collection of complementary colors, or an explosion of vibrant contrasts.

Once you have chosen your container, dress it with a bow if desired, then undo your parcel from the florist and begin the wonderful journey of creating a visual masterpiece from an armful of stems, leaves and petals. Follow these basic steps for arranging a bouquet of flowers and you will see how easy it is to make something so pretty.

1. Always re-cut flower stems just before you put them into the container.

Cut at an angle, using a sharp knife rather than scissors, which tend to pinch the ends together. Rose stems should be cut in the sink under water but not under running tap water.

Also, cut off any leaves that will touch the water in the container.

Choose a container that is about ⅓ the height of the tallest flower(s). Fill the container ¾ with warm water. Position the greenery (we are using tree ferns) to form a base for the flowers.

2. Determine the height and shape of the arrangement by inserting the tallest of the flowers. In our arrangement, the lemon yellow chrysanthemums form a nice rounded shape while keeping the height long and lanky, like the vase.

This group may also include a flower that will be the focal point, such as the calla lily shown here.

3. Add the rest of the floral stems, keeping true to the desired shape.

We have added complementary deep purple and white carnations as a foundation for the more vibrant yellow chrysanthemums, while remembering to keep the eye moving upward to the elegant calla lily.

4. For the final touch, add any shorter floral stems or filler flowers such as statice or baby's breath.

We have chosen a very subtle dark purple statice to fill in the lower gaps. The result is a voluminous arrangement that maintains its tall, angular look.

Candle Creativity

Candles give off warm light, illuminating dark corners, and offering a peaceful alternative to the harsh glare of electric lights. The ambiance set by a candle cannot be duplicated in any other manner. You can buy a variety of candles in just about every shade imaginable, which allows you to add color, scent and visual accents on the coffee table, at each place setting, in groupings of three or more, floating in a bowl, or in stately holders.

There are traditional taper candles as well as pillar (or column) candles, tea lights, votives, dipped tapers and rolled beeswax. Candles also come in every shape possible —bees, bears, trees and angels, and many, many more. But most people choose not to burn these candles. Pillars come in various designs—fluted, five-sided or more, and pyramid.

Tapers may be the kind that drip and slowly melt around the holder on to the table or mantel surface, or they may be dripless. Both offer an elegant look, but you may want to be cautious about where you place candles that drip, as they can damage some surfaces.

Many candles are scented but be careful where they will sit. Place them slightly away from conversation areas, or in the guest bathroom. Also be aware of mixing scents from flowers, candles and potpourri. Aromas may clash, creating an unpleasant fragrance you weren't expecting.

Unscented candles also help to clear odors that might be present from smoke, perfumes, cologne or food odors such as fish. Salt in a container also helps to absorb unwanted or overpowering odors. Here is a simple and easy candle/deodorizer all in one:

Select a well-rounded medium to large orange. Cut it in half. Scoop out the orange, pulp and first layer of white pith, leaving a dry white interior.

Fill almost to the top with table salt and level off. Take a tea light (remove it from its metal holder if it is in one) and gently twist it into the center of the salt. Repeat with the second half of the orange. Place strategically around the room.

Candle Types

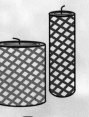

Beeswax
Burn quite quickly because of the large air holes. Pure beeswax burns more evenly than paraffin mixtures.

Dipped Taper
6 to 10 inches (15 to 25 cm) high
$\frac{1}{2}$ to 1 inch (12 mm to 2.5 cm) wide
Burns $1\frac{1}{2}$ to 9 hours

Floater
2 to 3 inches (5 to 7.5 cm) wide
Burns about 4 hours

Pillar
7 to 10 inches (17.5 to 25 cm) high
2 to 3 inches (5 to 7.5 cm) wide
Burns 70 to 100 hours

Taper
6 to 15 inches (15 to 38 cm) high
Burns 5 to 13 hours

Tea Light
Approximately $1\frac{1}{2}$ inches (3.8 cm) wide
Burns 4 to 5 hours

Votive
$1\frac{1}{2}$ to 2 inches (3 to 5 cm)
Burns 8 to 10 hours

Candle Burning & Storage

Here are some facts that will help ensure proper candle burning and storage:

- Never leave a burning candle unattended!

- Any kind of draft or breeze around a candle (or moving the candle) will cause it to drip. If air movement is unavoidable, protect the candle in a glass or hurricane shade.

- Always cut the wick of a new candle to about ¼ inch (6 mm), then light it for a minute or so. Blow it out and then it will be much easier to light just as your first guests arrive. Trim wick each time you relight it to prevent sputtering and smoking.

- Keep pillar candles lit for a minimum of one hour for every 1 inch (2.5 cm) in diameter to prevent a "well" or crater from forming. After extinguishing the candle, gently press the softened edges inward. If a crater is unavoidable, one makeshift remedy is to remove a tea light from its metal container and set it in the crater; it will give the appearance that the larger candle is burning.

- Store votive candles in an airtight container in the fridge to retain their scent.

- Store colored candles wrapped individually in tissue paper to prevent dyes from staining the other candles. White candles should be wrapped and stored in a dark place to prevent yellowing. All candles should be stored in a dry place away from sunlight or other heat sources.

- Extinguish a candle with a candle snuffer or place your open palm behind the flame and gently blow it out. The ensuing curl of smoke that emits a strong sulfurous odor into the air can be quickly extinguished by licking the tips of your thumb and forefinger, pinching the wick and releasing it quickly.

Use a wide open bowl or other dish to float fresh flower heads and floater candles. These gerbera daisies are breathtaking. The floaters seemed very plain beside the colorful flowers so we scattered tiny metallic stars on the top of each candle.

Craft sand is reasonably inexpensive and comes in a variety of colors. Sand provides a sturdy base for taper or pillar candles. You can then be creative in deciding what to put around them.

Wet the sand and add flower heads (we used yellow carnations), or choose items that will enhance a theme you might be using for the event. The variety of seashells we have set around the taper candles would be the crowning glory at a seafood buffet table. Cover the surface of the sand with scented potpourri (but be sure to use unscented tapers), marbles, small paper flags, or the little umbrellas used to garnish drinks. Use your imagination—it's so easy!

Fondue

If you are interested in offering your guests a dining experience a little bit out of the ordinary, consider the spectacular and impressive presentation of a fondue dinner. As you gather around the table, your guests will find themselves in an intimate and casual dining environment, perfect for encouraging conversation and fellowship.

As a centerpiece, fondue makes a wonderful focal point. The ensuing meal and the conversation are certain to stimulate and satisfy! Everything is simple to prepare ahead of time so that you, as host, can take full advantage of a relaxing evening with friends.

Fondue offers you the opportunity to serve appetizers, main courses, and desserts using this unique style of preparation, and the recipes here are certain to inspire. There are sweet and savory sauces to enhance the flavor of cooked meat, smooth and creamy cheese sauces to dress up practically any vegetable or bread, and of course, the irresistible flavors of chocolate or caramel sauces, accompanied by fresh fruit.

Fondue Equipment

Chocolate Fondue Pot

Tea Lights (Cheese or Chocolate)

Dipping Forks (long & short)

Cheese Fondue Pot

Gel Fuel (Oil or Broth)

Dipping Basket

Liquid Fuel & Burner (Oil or Broth)

Oil or Broth Fondue Pot

Pizza In A Pot Fondue

Pizza In A Pot Fondue

Tastes just like pizza—without the crust. ☺ Prepare the fondue dippers and grate the cheese the day before. Scramble-fry the ground beef, onion and garlic the day before as well and refrigerate.

Lean ground beef	¼ lb.	113 g
Finely diced onion	¼ cup	60 mL
Garlic clove, minced (or ¼ tsp., 1 mL, garlic powder)	1	1
All-purpose flour	1 tbsp.	15 mL
Condensed tomato soup	10 oz.	284 mL
White (or alcohol-free) wine	⅔ cup	150 mL
Grated Swiss cheese	1 cup	250 mL
Grated mozzarella cheese	1 cup	250 mL
Dried sweet basil	1 tsp.	5 mL
Ground oregano	1 tsp.	5 mL
Pepper, sprinkle		

Scramble-fry ground beef, onion and garlic in non-stick frying pan until browned. Drain well.

Mix in flour. Stir in tomato soup until boiling.

Add remaining 6 ingredients. Stir until cheese is melted. Pour into fondue pot over low flame. Makes 2½ cups (625 mL) fondue sauce.

2 tbsp. (30 mL) sauce: 62 Calories; 4 g Protein; 3.1 g Total Fat ; 3 g Carbohydrate; 145 mg Sodium

Dippers: Garlic bread cubes, bell pepper pieces, mushrooms, tomato wedges, wiener chunks, summer sausage chunks.

Pictured on this page.

Steak Fondue

Serve with Teriyaki Sesame Sauce, page 18, or Chili Horseradish Dip, page 18. ☺ A great make-ahead marinade. Slice beef while slightly frozen.

Marinade:

Sherry (or alcohol-free sherry)	¹/₂ cup	125 mL
Fancy (or cooking) molasses	¹/₄ cup	60 mL
Lemon juice	1 tbsp.	15 mL
Soy sauce	1 tbsp.	15 mL
Cooking oil	1 tbsp.	15 mL
Ketchup	1 tbsp.	15 mL
Ground ginger	¹/₂ tsp.	2 mL
Hot pepper sauce	¹/₄ tsp.	1 mL
Garlic powder	¹/₄ tsp.	1 mL
Flank steak, cut on diagonal into long, thin, 4 inch (10 cm) strips	1¹/₂ lbs.	680 g

Cooking oil, to fill ²/₃ of fondue pot (or use Oriental Broth Fondue, this page)

Marinade: Combine first 9 ingredients in bowl. Mix well.

Add meat strips. Cover. Marinate in refrigerator overnight. Drain. Thread onto bottom 3 inches (7.5 cm) of 10 inch (25 cm) wooden skewers that have been soaked in water for 10 minutes. Makes 35 to 40 beef skewers.

Heat second amount of cooking oil in saucepan to boiling. Carefully pour into fondue pot. Keep oil hot over medium-high flame or keep broth hot over high flame.

1 cooked skewer: 48 Calories; 4 g Protein; 2.8 g Total Fat; 1 g Carbohydrate; 29 mg Sodium

Pictured above.

Oriental Broth Fondue

Serve with individual bowls of hot cooked rice. ☺ Cut vegetables in the morning. Slice beef while slightly frozen. Refrigerate until serving time.

Oriental Broth:

Condensed beef (or chicken) broth	2 × 10 oz.	2 × 284 mL
Water	2 cups	500 mL
Ground ginger	¹/₂ tsp.	2 mL
Garlic powder, sprinkle		

Oriental Broth: Combine all 4 ingredients in saucepan. Bring to a boil. Pour into fondue pot over high flame. Makes 4¹/₂ cups (1.1 L) broth fondue.

1 tbsp. (15 mL) broth: 3 Calories; trace Protein; 0.1 g Total Fat; trace Carbohydrate; 50 mg Sodium

Dippers: Pork tenderloin, cut into thin strips; beef tenderloin, cut into thin strips; boneless chicken breast, skin removed, cut into thin strips; small cooked shrimp, peeled and deveined; lightly steamed fresh button mushrooms, pea pods, fresh or frozen; broccoli florets, cauliflower florets, green, red or yellow pepper pieces; sliced green onions.

Pictured above.

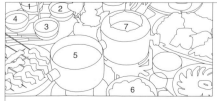

3. Chili Horseradish Dip, page 18
4. Sweet And Sour Sauce, page 18
5. Steak Fondue, page 17
6. Mexi Meatballs, page 18
7. Oriental Broth Fondue, page 17

1. Mango Chutney Sauce, page 18
2. Teriyaki Sesame Sauce, page 18

Mexi Meatballs

A nice spicy meatball. Best to use a dipping basket to cook these as a fork will break them up. ☺ Assemble these the morning of or day before and keep refrigerated.

Large egg, fork-beaten	1	1
Chili sauce	3 tbsp.	50 mL
Onion flakes	½ tsp.	2 mL
Dried crushed chilies	¼ tsp.	1 mL
Garlic powder	⅛ tsp.	0.5 mL
Bread slice, processed into crumbs	1	1
Lean ground beef	¾ lb.	340 g

Place first 6 ingredients in bowl. Stir together well.

Add ground beef. Mix well. Shape into 48 one half inch (12 mm) meatballs. This is easier to do by dividing mixture into 4 equal portions then dividing each portion into 2, making 8 portions in all. Now divide each portion into 6 balls. Chill until needed. Cook in hot oil in fondue pot. Makes 4 dozen meatballs, about ¾ inch (2 cm) size.

1 cooked meatball: 27 Calories; 2 g Protein; 2.1 g Total Fat; 1 g Carbohydrate; 24 mg Sodium

Pictured on page 17.

Chili Horseradish Dip

Orange-red with dark flecks of celery. ☺ Make ahead and refrigerate for up to one week.

Chili sauce	½ cup	125 mL
Prepared horseradish	¼ cup	60 mL
White vinegar	1 tbsp.	15 mL
Granulated sugar	1 tsp.	5 mL
Celery seed	1 tsp.	5 mL
Worcestershire sauce	1 tsp.	5 mL
Garlic salt	¼ tsp.	1 mL

Mix all 7 ingredients in bowl. Chill for several hours so flavors can blend. Makes generous ¾ cup (175 mL) dip.

1 tbsp. (15 mL) dip: 16 Calories; trace Protein; 0.1 g Total Fat; 4 g Carbohydrate; 192 mg Sodium

Pictured on page 17.

Mango Chutney Sauce

Dark-colored with an excellent flavor. Serve warm or cold with pork or beef. ☺ Make ahead and refrigerate for up to one week.

Mango chutney, chopped	1 cup	250 mL
Granulated sugar	½ cup	125 mL
Lemon juice	3 tbsp.	50 mL

Measure all 3 ingredients into saucepan. Bring to a boil, stirring often. Boil slowly until thickened and syrupy. Makes 1⅓ cups (325 mL) dipping sauce.

1 tbsp. (15 mL) sauce: 31 Calories; trace Protein; trace Total Fat; 8 g Carbohydrate; trace Sodium

Pictured on page 17.

Teriyaki Sesame Sauce

Serve warm or cold with any type of meat or vegetable. ☺ Make up to one week in advance.

Low-sodium soy sauce	½ cup	125 mL
Garlic powder	¼ tsp.	1 mL
White wine (or apple juice)	¼ cup	60 mL
Brown sugar, packed	2 tbsp.	30 mL
Cornstarch	1 tbsp.	15 mL
Toasted sesame seeds	2 tbsp.	30 mL

Combine soy sauce, garlic powder and white wine in small saucepan.

Stir sugar and cornstarch together in small bowl. Add to liquid mixture in saucepan and heat on medium, stirring frequently, until mixture is thickened and clear.

Add sesame seeds. Makes ¾ cup (175 mL) dip.

1 tbsp. (15 mL) sauce: 30 Calories; 1 g Protein; 0.7 g Total Fat; 4 g Carbohydrate; 418 mg Sodium

Pictured on page 17.

Sweet And Sour Sauce

Mild flavor. Serve with beef or pork. ☺ Make ahead and refrigerate for up to one week.

White vinegar	½ cup	125 mL
Water	½ cup	125 mL
Granulated sugar	1 cup	250 mL
Salt	¼ tsp.	1 mL
Finely chopped green pepper	1 tbsp.	15 mL
Finely chopped red pepper	2 tbsp.	30 mL
Cornstarch	1½ tbsp.	25 mL
Water	1½ tbsp.	25 mL
Paprika	1 tsp.	5 mL

Combine first 6 ingredients in saucepan. Bring to a boil, stirring occasionally. Simmer, uncovered, for 7 to 10 minutes.

Stir cornstarch into second amount of water in small cup. Add paprika. Mix. Stir into boiling vinegar mixture until boiling and thickened. Makes 1 cup (250 mL) dipping sauce.

1 tbsp. (15 mL) sauce: 53 Calories; trace Protein; trace Total Fat; 14 g Carbohydrate; 41 mg Sodium

Pictured on page 17.

1. Apricot Dessert Dippers, page 21
2. Meringue Fingers, page 21
3. Chocolate Fondue, page 20
4. Caramel Fondue, page 20

Casual Beer Fondue

Mild cheese taste. Beer adds a yeasty flavor.
⏱ *Grate the cheese the day before and keep refrigerated. Prepare the dippers ahead of time.*

Hard margarine (or butter)	3 tbsp.	50 mL
All-purpose flour	3 tbsp.	50 mL
Beer	1½ cups	375 mL
Grated medium Cheddar cheese	2 cups	500 mL
Grated Gouda (or Edam) cheese	2 cups	500 mL
Onion flakes	2 tsp.	10 mL
Dry mustard	1 tsp.	5 mL
Garlic powder, just a pinch		

Melt margarine in saucepan. Mix in flour. Stir in beer until boiling and thickened.

Add next 5 ingredients. Stir until cheese is melted. Pour into fondue pot over low flame. Makes 2⅔ cups (650 mL) fondue sauce.

2 tbsp. (30 mL) sauce: 112 Calories; 6 g Protein; 8.4 g Total Fat; 2 g Carbohydrate; 181 mg Sodium

Dippers: Cubes of rye or sourdough bread, broccoli and cauliflower florets cooked tender-crisp and cherry tomatoes.

Pictured on page 21.

Cheesy Artichoke Fondue

Try this and the variation. ⏱ *Make ahead and reheat on stove top when ready to fondue. Add a bit of milk to thin if needed.*

Hard margarine (or butter)	3 tbsp.	50 mL
All-purpose flour	3 tbsp.	50 mL
Homogenized (whole) milk	1¼ cups	300 mL
Canned artichoke hearts, drained and chopped	14 oz.	398 mL
Sherry (or alcohol-free sherry)	¼ cup	60 mL
Herbed cream cheese	4 oz.	125 g
Bacon slices, cooked crisp and crumbled	2	2
Pepper, sprinkle		

Melt margarine in heavy saucepan. Mix in flour. Stir in milk until boiling and thickened.

Add remaining 5 ingredients. Stir until cheese is melted. Pour into fondue pot over low flame. Makes 2 cups (500 mL) fondue sauce.

2 tbsp. (30 mL) sauce: 76 Calories; 2 g Protein; 5.8 g Total Fat; 4 g Carbohydrate; 111 mg Sodium

Pictured on page 21.

Variation: Omit herbed cream cheese. Add 1 cup (250 mL) grated Swiss cheese or grated sharp Cheddar cheese.

Dippers: Crusty bread chunks, cooked shrimp and scallops, cooked chicken chunks.

Chocolate Fondue

Just a hint of liqueur flavor. If using canned fruit for dippers, drain well, then carefully pat with paper towel. ⏱ *Cut up fresh fruit in advance and place in freezer for about 30 minutes to chill if desired. The chocolate will solidify slightly on the chilled fruit.*

Good quality milk chocolate, cut up	8 oz.	250 g
Bittersweet chocolate baking squares, broken up	4 × 1 oz.	4 × 28 g
Whipping cream	1 cup	250 mL
Tia Maria liqueur (or Cognac)	2 tbsp.	30 mL

Combine all 4 ingredients in heavy saucepan. Heat on low, stirring often, until chocolate melts and is blended. Pour into chocolate fondue pot. Keep warm over low flame. Makes 1⅓ cups (325 mL) fondue sauce.

2 tbsp. (30 mL) sauce: 246 Calories; 3 g Protein; 20.2 g Total Fat; 17 g Carbohydrate; 27 mg Sodium

Dippers: Meringue Fingers, page 21, marshmallows, small crêpes, small pretzels, fresh strawberries, mandarin orange segments, pineapple chunks, peeled cantaloupe chunks, peeled melon chunks, green grapes.

Pictured on page 19.

Caramel Fondue

Perfect consistency for dipping. ⏱ *Unwrap the caramels and prepare the dippers before dinner, or make the sauce and freeze. Reheat just before you are ready to sit down for dessert.*

Light cream (half-and-half)	⅔ cup	150 mL
Chewy caramel candies (about 53)	1 lb.	454 g

Place cream and caramels in heavy saucepan. Heat on low, stirring constantly, until melted and smooth. Pour into fondue pot over low flame. Makes 1¾ cups (425 mL) fondue sauce.

2 tbsp. (30 mL) sauce: 138 Calories; 2 g Protein; 4.4 g Total Fat; 24 g Carbohydrate; 87 mg Sodium

Variation: Use chocolate caramels or a mixture of both.

Dippers: Marshmallows, banana chunks, large pieces of brownies or pound cake.

Pictured on page 19.

Meringue Fingers

Dip one end of these fancy meringues into Chocolate Fondue, page 20, or Caramel Fondue, page 20. ☺ Freeze for up to one month, or keep in a sealed container for up to two weeks.

Egg whites (large), room temperature	3	3
Granulated sugar	¾ cup	175 mL
Food coloring, to tint a pretty pastel shade (optional)		

Beat egg whites together in bowl until soft peaks form. Gradually add sugar while continuing to beat until stiff. Spoon into piping bag or small plastic bag (cut off 1 corner when ready to pipe). Pipe 3 inch (7.5 cm) fingers on foil-lined baking sheet. Bake in 250°F (120°C) oven for about 2 hours until dry and crisp. Leave in oven until cool. Peel foil away. Makes 30 meringues.

1 meringue: 22 Calories; trace Protein; 0 g Total Fat; 5 g Carbohydrate; 5 mg Sodium

Pictured on page 19.

Meringue Finger Treats

Drizzle cooled meringues with melted semisweet chocolate and serve as cookies.

Apricot Dessert Dippers

Pierce with fondue fork and swirl quickly through Chocolate Fondue, page 20, or Caramel Fondue, page 20. ☺ Keep frozen for up to several months until immediately before serving as they become soft and moist when thawed.

Frozen pound cake, cut into ¼ inch (6 mm) slices	10¾ oz.	298 g
Envelope dessert topping, not prepared	1	1
Milk	⅓ cup	75 mL
Almond flavoring	½ tsp.	2 mL
Jars strained apricots (baby food)	2 x 4½ oz.	2 x 128 mL

Line 8 x 8 inch (20 x 20 cm) pan with foil. Cover with ⅓ of cake slices, trimmed to fit, to cover bottom of pan in single layer.

Beat dessert topping, milk and flavoring together. Directions will call for ½ cup (125 mL) milk but use lesser amount. Beat until stiff.

Fold apricots into topping. Spread ½ of topping mixture over cake in pan. Cover with ⅓ of cake slices. Spread with remaining topping mixture. Top with remaining ⅓ of cake slices. Cover. Freeze until ready to use. Remove from pan. Peel off foil. Cut into 1 inch (2.5 cm) squares. Makes 64 dippers.

1 dipper: 27 Calories; trace Protein; 1.2 g Total Fat; 4 g Carbohydrate; 10 mg Sodium

Pictured on page 19.

Cheesy Artichoke Fondue, page 20

Casual Beer Fondue, page 20

Garnishes & Presentation

In addition to adding wonderful visual flair to your dishes, did you know that creating and using garnishes is also fun and simple? Here's your chance to actually "play" with your food.

While garnishes are usually added as decoration, many will argue that a visually pleasing presentation of food can actually change our perception of its flavor. In other words, the better a dish looks, the better it tastes.

A few well-placed garnishes can offer an elegant, gourmet look to even the simplest dishes, like meatloaf. The end result is, of course, that your guests recognize the extra effort you made on their behalf, and that makes them feel special.

As you plan your grocery list, take a look at some of these eye-catching, yet simple ideas for spicing up the presentation of your food. Garnishes aren't the only way to enhance the look of your food. The shape and color of bowls, trays or other serving dishes can add interesting effects. These creative garnishes and presentation ideas are guaranteed to inspire rave reviews from your guests.

Crinkle Tool

Found in kitchen shops and grocery stores, this tool is a must in every kitchen. Use it on cucumbers and carrots when preparing a vegetable tray but also use it when slicing carrots for a stew, casserole, or even just cooked carrots. It can even be used to dress up a block of margarine or butter. Wow!

Roses

The rose garnishes on this page are absolutely exquisite-looking, and guess what—they are really easy to make! The red rose is made from the peel of a tomato. The orange rose is formed using the peel of a thin-skinned orange. The caramel-colored rose is made from just that—caramels! The yellow rose (in fruit bowl on page 24) is made from chewy-type candies. Just warm the candy or caramels in the microwave for a few seconds. Place on the counter and sprinkle with granulated sugar. Press slightly with the palm of your hand and then roll flat. Shape into semicircles using a small paring knife. Roll one up tightly to form the center. Place each remaining "petal" in a staggered fashion around the center. Use the chocolate caramels to form "leaves."

Green Onion Curls

Green onion curls are often the finishing touch on vegetable trays, rice dishes and some casseroles. Cut the white onion off, leaving just a touch of white, and then leave about 2 to 3 inches (5 to 7.5 cm) of the green portion at the other end. Use a paring knife to cut a number of vertical slits into the green stems. Submerge in cold water in the fridge until ready to use. For a tighter, curlier effect, open a pair of scissors and pull the sharp edge along the slits (as you would gift ribbon) to make it curl.

Strawberry Fan

Choose firm, nicely-shaped red strawberries with leaves. Wash and dry. Using a sharp paring knife, slice strawberries vertically from bottom to top, being careful not to cut right through. Make 4 to 7 parallel cuts. Gently spread slices apart to make fan.

Citrus Stripper

This is another tool that is a must in every kitchen. Use the citrus stripper to remove strips of peel, creating "stripes" on radishes, mushrooms, cucumbers, oranges or lemons. Remove strips of lemon or orange peel and use the peel to "tie up" bundles of cooked asparagus spears (below), julienne carrots or cinnamon sticks (below). Strips can also be used to form knots or twists for garnishing vegetable dishes (below), pies, cheesecakes and other fancy desserts.

Cinnamon Stick Stack

Choose 3 to 5 cinnamon sticks similar in length. Wash and dry smooth-skinned orange or lemon. Using citrus stripper, cut a long, continuous coil of peel from about ½ the orange or lemon. Wrap the peel around cinnamon sticks. Tie into knot. Perfect to garnish a punch.

Lemon Peel Spiral

Choose a firm, smooth-skinned lemon. Wash and dry. Use the citrus stripper to remove a long continuous coil of lemon peel from entire length of lemon. Twist into spiral design. Use to garnish cakes, beverages or vegetables.

Garnishing With Chocolate

Chocolate Curls

Melt chocolate baking squares. Spread on cookie sheet to ⅛ inch (3 mm) thickness. If cookie sheet has sides, use it upside down. Chill in refrigerator for 7 to 10 minutes. It should be just firm. Put backside of lifter under edge and push forward. Chocolate will curl. Transfer curls to plate using wooden pick. For smaller curls, place the edge of a chef's knife, or smaller paring knife on the chocolate and pull towards you.

Chocolate Leaves

Wash and dry non-toxic leaves that have veins in them (e.g. rose leaves, mint leaves). Brush underside with melted chocolate. Place on waxed paper. Let harden at room temperature. Repeat to make ⅛ inch (3 mm) thick. Let set until dry and hard. Carefully peel leaf away from chocolate.

Chocolate Filigrees

Draw desired shape(s) on paper. Place waxed paper over drawings and tape in place. Pipe melted chocolate over lines that are easily seen through waxed paper. Let stand until dry and hard. Carefully lift chocolate design off waxed paper.

Feathered Design

Pipe contrasting sauce or icing in parallel lines or circles over sauce or icing. Draw a knife or skewer through lines at even intervals. For variation, draw knife in opposite directions every other line.

Getting creative with room decorations is one technique for impressing your guests, and adding flair to your food with a garnish or two is always worthy of compliments, but don't stop there. What about the serving dishes? A bowl is fine—but soup served in a hollowed-out round loaf is incredible! Dip served in a small bowl works well, but dip served in a carved cantaloupe (see photo on page 25) is fabulous!

Don't just put fruit in a bowl and call it your centerpiece —frost it first!

Place the washed and paper towel-dried fruit on a piece of waxed paper or cutting board. Brush with beaten egg white then sprinkle with berry sugar. Granulated sugar works fine too but may clump a bit more. Carefully place in your bowl, trying not to disturb the "frost." Warning— frosted fruit is not edible because of the raw egg white that has been sitting at room temperature during your event.

You can also use edible flower heads or their petals which can garnish a salad or, as shown below, an iced cake. A bowl of frosted flowers is just as stunning as the fruit.

Here is a great idea for serving snack mix in a more flamboyant vessel than a wooden nut dish. Simply take crêpe paper and a plastic Hawaiian lei and form into a bowl. Form the base, then gather the ends and wind the leis around. Tape and staples aren't needed. See photo on page 85 too.

If you look at the photo on page 26/27 you will notice the Mustard Dip, page 26, is surrounded by a breathtaking display of herbs. Our Herbal Halo, page 182, is very easy to make. It can be made several days in advance and stored, wrapped, in the refrigerator.

Spring Dip

A great duo with fresh vegetables, cut into bite-size pieces.
☺ Can be made up to two days ahead.

Chopped onion	¹/₃ cup	75 mL
Medium carrot, chopped	¹/₂	¹/₂
Green or red pepper, chopped	¹/₂	¹/₂
White vinegar	2 tbsp.	30 mL
Low-fat salad dressing (or mayonnaise)	1 cup	250 mL
Process cheese spread	¹/₂ cup	125 mL

Measure first 5 ingredients into blender. Process until smooth.

Add cheese. Process until smooth. Pour into bowl. Makes 2 cups (500 mL) dip.

1 tbsp. (15 mL) dip: 35 Calories; 1 g Protein; 2.8 g Total Fat; 2 g Carbohydrate; 123 mg Sodium

Pictured below.

Spring Dip

Fruit Dip

Fruit Dip

Creamy yellow color. Smooth. Dip your favorite fruits in this simple quick mixture. ☺ Make the night before if desired.

Non-fat vanilla yogurt	1 cup	250 mL
Brown sugar, packed	2 tbsp.	30 mL
Frozen concentrated orange juice	1¹/₂ tsp.	7 mL

Stir yogurt, brown sugar and juice together in bowl. Makes 1 cup (250 mL) dip.

1 tbsp. (15 mL) dip: 15 Calories; 1 g Protein; trace Total Fat; 3 g Carbohydrate; 12 mg Sodium

Pictured above.

Buffet Trays

Keeping the basics for a few dips on hand, along with some deli meats well wrapped in the freezer, can allow for quick and easy impromptu entertaining. Just take a bit of extra time to arrange the food on trays. Here are a few tips:

1. Try to keep slices of the same items exactly the same size.

2. Arrange the slices or pieces on the tray using symmetrical balance, that is, do on the left side what you do on the right side and vice versa.

3. Vary light and dark colors for a visually pleasing balance.

4. Use doilies or napkins as a base to add spots of color.

Shrimp Dip

Good taste of shrimp and Italian spices. Great with fresh vegetables and crackers. ☺ Make up to 24 hours ahead.

Cream cheese, softened	8 oz.	250 g
Low-fat sour cream	1 cup	250 mL
Envelope Italian dressing mix	1 × ³/₄ oz.	1 × 21 g
Cooked tiny shrimp, mashed	1 cup	250 mL

Mix cream cheese, sour cream and dressing mix in bowl until smooth.

Add shrimp. Stir. Chill at least 2 hours before serving. Makes 2¹/₂ cups (625 mL) dip.

1 tbsp. (15 mL) dip: 31 Calories; 1 g Protein; 2.6 g Total Fat; 1 g Carbohydrate; 72 mg Sodium

Pictured on page 26/27.

Cookie Fruit Dip

Serve with assorted fruit cut in spears, chunks or slices, or ice cream wafers. ☺ Can be made the day before.

Sour cream	1 cup	250 mL
Liquid honey	2 tbsp.	30 mL
Coconut (or oatmeal) cookies, crushed into crumbs	3	3

Stir sour cream and honey together well. Add cookie crumbs. Stir. Chill several hours in refrigerator. Makes 1¹/₄ cups (300 mL) dip.

2 tbsp. (30 mL) dip: 74 Calories; 1 g Protein; 4.5 g Total Fat; 8 g Carbohydrate; 12 mg Sodium

Pictured on page 27.

Mustard Dip

Best served warm but can also be served cold. ☺ Make the day before and reheat in microwave just before serving.

Brown sugar, packed	1 cup	250 mL
All-purpose flour	3 tbsp.	50 mL
Salt	¼ tsp.	1 mL
Water	⅔ cup	150 mL
White vinegar	6 tbsp.	100 mL
Prepared mustard	3 tbsp.	50 mL

Measure brown sugar, flour and salt into saucepan. Stir together well.

Mix in water, vinegar and mustard. Heat, stirring often, until boiling and thickened. Serve warm. Makes 1¾ cups (425 mL) dip.

1 tbsp. (15 mL) dip: 34 Calories; trace Protein; trace Total Fat; 9 g Carbohydrate; 46 mg Sodium

Pictured on page 27 and on page 45.

Guacamole

Serve with corn chips. ☺ Since this freezes well, make it when you have nice ripe avocados.

Avocados, peeled and cut up	4	4
Lemon juice	¼ cup	60 mL
Salad dressing (or mayonnaise)	½ cup	125 mL
Chopped onion	¼ cup	60 mL
Chili powder	1 tsp.	5 mL
Garlic powder	½ tsp.	2 mL
Cayenne pepper	¼ tsp.	1 mL
Salt	1 tsp.	5 mL
Pepper	¼ tsp.	1 mL
Medium tomatoes, diced	2	2

Put first 9 ingredients into blender. Process until smooth. Turn into bowl. May be frozen at this point. Thaw well before using.

Sprinkle with tomato for garnish or stir into dip. Makes 2 cups (500 mL) dip, before adding tomato.

1 tbsp. (15 mL) dip (with tomato): 60 Calories; 1 g Protein; 5.6 g Total Fat; 3 g Carbohydrate; 109 mg Sodium

Pictured on page 27.

Menu Suggestions

As you plan your menu, consider the number of guests you expect and the kind of food appropriate for the occasion. Will your guests arrive around the same time, or are some due to arrive later?

We offer these menu selections to help your entertaining run smoothly. If you prefer, feel free to add or change a recipe to another that is more suitable to your taste. As you make your selections, keep in mind a nice balance of color, flavor, hot and cold dishes.

Our ultimate goal is to help you spend less time in the kitchen so you can spend more time with your guests!

Romance Is In The Air
(dinner for 2)

Salmon Mousse (½ recipe), page 48
(served with assorted crackers)
Oriental Broth Fondue, page 17
(served with rice)
Chocolate Fondue, page 20
Meringue Fingers, page 21
Raspberry Liqueur, page 56

Brunch For 10

Chicken Bunwiches, page 74
Mac 'N' Cheese Surprise, page 71
Breakfast Strata, page 71
Peach Melba Salad, page 147
Chocolate Orange Bread, page 65

Family Get-Together
(dinner for 8)

Turkey Roast, page 137
Stuffing Patties, page 167
Mashed Potatoes, page 168
Nutty Glazed Carrots, page 161
Coleslaw, page 148
Banana Cream Pie, page 144

Summer Supper
(dinner for 8)

Mixed Grill, page 130
Eggplant Parmigiana, page 163
Spicy Baked Potatoes And Onions, page 167
Cool Fruit Delight, page 103
Rhubarb Punch, page 53

An Evening Of Video
(nibblies for 8)

Little Smokies, page 36
Oven Hot Dip, page 42
(served with tortilla chips)
Nifty Nibbles, page 45
Cereal Party Mix, page 84
Caramel Popcorn, page 84

Gather The Gang
(buffet for 20)

Saucy Meatballs, page 36
Cold Party Salmon, page 104
Quick Potato Casserole, page 169
Baked Beans, page 164
Mixed Green Salad, page 146
Raspberry Salad, page 149
Dessert Special, page 98

Let's Party
(finger food buffet for 16)

Saucy Wings, page 38
Chafing Dish Sausage, page 37
Chicken Buns, page 37
Stack O' Cheese, page 50
(served with assorted crackers)
Chili Rolls, page 50

Mexican Madness
(dinner for 6)

Quesadilla Starters, page 39
Tostadas, page 39
Black Bean Soup, page 154
Crab Enchiladas, page 106
Rice Elegant, page 170
Saucy Bananas, page 97

Pasta Party
(buffet for 10)

Bruschetta, page 34
Italian Vegetable Bowl, page 162
Lasagne, page 124
Smoky Pasta, page 110
Ham And Pasta Bake, page 129

Oriental Offerings
(dinner for 6)

Crab Finger Puffs, page 46
Beef With Ginger, page 116
Braised Vegetables (½ recipe), page 162
Noodles And Soup, page 150
Shrimp Fried Rice, page 169

Oceans Of Fun
(seafood dinner for 8)

Crab Appetizers, page 48
Clam Chowder, page 152
Coulibiac, page 105
Shrimp Casserole, page 108
Shrimpy Rice Salad, page 145

Book Club Night
(nibblies for 10)

Cheesy Ham Ball, page 51
(served with assorted crackers)
Bagel Bites, page 44
Glazed Munchies, page 85
Jam Pie, page 141

The In-Laws Are Coming!
(dinner for 4)

Velvet Potato Soup, page 150
Herb Biscuits, page 62
Beef Medallions, page 119
Onion Rice, page 170
Broccoli Casserole, page 161
Almond Dessert, page 99

Teenage Bash
(buffet for 14)

Salsa Dip, page 42
(served with tortilla chips)
Corn Pups, page 36
Veggie Pizza Squares, page 44
Potato Skins, page 35
Oven Wings, page 38
Boiled Butterscotch Cookies, page 87
Chipped Dumplings, page 103
Turtle Squares, page 158

Bridal or Baby Shower
(light lunch for 15)

Zucchini Bites, page 43
Pretzel Salad, page 149
Rice Artichoke Salad, page 147
Angel Roll, page 81
Cranberry Bowl, page 54
(tea and/or coffee)

Napkin Folding

With all the details you have to think about, you are probably wondering about
the necessity of including creatively-folded napkins at your dinner table.

Think about their presence at a table in a restaurant. If the napkin merely sits by your plate, that's fine.
But if it has been stylishly folded on your plate, you notice it as something a little extra special.

The same holds true for your dinner table. It's not necessary to add this one bit
of decoration, but if time allows, it's a fun way to do something unique and showy.
Now is a perfect time to try it, and your guests are certain to be impressed.

For the Buffet Table

Buffet Envelope

(2 large cloth napkins: 1 patterned, 1 solid; same size)

1. Place napkins on top of each other, staggering right and left edges to create a 2 inch (5 cm) stripe of one color on left side.

2. Fold both napkins in half together with folded edge along top. Place up to 3 pieces of silverware in center of napkin and pointing toward stripe.

3. Fold the bottom edge up to the center, partially covering the silverware. Fold top edge down to almost meet bottom edge.

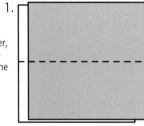

1.

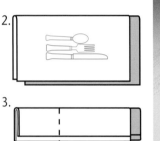

2.

3.

4. Fold left edge to center.

5. Fold right edge toward center as well, and tuck left edge under first two layers of stripe.

4.

5.

Buffet Pocket

(1 large cloth napkin)

1. Fold napkin in half with folded edge along bottom.

2. Fold front flap down to meet bottom edge.

3. Turn napkin over. Fold right edge to center of napkin.

4. Fold new right edge over again to center.

5. Fold once more to make a rectangle with a pocket.

1.

2.

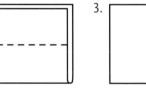

3.

4.

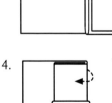

5.

Buffet Wrap

(1 large cloth napkin)

1. Fold napkin into quarters. Place up to 3 pieces of silverware in center of square. Fold in two side points to form two small triangles.

2. Bring two side folds over cutlery to cover it completely.

3. Secure bundle with ribbon or raffia tied in a bow.

1.

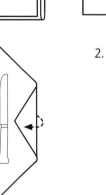

2.

3.

For the Dinner Table

Bouquet

(1 soft cloth napkin; equal color value on both sides)

1. Lay napkin open and flat. Bring bottom right corner up to and beyond center point of top edge, forming 2 equal triangles on either side.

2. Place napkin ring at center of diagonal bottom edge. Loosely draw napkin through ring.

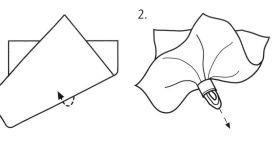

3. Continue to pull napkin through ring until halfway up its length. Gently open out sides.

3.

Fireworks

(1 stiff cloth or paper napkin)

1. Fold napkin down into a triangle.

2. Fold top right corner down to meet bottom point.

3. Fold right corner down to meet center line of diamond to form a right angle. Repeat with left corner.

4. Fold napkin back along vertical center line. Turn napkin upside down.

5. Hold folds together with one hand. Draw the bottom point through napkin ring. Pull folds out slightly.

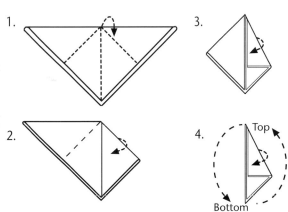

Top

Bottom

5.

Fancy Fan

(1 large stiff cloth or paper napkin)

1. Make accordion pleats along entire length of open napkin, starting at the edge nearest you.

2a. Place one hand firmly over center of completed pleats.

2b. Fold napkin in half.

3. Tie a bow halfway up the pleats and fan out the top to make a parasol.

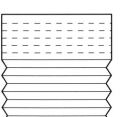

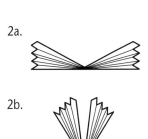

3.

Standing Fan

(1 large stiff cloth or paper napkin)

1. Fold napkin in half, vertically, to form rectangle.

2. Accordion pleat from bottom, folding ¾ of napkin's length.

3. Fold napkin in half with pleats on outside bottom edge.

4. Fold unpleated corner toward center fold to form triangle. Tuck edge of triangle into first pleat.

5. Stand napkin on pleated edge and release fan.

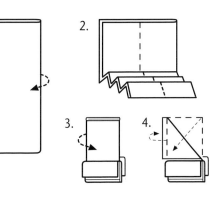

5.

Appetizers

Entertaining can be made easy with the right selection of simple and quick-to-prepare appetizers. Whether hosting a formal dinner or simply inviting neighbors over for a last minute get-together, it is a thoughtful and welcome gesture to offer your guests a variety of impressive appetizers such as these.

Keep an assortment readily available in your freezer for when unexpected company arrives. If dinner is included as part of your event, then these quick bites offer guests a small taste of what is to come.

Corned Beef Canapés

Pretty pink and orange spread on dark bread slices.
🕐 These can be prepared several hours ahead and broiled when ready to serve.

Canned corned beef, mashed	12 oz.	340 g
Grated sharp Cheddar cheese	2 cups	500 mL
Worcestershire sauce	1 tbsp.	15 mL
Garlic powder	1/4 tsp.	1 mL
Onion powder	1/2 tsp.	2 mL
Low-fat salad dressing (or mayonnaise)	6 tbsp.	100 mL
Small cocktail-size bread slices (such as pumpernickel)	54	54

Mix first 6 ingredients well in bowl. Makes 2 1/4 cups (560 mL) spread.

Spread 2 tsp. (10 mL) filling on each bread slice. At this point, these can be placed in refrigerator for 2 hours or longer before serving. Place on ungreased baking sheet. Broil 4 to 6 inches (10 to 15 cm) from heat for about 4 minutes until bubbly and cheese is melted. Makes 54 canapés.

1 canapé: 56 Calories; 3 g Protein; 2.9 g Total Fat; 4 g Carbohydrate; 147 mg Sodium

Pictured on page 33.

Shrimp Canapés

An attractive contrast of dark and light. 🕐 Shrimp spread will keep well in the refrigerator if made a day or two ahead. Extra canapés can quickly be made and added to an empty tray.

Onion flakes	1 tbsp.	15 mL
Low-fat salad dressing (or mayonnaise)	2 tbsp.	30 mL
Lime juice	1 tbsp.	15 mL
Dill weed	1/8 tsp.	0.5 mL
Light spreadable cream cheese	8 oz.	250 g
Cooked tiny shrimp	1 1/4 lbs.	560 g
Small cocktail-size bread slices (such as pumpernickel)	54	54

Mix first 5 ingredients in bowl.

Stir in shrimp. Refrigerate for 24 hours. Makes 1 1/2 cups (375 mL) spread.

Spread about 1 1/2 tsp. (7 mL) shrimp mixture on each bread slice. Makes 54 canapés.

1 canapé: 41 Calories; 4 g Protein; 1.2 g Total Fat; 4 g Carbohydrate; 106 mg Sodium

Pictured on page 33.

Zippy Canapés

Pretty as a picture with red, green and white on dark bread. 🕐 Spread freezes well.

Light cream cheese, softened	8 oz.	250 g
Chopped chives	2 tbsp.	30 mL
Seasoning salt	1/2 tsp.	2 mL
Finely chopped pimiento	1 tbsp.	15 mL
Small cocktail-size bread slices (such as pumpernickel)	48	48

Mix cream cheese, chives and seasoning salt well. Add pimiento. Mix. Makes 1 cup (250 mL) spread.

Spread or pipe 1 tsp. (5 mL) cream cheese mixture on each bread slice. Makes 48 canapés.

1 canapé: 28 Calories; 1 g Protein; 1.0 g Total Fat; 4 g Carbohydrate; 104 mg Sodium

Pictured on page 33.

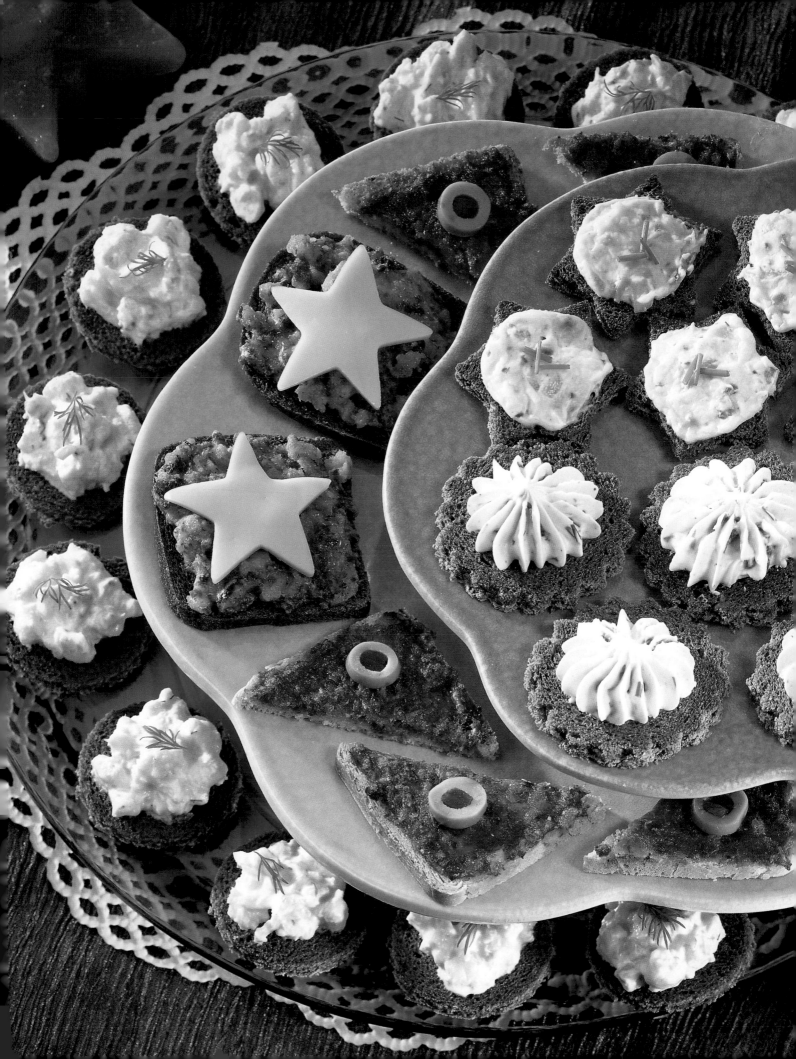

Mushroom Canapés

Spread has a smooth, creamy texture.
⊕ The mushroom spread can be prepared up to two days ahead and refrigerated until ready to use.

Hard margarine (or butter)	1½ tsp.	7 mL
Finely chopped onion	¾ cup	175 mL
Finely chopped fresh mushrooms	1½ cups	375 mL
Cream cheese, softened	2 × 8 oz.	2 × 250 g
Large egg	1	1
Paprika	⅛ tsp.	0.5 mL
Onion powder	⅛ tsp.	0.5 mL
Salt	⅛ tsp.	0.5 mL
Parsley flakes	⅛ tsp.	0.5 mL
Small cocktail-size bread slices (such as pumpernickel)	64	64

Heat margarine in frying pan. Add onion and mushrooms. Sauté until soft and moisture is evaporated.

Beat cream cheese, egg, paprika, onion powder, salt and parsley together well. Add mushroom mixture. Mix. Makes 2 cups (500 mL) filling.

Spread about 1½ tsp. (7 mL) mixture on each bread slice. Place on ungreased baking sheet. Broil until golden. Serve hot. Makes 64 canapés.

1 canapé: 48 Calories; 1 g Protein; 3.0 g Total Fat; 4 g Carbohydrate; 71 mg Sodium

Pictured on page 33.

Cheesy Meat Canapés

Recipe can easily be halved. ⊕ Keep these ingredients on hand for a quick and delicious last minute appetizer.

Ground beef	1 lb.	454 g
Sausage meat	1 lb.	454 g
Process cheese loaf (such as Velveeta), cut up	1 lb.	454 g
Small cocktail-size bread slices (such as pumpernickel)	64	64

Scramble-fry ground beef and sausage meat together. Drain well.

Add cheese. Stir constantly until melted. Makes 4 cups (1 L) spread.

Spread 1 tbsp. (15 mL) on each bread slice. May be frozen at this point. Place on ungreased baking sheet. Bake in 350°F (175°C) oven for 15 minutes until hot. Makes 64 canapés.

1 canapé: 66 Calories; 4 g Protein; 3.9 g Total Fat; 4 g Carbohydrate; 184 mg Sodium

Pictured on page 33.

Bruschetta

Once the tomatoes are diced, this assembles quickly.
⊕ Prepare ingredients in the morning and refrigerate.

Seeded and diced plum tomatoes	3 cups	750 mL
Garlic cloves, minced (or ½ tsp., 2 mL, garlic powder)	2	2
Olive (or cooking) oil	⅓ cup	75 mL
Dried sweet basil	1 tbsp.	15 mL
Salt	1 tsp.	5 mL
Baguette, cut into 1 inch (2.5 cm) slices	1	1
Grated Parmesan cheese (or ½ cup, 125 mL, mozzarella cheese)	¼ cup	60 mL

Combine first 5 ingredients in bowl. Cover. Let stand for at least 1 hour so flavors can blend.

Arrange baguette slices on ungreased baking sheet. Broil to toast 1 side. Turn slices over. Use a fork to spread tomato mixture on each slice. Spoon remaining juice over slices.

Sprinkle with Parmesan or mozzarella cheese. Try a few with each. Broil for 5 minutes until cheese is melted and bread edges are crisp. Makes 20 slices.

1 slice: 111 Calories; 3 g Protein; 5 g Total Fat; 14 g Carbohydrate; 294 mg Sodium

Pictured below.

Bruschetta

Top Left: Little Smokies, page 36   Bottom Left: Potato Skins, below   Top Right: Corn Pups, page 36   Bottom Right: Aloha Kabobs, below

Potato Skins

Serve these spicy wedges with sour cream for dipping.
🕐 These can be prepared earlier in the day and
covered. Bake just before serving.

Medium baking potatoes	4	4
Cooking oil	2 tbsp.	30 mL
Seasoning salt	1 tsp.	5 mL
Pepper	¼ tsp.	1 mL
Paprika	1 tsp.	5 mL
Ground thyme	⅛ tsp.	0.5 mL

Bake potatoes in 400°F (205°C) oven for 45 to 60 minutes until tender. Cool for 15 minutes. Cut in half lengthwise. Cut each half in half lengthwise again, making a total of 16 wedges. Scoop out potato from wedges, leaving each shell ¼ inch (6 mm) thick.

Mix remaining 5 ingredients in small cup. Brush inside of each potato shell with oil mixture. Arrange on ungreased baking sheet. Bake in 400°F (205°C) oven for 20 to 25 minutes. Makes 16 potato skins.

1 potato skin: 21 Calories; trace Protein; 1.8 g Total Fat; 1 g Carbohydrate; 86 mg Sodium

Pictured above.

Aloha Kabobs

Pretty yellow and red. 🕐 In the morning, arrange
meat and pineapple cubes on skewers. Brush with
sauce and refrigerate. Broil when ready to serve.

Canned processed meat, cut into ¾ inch (2 cm) cubes	12 oz.	340 g
Canned pineapple chunks, drained, blotted dry	14 oz.	398 mL
Soy sauce	2 tbsp.	30 mL
White vinegar	1 tbsp.	15 mL
Brown sugar, packed	1 tbsp.	15 mL

Place 1 cube each of meat and pineapple on a round wooden toothpick. Repeat. Arrange on ungreased baking sheet with sides.

Stir soy sauce, vinegar and sugar together in small bowl. Brush all sides of kabobs. Broil until hot, turning several times. Makes 20 kabobs.

1 kabob: 67 Calories; 2 g Protein; 5.2 g Total Fat; 3 g Carbohydrate; 324 mg Sodium

Pictured above.

Saucy Meatballs

A sure hit! Serve with cocktail picks for dipping into the tangy sauce. ☉ Have these soft and moist meatballs ready in the refrigerator or freezer. Reheat for company.

Water	½ cup	125 mL
Salt	¾ tsp.	4 mL
Pepper	¼ tsp.	1 mL
Prepared horseradish	2 tsp.	10 mL
Bread slices, processed into crumbs	4	4
Large egg, fork-beaten	1	1
Lean ground beef	1 lb.	454 g
Sauce:		
Ketchup	⅓ cup	75 mL
Corn syrup	¼ cup	60 mL
Soy sauce	2 tbsp.	30 mL
Worcestershire sauce	½ tsp.	2 mL
Prepared mustard	1 tsp.	5 mL

Mix first 5 ingredients in bowl. Stir well. Stir in egg.

Add ground beef. Mix. Shape into ¾ inch (2 cm) meatballs. Arrange on ungreased baking sheet with sides. Bake in 450°F (230°C) oven for 10 to 15 minutes. Makes 45 meatballs.

Sauce: Measure all 5 ingredients into large saucepan. Heat and stir until hot. Pour over hot meatballs in serving dish. Makes ½ cup (125 mL) sauce.

1 meatball (with sauce): 49 Calories; 2 g Protein; 1.7 g Total Fat; 6 g Carbohydrate; 141 mg Sodium

Pictured below.

Saucy Meatballs

Little Smokies

These will be the first appetizers to disappear. ☉ Make ahead and reheat when needed. These freeze well.

Red or black currant jelly	1 cup	250 mL
Prepared mustard	⅔ cup	150 mL
Canned cocktail sausages (see Note)	2 × 4 oz.	2 × 113 g

Stir jelly and mustard together in saucepan. Add smokies. Heat, stirring occasionally until simmering. Cover. Simmer for about 1 hour. Serve warm with cocktail picks or round wooden picks. Makes 28 smokies.

1 smokie (with sauce): 58 Calories; 1 g Protein; 2.3 g Total Fat; 9 g Carbohydrate; 155 mg Sodium

Pictured on page 35.

Note: 2 packages of small link smokies may be used in place of canned sausages. Regular smokies may be used in slices. Makes 32 smokies.

Corn Pups

Serve hot with ketchup and mustard. ☉ These freeze well. Simply reheat on a baking sheet in a 350°F (175°C) oven until heated through.

Pancake mix	1 cup	250 mL
Yellow cornmeal	⅔ cup	150 mL
Granulated sugar	1 tbsp.	15 mL
Large egg, fork-beaten	1	1
Milk	¾ cup	175 mL
Cooking oil	2 tbsp.	30 mL
Canned cocktail sausages, cut in half and patted dry (or 8 wieners, each cut into 5 pieces)	3 × 4 oz.	3 × 113 g

Cooking oil, for deep-frying

Stir pancake mix, cornmeal and sugar together in bowl.

Add egg, milk and cooking oil. Stir well.

Insert round wooden pick in end of each sausage, leaving about 1 inch (2.5 cm) exposed. Dip each sausage into cornmeal mixture using spoon to help cover completely.

Put sausages into hot 375°F (190°C) cooking oil in deep fryer. Cook, turning to brown both sides until coating is evenly golden. Remove with slotted spoon. Drain on paper towel. Makes 42 appetizers.

1 appetizer: 101 Calories; 2 g Protein; 6.7 g Total Fat; 8 g Carbohydrate; 194 mg Sodium

Pictured on page 35.

Chafing Dish Sausage

Chafing Dish Sausage

If you don't have a chafing dish, transfer to a warmed casserole dish. Serve with cocktail picks. ☺ Cook these ahead. When ready to serve, reheat in saucepan and place in chafing dish at the last minute.

Ketchup	¾ cup	175 mL
Brown sugar, packed	¾ cup	175 mL
Worcestershire sauce	2 tsp.	10 mL
Garlic powder	¼ tsp.	1 mL
Onion powder	¼ tsp.	1 mL
Water	¾ cup	175 mL
Water	1 tbsp.	15 mL
Cornstarch	2 tsp.	10 mL
Garlic (or other) sausage, sliced ¼ inch (6 mm) thick	2 lbs.	900 g

Measure first 6 ingredients into large saucepan. Stir. Heat until boiling.

Mix second amount of water with cornstarch in small cup. Stir into boiling liquid until sauce is slightly thickened.

Add sausage to sauce. Simmer for 10 to 15 minutes. Transfer to chafing dish. Makes 5⅓ cups (1.3 L).

¼ cup (60 mL) sausage (with sauce): 129 Calories; 6 g Protein; 8.7 g Total Fat; 6 g Carbohydrate; 554 mg Sodium

Pictured above.

Chicken Buns

Even the kids will like these "surprise packages." ☺ Make ahead then reheat for five to ten minutes.

Light cream cheese, softened	2 oz.	57 g
Hard margarine (or butter), softened	1 tbsp.	15 mL
Chopped chives	2 tsp.	10 mL
Canned flakes of chicken, drained	6½ oz.	184 g
Water	1 tbsp.	15 mL
Chicken bouillon powder	⅛ tsp.	0.5 mL
Salt, sprinkle		
Pepper, sprinkle		
Refrigerator country-style biscuits (10 per tube)	1 × 12 oz.	1 × 340 g
Egg white (large), fork-beaten	1	1
Grated Parmesan cheese	1 tbsp.	15 mL
Fine dry bread crumbs	2 tbsp.	30 mL

Mash cream cheese, margarine and chives together in bowl.

Add next 5 ingredients. Mix well.

Cut each biscuit in half. Press, with floured hands, into 3½ inch (9 cm) circles on lightly floured surface. Place about 2 tsp. (10 mL) of filling in center of each. Dampen outer edge of circles with water. Gather up edges and pinch together to form a flattened round shape.

Brush tops with egg white.

Mix Parmesan cheese and bread crumbs in bowl. Sprinkle over top. Arrange on ungreased baking sheet. Bake in 350°F (175°C) oven for 12 to 15 minutes until lightly browned. Makes 20 buns.

1 bun: 77 Calories; 4 g Protein; 2.9 g Total Fat; 9 g Carbohydrate; 241 mg Sodium

Pictured below.

Chicken Buns

Oven Wings

Saucy Wings

Dark golden thick coating with a real sheen. Remove skin or leave as is. ⊕ Make ahead and freeze. Reheat to serve.

Chicken drumettes (or whole chicken wings)	3 lbs.	1.4 kg
Pineapple juice	¾ cup	175 mL
Low-sodium soy sauce	¼ cup	60 mL
Lemon juice	3 tbsp.	50 mL
Brown sugar, packed	½ cup	125 mL
Granulated sugar	⅓ cup	75 mL
Ground ginger	1 tsp.	5 mL
Garlic salt	¼ tsp.	1 mL
All-purpose flour	6 tbsp.	100 mL

Arrange drumettes on foil-lined baking sheet with sides. If using whole wings, discard wing tips and cut wings apart at joint. Bake in 350°F (175°C) oven for 30 minutes.

Heat pineapple juice, soy sauce and lemon juice in saucepan until boiling.

Mix remaining 5 ingredients well in bowl. Stir into boiling liquid until sauce returns to a boil and thickens. Remove from heat. Brush wings generously with sauce. Bake, brushing with sauce every 10 minutes, for about 30 minutes until tender. Serve hot. Makes about 24 drumettes or 36 wing pieces.

1 drumette (with skin): 114 Calories; 6 g Protein; 5.1 g Total Fat; 11 g Carbohydrate; 148 mg Sodium

Pictured below.

Oven Wings

Remove skin or leave as is. Either way, the color is dark and rich. ⊕ Make ahead and freeze. Reheat to serve.

Chicken drumettes (or whole chicken wings)	3 lbs.	1.4 kg
Soy sauce	¾ cup	175 mL
Water	¾ cup	175 mL
Brown sugar, packed	⅓ cup	75 mL
Chopped red pepper	1	1
Chopped green pepper	1	1
Chopped onion	1 cup	250 mL
Seasoning salt	½ tsp.	2 mL

Arrange drumettes on foil-lined baking sheet with sides. If using whole wings, discard wing tips and cut wings apart at joint.

Stir remaining 7 ingredients together in bowl. Pour over chicken. Bake, uncovered, in 350°F (175°C) oven for about 1 hour until tender. Remove with slotted spoon or tongs to platter. Makes about 24 drumettes or 36 wing pieces.

1 drumette (with skin): 92 Calories; 5 g Protein; 5.1 g Total Fat; 5 g Carbohydrate; 598 mg Sodium

Pictured above.

Saucy Wings

Green Chili Snacks

A simple, delicious one-bowl recipe. ☺ Serve warm or make ahead and serve cold. These freeze well.

Creamed cottage cheese	1 cup	250 mL
All-purpose flour	1/3 cup	75 mL
Baking powder	1/2 tsp.	2 mL
Baking soda	1/2 tsp.	2 mL
Salt	1/2 tsp.	2 mL
Large eggs	4	4
Hard margarine (or butter), softened	3 tbsp.	50 mL
Grated sharp Cheddar cheese	1 1/2 cups	375 mL
Canned chopped green chilies, drained	4 oz.	114 mL

Put first 7 ingredients into bowl. Beat on medium to mix.

Stir in cheese and green chilies. Turn into greased 8 × 8 inch (20 × 20 cm) dish. Bake in 350°F (175°C) oven for 45 to 55 minutes. Cuts into 25 pieces.

1 piece: 68 Calories; 4 g Protein; 4.7 g Total Fat; 2 g Carbohydrate; 193 mg Sodium

Pictured on page 40.

Tostadas

Pretty little morsels of red, green and white. A taste of Mexico. ☺ Have all ingredients ready in the morning. Spread on chips shortly before serving so they don't get soggy.

Round tortilla chips	20	20
Canned jalapeño bean dip (or refried beans), heated	10 1/2 oz.	298 mL
Sour cream	1/2 cup	125 mL
Mild or medium salsa	1/2 cup	125 mL
Sliced green onion	2 tbsp.	30 mL
Grated Monterey Jack cheese	1/2 cup	125 mL

Arrange tortilla chips on ungreased baking sheet with sides. Spread layers on each as follows: 1 tbsp. (15 mL) bean dip, 1 tsp. (5 mL) sour cream, 1 tsp. (5 mL) salsa, 1/4 tsp. (1 mL) green onion, 1 tsp. (5 mL) cheese. May be served as is or baked in 350°F (175°C) oven for about 5 minutes until cheese is melted. Makes 20 tostadas.

1 tostada: 68 Calories; 1 g Protein; 3.4 g Total Fat; 7 g Carbohydrate; 184 mg Sodium

Pictured on page 40.

1. Oven Hot Dip, page 42
2. Quesadilla Starters, page 39
3. Tostadas, page 39
4. Salsa Dip, page 42
5. Green Chili Snacks, page 39
6. Cranberry Bowl, page 54

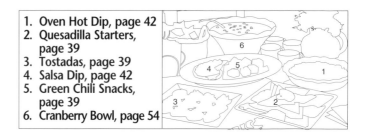

Quesadilla Starters

Here's an appetizer that doesn't crumble when you bite into it. Good hot or cold. ☺ Prepare in the morning. Brown when ready to serve. Do not freeze.

Grated Monterey Jack cheese	2 cups	500 mL
Canned chopped green chilies, drained	4 oz.	114 mL
Finely chopped onion	1/3 cup	75 mL
Medium avocado, peeled, seeded and chopped (optional)	1	1
Large tomato, finely diced	1	1
Flour tortillas, 8 inch (20 cm)	6	6
Cooking oil	2 tbsp.	30 mL

Have first 5 ingredients ready, each in separate containers.

Scatter 1/3 cup (75 mL) cheese over half of each tortilla. Divide green chilies, onion, avocado and tomato among the tortillas. Moisten edges with water. Fold tortilla over filled half. Press edges with fork to seal. Cover with damp towel to keep moist.

Heat 1 tbsp. (15 mL) cooking oil in frying pan. Add 3 folded tortillas. Brown each side slowly for 3 minutes until cheese is melted. Repeat with remaining 3 tortillas. Cut each into 4 wedges. Makes 24 wedges.

1 wedge: 105 Calories; 4 g Protein; 4.4 g Total Fat; 12 g Carbohydrate; 122 mg Sodium

Pictured on page 41.

Freeze main dishes and desserts in individual portions or slices so that you can remove only as many servings as you need for unexpected guests.

Salsa Dip

Serve with tortilla chips for dipping. ☺ *While this can be made ahead, do not freeze. Store in refrigerator.*

Medium tomatoes, peeled and diced	3	3
Green onions, chopped	3	3
Canned chopped green chilies, with liquid	4 oz.	114 mL
Chopped ripe pitted olives	¼ cup	60 mL
Cooking oil	2 tbsp.	30 mL
White vinegar	1½ tbsp.	25 mL
Garlic powder	½ tsp.	2 mL
Salt	½ tsp.	2 mL
Pepper	⅛ tsp.	0.5 mL

Combine all 9 ingredients in bowl. Cover. Chill at least 2 hours before serving. Makes 3 cups (750 mL) dip.

1 tbsp. (15 mL) dip: 8 Calories; trace Protein; 0.6 g Total Fat; 1 g Carbohydrate; 32 mg Sodium

Pictured on page 40.

Oven Hot Dip

Lots of red, green and orange showing. Serve with tortilla chips. ☺ *This may be assembled and refrigerated until ready to heat and serve.*

Cream cheese, softened	8 oz.	250 g
Commercial pizza sauce	½ cup	125 mL
Dried whole oregano	½ tsp.	2 mL
Garlic powder	¼ tsp.	1 mL
Dried sweet basil	¼ tsp.	1 mL
Onion powder	¼ tsp.	1 mL
Chili powder (optional)	½-1 tsp.	2-5 mL
Finely chopped red pepper	½ cup	125 mL
Finely chopped green pepper	½ cup	125 mL
Sliced green onion	¼ cup	60 mL
Grated sharp Cheddar cheese	½ cup	125 mL
Grated mozzarella cheese	½ cup	125 mL

Mix first 7 ingredients well in bowl. Turn into 9 inch (22 cm) ungreased glass pie plate. Spread evenly.

Sprinkle with red pepper, green pepper, green onion, Cheddar cheese and mozzarella cheese. May be chilled at this point. Bake in 350°F (175°C) oven for 20 minutes. Makes about 3 cups (750 mL) dip.

1 tbsp. (15 mL) dip: 31 Calories; 1 g Protein; 2.6 g Total Fat; 1 g Carbohydrate; 40 mg Sodium

Pictured on page 41.

Ripe Olive Snacks, page 43   Forest Mushrooms, below

Forest Mushrooms

Glistening little nuggets. ☺ *Make the day before, or even three or four days ahead, for best flavor.*

Marinade:		
Ketchup	½ cup	125 mL
Tarragon (or white) vinegar	¼ cup	60 mL
Granulated sugar	2 tsp.	10 mL
Garlic powder	½ tsp.	2 mL
Salt	½ tsp.	2 mL
Onion powder	¼ tsp.	1 mL
Water	½ cup	125 mL
Cooking oil	1 tbsp.	15 mL
Canned whole mushrooms, drained	3 × 10 oz.	3 × 284 mL

Marinade: Combine first 8 ingredients in bowl. Mix well.

Add mushrooms. Stir. Cover. Let stand in refrigerator overnight. Remove mushrooms with slotted spoon. Discard marinade. Place cocktail pick in center of each. Makes about 90 mushrooms.

3 mushrooms: 9 Calories; trace Protein; 0.3 g Total Fat; 2 g Carbohydrate; 111 mg Sodium

Pictured above.

Ripe Olive Snacks

Use submarine buns, sliced, if you prefer a softer crust. ☺ Filling can be spread over sliced buns, arranged on baking sheet, covered and refrigerated. Just remove wrap and heat in oven.

Canned ripe pitted olives, drained and chopped, reserve slices for garnish	14 oz.	398 mL
Grated medium or sharp Cheddar cheese	1 cup	250 mL
Salad dressing (or mayonnaise)	¼ cup	60 mL
Sliced green onion	¼ cup	60 mL
Medium tomato, seeded and diced	1	1
Curry powder	¼ tsp.	1 mL
Baguette, cut into 1 inch (2.5 cm) slices	1	1

Mix first 6 ingredients well in bowl.

Divide olive mixture evenly among the bread slices. Garnish with reserved olive slices. Place on ungreased baking sheet. Bake in 350°F (175°C) oven for 15 minutes. Serve hot. Makes 20 snacks.

1 snack: 120 Calories; 4 g Protein; 5.4 g Total Fat; 14 g Carbohydrate; 288 mg Sodium

Pictured on page 42.

Zucchini Bites

An easy one-bowl recipe with mild Parmesan flavor. ☺ These freeze very well. Cut while still partially frozen.

Large eggs	4	4
Cooking oil	⅓ cup	75 mL
Chopped onion	¾ cup	175 mL
Grated Parmesan cheese	½ cup	125 mL
Parsley flakes	1½ tsp.	7 mL
Seasoning salt	½ tsp.	2 mL
Dried whole oregano	½ tsp.	2 mL
Garlic powder	½ tsp.	2 mL
Salt	½ tsp.	2 mL
Pepper	⅛ tsp.	0.5 mL
Thinly sliced small zucchini, with peel	3 cups	750 mL
Biscuit mix	1 cup	250 mL

Beat eggs in bowl. Stir in remaining 11 ingredients in order given. Turn into greased 9 x 13 inch (22 x 33 cm) pan. Bake in 350°F (175°C) oven for about 35 minutes until golden. Let stand for 2 minutes before cutting. Cuts into 54 squares.

1 square: 31 Calories; 1 g Protein; 2.2 g Total Fat; 2 g Carbohydrate; 77 mg Sodium

Pictured below.

Veggie Pizza Squares, page 44   Cheese Nuggets, page 52   Zucchini Bites, above

Veggie Pizza Squares

Lots of color, depending on what veggies you choose.
🕐 *Bake the crust the day before. Prepare the topping and vegetables in the morning. Assemble just before serving.*

Refrigerator crescent-style rolls (8 per tube)	11½ oz.	325 g
Topping:		
Non-fat spreadable cream cheese	8 oz.	225 g
Low-fat salad dressing (or mayonnaise)	½ cup	125 mL
Envelope ranch-style salad dressing mix	1 × 1 oz.	1 × 28 g
Vegetables:		
Finely chopped celery	2 tbsp.	30 mL
Finely chopped red pepper	⅓ cup	75 mL
Finely chopped green pepper	⅓ cup	75 mL
Finely chopped radish	3 tbsp.	50 mL
Finely chopped green onion	3 tbsp.	50 mL
Finely chopped fresh mushrooms	3 tbsp.	50 mL
Finely chopped cauliflower	3 tbsp.	50 mL
Finely chopped broccoli	3 tbsp.	50 mL
Grated carrot	3 tbsp.	50 mL

Separate crescent rolls and press into lightly greased 9 x 13 inch (22 x 33 cm) pan, covering bottom to form crust. Bake in 350°F (175°C) oven for 10 to 12 minutes until lightly browned. Cool.

Topping: Mix all 3 ingredients well in bowl. Spread over cooled crust.

Vegetables: The vegetables given are a guide. You will need a total of about 2 cups (500 mL). Be sure to include some red color for appearance. Mix well. Sprinkle over topping. Press vegetables into topping. Refrigerate. Cuts into 48 squares.

1 square: 33 Calories; 1 g Protein; 1.1 g Total Fat; 5 g Carbohydrate; 121 mg Sodium

Pictured on page 43.

To clean the garbage disposal in your sink, pour ½ cup (125 mL) salt into the disposal. Turn it on for several seconds, with the water running. To freshen the odor in the disposal, grind orange or lemon peels, with the water running, until well ground.

Bottom Left: Crab Finger Puffs, page 46   Top Left: Bagel Bites, page 44

Bagel Bites

Extra quick to whip up. Simply cut bagels into small portions, spread and serve. 🕐 *Make either, or both, toppings in the morning to allow flavors to blend.*

Pumpernickel (or other) bagels	3	3
Dill Topping:		
Cream cheese, softened	4 oz.	125 g
Dill weed	¼ tsp.	1 mL
Olive Topping:		
Processed cheese spread	½ cup	125 mL
Pimiento-stuffed olives, cut into 3 slices each	8	8

Cut each bagel into 8 wedges.

Dill Topping: Mash cream cheese and dill weed together until creamy. Spread dab on each bagel wedge. Makes 24 bites.

Olive Topping: Spread each bagel wedge with cheese. Lay 1 olive slice on top. Makes 24 wedges.

1 wedge with 1 tsp. (5 mL) dill topping: 50 Calories; 1 g Protein; 2 g Total Fat; 6 g Carbohydrate; 105 mg Sodium

Pictured above.

Center: Mustard Dip, page 26   Top Right: Nifty Nibbles, below   Bottom Right: Little Ham Bites, below

Nifty Nibbles

These have a bite to them that can be made milder by using less cayenne pepper.
☺ Make ahead and freeze.

Hard margarine (or butter), softened	½ cup	125 mL
Envelope dry onion soup mix, stirred before dividing	½ × 1½ oz.	½ × 42 g
Grated sharp Cheddar cheese	1 cup	250 mL
Cayenne pepper	¼ tsp.	1 mL
All-purpose flour	1 cup	250 mL

Cream first 4 ingredients together in bowl.

Mix in flour. If too sticky to roll, add a bit more flour. Roll out ¼ inch (6 mm) thick on lightly floured surface. Cut with your favorite cookie cutter. Arrange on ungreased baking sheet with sides. Bake in 350°F (175°C) oven for 8 to 10 minutes. Makes about 40 appetizers, using a 1¾ inch (4.5 cm) cookie cutter.

1 appetizer: 47 Calories; 1 g Protein; 3.5 g Total Fat; 3 g Carbohydrate; 94 mg Sodium

Pictured above.

Little Ham Bites

Serve hot with picks and Mustard Dip, page 26. Excellent flavor with or without the dip. ☺ Make these ahead and refrigerate until ready to bake. These freeze well.

Canned flakes of ham, drained	6½ oz.	184 g
Ground pork	½ lb.	225 g
Chopped green onion	¼ cup	60 mL
Water chestnuts, finely chopped	½ cup	125 mL
Fine dry bread crumbs	¼ cup	60 mL
Large egg, fork-beaten	1	1
Water	3 tbsp.	50 mL
Garlic powder	¼ tsp.	1 mL

Measure all 8 ingredients into bowl. Mix well. Form into 1 inch (2.5 cm) balls. Arrange on ungreased baking sheet with sides. Bake in 375°F (190°C) oven for 10 to 15 minutes until cooked through. May also be browned in 2 tbsp. (30 mL) hot cooking oil in frying pan. Makes about 60 appetizers.

1 appetizer: 17 Calories; 1 g Protein; 0.9 g Total Fat; 1 g Carbohydrate; 49 mg Sodium

Pictured above.

Crab Finger Puffs

Golden, crispy packets. ☉ Ideal to prepare in the morning and bake just before serving.

Light cream cheese, softened	8 oz.	250 g
Grated onion	2 tbsp.	30 mL
Canned crabmeat, drained and cartilage removed	4.2 oz.	120 g
Fine dry bread crumbs	2 tbsp.	30 mL
Salt	¼ tsp.	1 mL
Garlic powder	¹⁄₁₆ tsp.	0.5 mL
Package wonton wrappers	1 lb.	454 g

Cooking oil, for deep-frying

Mash cream cheese in bowl. Work in onion, crabmeat, bread crumbs, salt and garlic powder.

Place 1 tsp. (5 mL) mixture in center of each wonton wrapper. Dampen edges of wonton with water. Fold 1 corner at a time to center, pressing to seal well. Cover with damp tea towel until ready to cook.

Deep-fry in hot 375°F (190°C) cooking oil for about 2 minutes until browned. Drain on paper towel. Cool. Refrigerate in covered container. To serve, arrange on ungreased baking sheet. Heat in 450°F (230°C) oven for about 4 minutes until hot. Makes 54 puffs.

1 puff: 52 Calories; 1 g Protein; 3.7 g Total Fat; 3 g Carbohydrate; 109 mg Sodium

Pictured on page 44.

Whenever possible, make canapés or other appetizers small enough to be eaten in one mouthful. This eliminates the need for plates and is less messy for your guests.

Little Green Munchkins

Makes a large number, but they are so good they will disappear fast. Recipe may be halved. ☉ To freeze, prepare and shape into balls.

Frozen chopped broccoli	2 × 10 oz.	2 × 300 g
Boiling water		
Large eggs	6	6
Onion flakes	2 tbsp.	30 mL
Parsley flakes	1 tsp.	5 mL
Poultry seasoning	½ tsp.	2 mL
Salt	½ tsp.	2 mL
Pepper	¼ tsp.	1 mL
Fine dry bread crumbs	2 cups	500 mL
Grated Parmesan cheese	1 cup	250 mL
Hard margarine (or butter), softened	½ cup	125 mL
Milk	¼ cup	60 mL

Cook broccoli in boiling water until tender. Drain well. Chop finely.

Beat eggs in bowl. Add next 5 ingredients. Beat.

Add bread crumbs, cheese, margarine and milk to egg mixture. Add broccoli. Mix well. Let stand for 10 minutes for easier rolling. Shape into balls using 1 tbsp. (15 mL) for each. Arrange on greased baking sheet with sides. Bake in 350°F (175°C) oven for 15 minutes, or if frozen, for 20 minutes. Makes 85 munchkins.

1 munchkin: 35 Calories; 2 g Protein; 2.0 g Total Fat; 3 g Carbohydrate; 79 mg Sodium

Pictured on page 47.

1. Salmon Mousse, page 48
2. Burnt Sugar Brie, page 49
3. Cheese Flake Crisps, page 49
4. Little Green Munchkins, page 46
5. Cheese Log, page 52

Salmon Mousse

*If your entertaining is on a small scale, this may
be easily divided in half. Serve on crackers or in
toast cups. ☺ Must be made ahead to set.*

Envelopes unflavored gelatin	2 × ¼ oz.	2 × 7 g
Water	1½ cups	375 mL
Non-fat sour cream	1 cup	250 mL
Low-fat salad dressing (or mayonnaise)	1 cup	250 mL
Dill weed	½ tsp.	2 mL
Onion powder	½ tsp.	2 mL
Celery salt	½ tsp.	2 mL
Canned salmon, drained, skin and round bones removed, flaked (red is best for color)	2 × 7½ oz.	2 × 213 g
Finely chopped English cucumber, with peel	1 cup	250 mL

Sprinkle gelatin over water in saucepan. Let stand for at
least 1 minute. Heat and stir until gelatin is dissolved.
Remove from heat. Cool.

Mix next 5 ingredients well in bowl. When gelatin has
cooled thoroughly but not thickened, add to sour cream
mixture. Mix. Refrigerate, stirring and scraping sides of
bowl occasionally while thickening.

Fold in salmon and cucumber. Pour into 5 cup (1.25 L)
mold. Chill until firm. Unmold onto serving plate.
Makes 5 cups (1.25 L) mousse.

1 tbsp. (15 mL) mousse: 19 Calories; 1 g Protein; 1.3 g Total Fat; 1 g Carbohydrate;
54 mg Sodium

Pictured on page 47.

Wooden cutting boards start to retain odors
after a while. To freshen, pour on a generous
amount of salt. Rub lightly with a damp cloth,
then rinse clean and dry.

Crab Appetizers

Crab Appetizers

*Very quick and easy. The red and white color is very
attractive. ☺ Have seafood sauce prepared in the refrigerator.
When ready to serve, arrange crackers in serving container
beside covered cheese. Assemble at a moment's notice.*

Seafood Sauce:		
Chili sauce	¾ cup	175 mL
Sweet pickle relish	3 tbsp.	50 mL
Prepared horseradish	½ tsp.	2 mL
Worcestershire sauce	½ tsp.	2 mL
Onion powder	⅛ tsp.	0.5 mL
Garlic powder	⅛ tsp.	0.5 mL
Cream cheese, room temperature	8 oz.	250 g
Canned crabmeat, drained and cartilage removed	4.2 oz.	120 g

Seafood Sauce: Stir first 6 ingredients together in bowl.
Makes 1 cup (250 mL) sauce.

Lay cream cheese on serving plate. Cover with crabmeat.
Pour sauce over all.

1 tbsp. (15 mL) cheese mixture with 1 tsp. (5 mL) sauce: 43 Calories; 2 g Protein;
3.5 g Total Fat; 2 g Carbohydrate; 123 mg Sodium

Pictured above.

Shrimp Tartlets

Hot party appetizers are the first to need refilling. ☺ These freeze well. Reheat in 325°F (160°C) oven for 15 to 20 minutes if thawed or 30 to 40 minutes if still frozen.

Pastry:

Hard margarine (or butter), softened	½ cup	125 mL
Cream cheese, softened	4 oz.	125 g
All-purpose flour	1 cup	250 mL

Filling:

Cooked tiny shrimp (or 1 can 4 oz., 113 g, rinsed and drained)	¾ cup	175 mL
Large egg	1	1
Chopped chives	1 tbsp.	15 mL
Onion powder	¼ tsp.	1 mL
Dill weed	¼ tsp.	1 mL
Salt	¼ tsp.	1 mL
Pepper	1/16 tsp.	0.5 mL
Milk	½ cup	125 mL
Grated Swiss cheese	1 cup	250 mL

Pastry: Mix margarine, cream cheese and flour in bowl until smooth. Divide into 24 equal balls. Press into ungreased mini-muffin or tart pans about 1½ inch (3.8 cm) wide at top. Press on bottom and up sides.

Filling: Divide shrimp among pastry-lined cups.

Put remaining 8 ingredients into blender. Process until smooth. Pour over shrimp. Bake in 350°F (175°C) oven for 20 to 25 minutes until set. Makes 24 tartlets.

1 tartlet: 103 Calories; 4 g Protein; 7.6 g Total Fat; 5 g Carbohydrate; 116 mg Sodium

Pictured below.

Shrimp Tartlets

Burnt Sugar Brie

Beautiful dark sauce over the white round of cheese. Serve with a cocktail and savory crackers. ☺ The sugar syrup can be made ahead, ready to pour over heated Brie at serving time.

Granulated sugar	1 cup	250 mL
Water	½ cup	125 mL
Brie cheese round	4 oz.	125 g

Spread sugar in large frying pan over medium-low. Stir occasionally as it melts. Heat until melted and a dark butterscotch color. Remove from heat.

Add ¼ of the water. It will sputter furiously. Stir. Add remaining water. Return to medium heat. Stir until dissolved and smooth. Cool. Pour into jar to store in cupboard. Makes ⅔ cup (150 mL) sugar syrup.

When ready to serve, place cheese on plate. Heat in microwave on high (100%) for 20 to 30 seconds. Pour ½ of sugar syrup over cheese, allowing it to run down sides. Pour remaining ½ over cheese, once your guests have started feasting, or keep remaining syrup for another time.

1 tbsp. (15 mL) Brie plus ½ tbsp. (7 mL) syrup: 95 Calories; 3 g Protein; 4.0 g Total Fat; 12 g Carbohydrate; 91 mg Sodium

Pictured on page 47.

Cheese Flake Crisps

Yellow and crunchy. Make these up in no time. ☺ These freeze well.

Container of sharp cold pack Cheddar cheese (such as Imperial)	8 oz.	250 g
Hard margarine (or butter), softened	1 cup	250 mL
All-purpose flour	2 cups	500 mL
Coarsely crushed flakes of corn cereal	2 cups	500 mL

Mash cheese and margarine together in bowl. Add flour. Mix.

Work in crushed cereal. Roll into 1¼ inch (3 cm) balls. Arrange on ungreased baking sheet. Press down with floured fork. Bake in 350°F (175°C) oven for about 15 minutes. Makes 24 crisps.

1 crisp: 186 Calories; 4 g Protein; 11.7 g Total Fat; 16 g Carbohydrate; 242 mg Sodium

Pictured on page 47.

Stack O' Cheese

Not only is this a a pretty conversation piece, but it is also a perfect hostess gift. Serve with a cocktail spreader and basketful of crackers. ☺ Place in plastic bag or container to store. Refrigerate or freeze. Allow to come to room temperature before serving.

Bottom Layer:

Cream cheese, softened	8 oz.	250 g
Grated sharp Cheddar cheese	1½ cups	375 mL
Worcestershire sauce	1 tsp.	5 mL
Onion powder	¼ tsp.	1 mL
Cayenne pepper	1/16 tsp.	0.5 mL

Middle Layer:

Cream cheese, softened	8 oz.	250 g
Grated Swiss Cheese	1½ cups	375 mL
Onion powder	¼ tsp.	1 mL

Top Layer:

Cream cheese, softened	8 oz.	250 g
Grated port wine (or claret Cheddar) cheese	1½ cups	375 mL
Finely chopped pecans	1 cup	250 mL

Bottom Layer: Combine all 5 ingredients in bowl. Mash together and mix well. Shape into 5½ inch (14 cm) circle on waxed paper. May be chilled briefly for easier shaping.

Middle Layer: Combine all 3 ingredients in clean bowl. Mash together and mix well. Shape into 5½ inch (14 cm) circle on waxed paper. Carefully place on bottom layer.

Top Layer: Mash together and mix both cheeses in clean bowl. Shape into 5½ inch (14 cm) circle on waxed paper. Carefully place on second layer.

Coat sides and top generously with pecans. Makes about 6 cups (1.5 L).

1 tbsp. (15 mL) serving: 55 Calories; 2 g Protein; 5.1 g Total Fat; 1 g Carbohydrate; 49 mg Sodium

Pictured on page 51.

Cheese Sticks

Chili Rolls

Pretty little pinwheels with a creamy filling. Wrap the rolls separately and remove from fridge as needed. ☺ These can be made one or two days ahead.

Cream cheese, softened	12 oz.	375 g
Low-fat salad dressing (or mayonnaise)	2 tbsp.	30 mL
Canned chopped green chilies, drained	4 oz.	114 mL
Onion powder	¼ tsp.	1 mL
Celery salt	¼ tsp.	1 mL
Finely chopped green onion	3 tbsp.	50 mL
Flour tortillas, 8 inch (20 cm)	6	6

Mix first 6 ingredients well in bowl.

Spread ⅓ cup (75 mL) cream cheese mixture over each tortilla. Roll up snugly like a jelly roll. Cover with plastic wrap. Chill. To serve, cut into ½ inch (12 mm) slices. Arrange on serving plate. Makes about 72 slices.

1 slice: 29 Calories; 1 g Protein; 2.0 g Total Fat; 2 g Carbohydrate; 35 mg Sodium

Pictured on page 51.

Cheese Sticks

A lovely golden yellow color. Easy to shape as you like. ☺ Make up to one week ahead and store in covered container, or freeze well in advance.

Grated sharp Cheddar cheese	1½ cups	375 mL
Hard margarine (or butter), softened	½ cup	125 mL
Water	¼ cup	60 mL
Dried whole oregano	½ tsp.	2 mL
Salt	¼ tsp.	1 mL
Cayenne pepper	⅛ tsp.	0.5 mL
All-purpose flour	1½ cups	375 mL

Place first 6 ingredients in bowl. Beat well.

Gradually work in flour. Roll out on lightly floured surface about ¼ inch (6 mm) thick. Cut into 3 x ¾ inch (7.5 x 2 cm) strips. Arrange on ungreased baking sheet with sides. Bake in 400°F (205°C) oven for 12 to 15 minutes until crisp. Makes 48 sticks.

1 stick: 48 Calories; 1 g Protein; 3.3 g Total Fat; 3 g Carbohydrate; 61 mg Sodium

Pictured on this page.

Left: Chili Rolls, page 50   Bottom Center: Cheese Bake, below   Top Center: Stack O' Cheese, page 50   Right: Cheesy Ham Ball, below

Cheese Bake

A rich treat. Serve hot as a spread with taco chips, toast points or crackers. Recipe can easily be halved. ☼ Cube and grate the cheeses in the morning. Cover and refrigerate until ready to assemble.

Process cheese loaf (such as Velveeta), cubed	1 lb.	454 g
Grated medium Cheddar cheese	2 cups	500 mL
Large eggs	4	4
Creamed cottage cheese	1 cup	250 mL
All-purpose flour	1 tbsp.	15 mL
Onion salt	¼ tsp.	1 mL

Scatter cheese cubes in greased 9 x 13 inch (22 x 33 cm) pan or 12 inch (30 cm) quiche dish. Sprinkle Cheddar cheese over top.

Measure remaining 4 ingredients into small bowl. Beat together well. Pour over cheese. Bake, uncovered, in 350°F (175°C) oven for 30 to 35 minutes. Makes about 5 cups (1.25 L).

1 tbsp. (15 mL) serving: 35 Calories; 2 g Protein; 2.6 g Total Fat; 1 g Carbohydrate; 124 mg Sodium

Pictured above.

Cheesy Ham Ball

This is a nice pink ball that doesn't require a coating. Serve with assorted crackers. ☼ Make ahead and refrigerate for up to two days, or freeze.

Canned flakes of ham, drained and broken up	2 × 6½ oz.	2 × 184 g
Cream cheese, softened	8 oz.	250 g
Low-fat salad dressing (or mayonnaise)	1 tbsp.	15 mL
Parsley flakes	2 tsp.	10 mL
Chopped chives	1 tbsp.	15 mL
Dry mustard	¼ tsp.	1 mL
Cayenne pepper	¼ tsp.	1 mL

Mix all 7 ingredients well in bowl. Shape into ball. Makes about 1⅔ cups (400 mL).

1 tbsp. (15 mL) serving: 81 Calories; 4 g Protein; 7.3 g Total Fat; trace Carbohydrate; 265 mg Sodium

Pictured above.

Blue Cheesecake

Garnish with sour cream. Serve with assorted crackers and breads, or serve in wedges as a first course.
⊕ This can be prepared the day before and refrigerated.

Fine dry bread crumbs	2 tbsp.	30 mL
Grated Parmesan cheese	1 tbsp.	15 mL
Bacon slices, diced	8	8
Finely chopped onion	1 cup	250 mL
Cream cheese, softened	3 × 8 oz.	3 × 250 g
Blue cheese, crumbled	4 oz.	113 g
Large eggs	4	4
Sour cream	½ cup	125 mL
Hot pepper sauce	¼ tsp.	1 mL

Stir bread crumbs and Parmesan cheese together in small bowl. Grease sides and bottom of 9 inch (22 cm) springform pan. Coat with crumb mixture, shaking off excess.

Sauté bacon in frying pan for 3 to 4 minutes. Add onion, continuing to sauté until onion is soft and bacon is cooked. Drain.

Beat cream cheese, blue cheese and 1 egg together in mixing bowl until smooth. Little bits of blue cheese will remain. Add remaining eggs, 1 at a time, beating only to blend. Add sour cream. Beat to mix. Mix in hot pepper sauce and bacon mixture. Pour into prepared pan. Bake in 325°F (160°C) oven for 1 to 1½ hours. Center will quiver slightly when pan is shaken. Immediately run sharp knife around top edge to allow it to settle evenly. Cool. Cover and refrigerate 4 to 5 hours or overnight. Serves 20.

1 serving: 197 Calories; 7 g Protein; 17.9 g Total Fat; 3 g Carbohydrate; 255 mg Sodium

Pictured below.

Blue Cheesecake

Cheese Log

Pale yellow with flecks of white. Spreads easily. ⊕ Make ahead and freeze. Roll in parsley just before serving.

Grated Edam (or Gouda) cheese	2 cups	500 mL
Non-fat sour cream	⅔ cup	150 mL
Prepared mustard	1 tsp.	5 mL
Worcestershire sauce	¼ tsp.	1 mL
Parsley flakes (or chopped nuts), for rolling (optional)		

Combine first 4 ingredients in bowl. Mash together. Shape into log.

Sprinkle parsley on waxed paper. Roll cheese log in parsley. Chill in plastic bag. Makes a 1¼ cups (300 mL) log.

1 tbsp. (15 mL) serving: 51 Calories; 4 g Protein; 3.8 g Total Fat; 1 g Carbohydrate; 140 mg Sodium

Pictured on page 47.

Cheese Nuggets

Simple layers of brown, yellow and white.
⊕ To make these ahead, a damp cloth should be placed over the squares, followed by plastic wrap or foil. This will keep them fresh until serving time.

Thin dark rye (or pumpernickel) bread slices	4	4
Hard margarine (or butter), softened	2 tbsp.	30 mL
White process cheese slices	2	2
Orange process cheese slice	1	1

Cut bread slices the same size as cheese slices. Butter 2 slices on 1 side of each. Butter remaining 2 slices on both sides. Stack as follows: 1 slice bread, buttered side up; 1 white cheese slice; 1 slice bread, buttered both sides; 1 orange cheese slice; 1 slice bread, buttered both sides; 1 white cheese slice; 1 slice bread buttered side down. Wrap in plastic. Chill. Cut into 16 squares. Push cocktail pick into each piece. Makes 16 nuggets.

1 nugget: 54 Calories; 2 g Protein; 3.3 g Total Fat; 4 g Carbohydrate; 145 mg Sodium

Pictured on page 43.

Beverages

As soon as you welcome your guests into your home and offer them a drink, you make them feel at ease. The kinds of beverages you choose to serve may depend upon the reason for the get-together, the formality of the event, or even just the weather outside. After all, sometimes a cup of rich hot chocolate at the end of a skating party can be more welcome than a frosty glass of iced tea. The following variety of beverage recipes allows you the chance to offer whatever is appropriate for the moment.

And don't just settle for the usual offering! This is a wonderful opportunity for you, as host, to suggest something a little bit unique—such as a flavorful homemade liqueur!

Cranberry Iced Tea

Ready to refresh you at a moment's notice. ☻ *Store in the refrigerator for up to two weeks.*

Boiling water	4 cups	1 L
Orange pekoe tea bags	4	4
Granulated sugar	½ cup	125 mL
Cranberry cocktail	2 cups	500 mL
Prepared orange juice	1 cup	250 mL
Lemon juice	¼ cup	60 mL

Pour boiling water over tea bags in saucepan or pitcher. Cover. Let steep for 5 minutes. Squeeze bags to release any tea. Remove tea bags.

Add sugar. Stir until dissolved. Add cranberry cocktail, orange juice and lemon juice. Chill. Makes about 7 cups (1.75 L) iced tea.

1 cup (250 mL) iced tea: 122 Calories; trace Protein; 0.1 g Total Fat; 31 g Carbohydrate; 8 mg Sodium

Pictured on page 61.

Rhubarb Punch

Beautiful clear ruby color. ☻ *Rhubarb juice can be made anytime and frozen. Simply thaw and add remaining ingredients.*

Finely chopped rhubarb	4 cups	1 L
Boiling water	6 cups	1.5 L
Prepared orange juice	2 tbsp.	30 mL
Lemon juice	2 tbsp.	30 mL
Granulated sugar	1 cup	250 mL
Water	1 cup	250 mL

Measure rhubarb into large bowl. Pour boiling water over top. Cover. Let stand overnight. Strain through cheesecloth into pitcher. Squeeze out juice. There should be about 7¾ cups (1.9 L).

Add orange juice and lemon juice.

Combine sugar and second amount of water in saucepan. Stir. Bring to a boil. Cool. Add to rhubarb juice. Stir. Taste for sweetness, adding a bit more sugar if needed. Chill to serve. Makes about 9 cups (2.25 L) punch.

1 cup (250 mL) punch: 99 Calories; trace Protein; trace Total Fat; 26 g Carbohydrate; 1 mg Sodium

Pictured below.

Grape Punch, page 54

Rhubarb Punch, above

Cranberry Bowl

Rose-colored. So easy and fast. ☺ *Combine and chill first three ingredients. Have garnishes ready in fridge. Add ginger ale just before serving.*

Frozen concentrated orange juice	½ × 12½ oz.	½ × 355 mL
Cranberry cocktail	6 cups	1.5 L
Pineapple juice	19 oz.	540 mL
Ginger ale	8 cups	2 L
Cranberries, fresh or frozen, for garnish		
Ice cubes		

Combine concentrated orange juice, cranberry cocktail and pineapple juice in punch bowl. Chill.

Just before serving, add ginger ale. Stir gently.

Float a few cranberries on top. Pour over ice cubes in glasses. Makes 16 cups (4 L) punch.

1 cup (250 mL) punch: 143 Calories; trace Protein; 0.1 g Total Fat; 36 g Carbohydrate; 14 mg Sodium

Pictured on page 40.

Coffee Punch

Rich mocha color. Mild coffee flavor with a hint of chocolate. ☺ *The first five ingredients can be prepared ahead of time and refrigerated. Add frozen yogurt when ready to serve.*

Cold strong coffee	5 cups	1.25 L
Chocolate sundae topping	1 cup	250 mL
Milk	8 cups	2 L
Granulated sugar	½ cup	125 mL
Vanilla	2 tsp.	10 mL
Frozen vanilla yogurt (or vanilla ice cream)	2 cups	500 mL

Combine first 5 ingredients in punch bowl. Stir until sugar dissolves.

Add frozen yogurt. Stir lightly. Makes 16 cups (4 L) punch.

1 cup (250 mL) punch: 189 Calories; 6 g Protein; 5.5 g Total Fat; 30 g Carbohydrate; 100 mg Sodium

Pictured on this page.

Coffee Punch, this page

Grape Punch

Soft purple color. Smooth drink. ☺ *Make ahead and keep in the refrigerator.*

White grape juice	4½ cups	1.1 L
Purple grape juice	½ cup	125 mL
Lemon-lime soft drink	2 cups	500 mL
Lime slices, for garnish		

Stir both grape juices together in punch bowl or pitcher. Add soft drink. Pour over ice in glasses.

Garnish with lime slice on edge of each glass. Makes 7 cups (1.75 L) punch.

1 cup (250 mL) punch: 132 Calories; 1 g Protein; 0.1 g Total Fat; 33 g Carbohydrate; 13 mg Sodium

Pictured on page 53.

Frappé, page 56   Mocha Mugs, below   Minted Hot Chocolate, below

Mocha Mugs

Delicious blend of coffee and chocolate. ☺ *Keep the mix on hand in covered container, ready to treat unexpected—or expected—guests.*

Granulated sugar	½ cup	125 mL
Vanilla	1 tsp.	5 mL
Skim milk powder	1 cup	250 mL
Powdered coffee whitener	2 tbsp.	30 mL
Cocoa	¼ cup	60 mL
Instant coffee granules, crushed	¼ cup	60 mL
Boiling water	1 cup	250 mL
Frozen whipped topping (in a tub), thawed (optional)		
Grated chocolate (optional)		

Combine sugar and vanilla in covered container. Shake well to mix.

Add next 4 ingredients. Stir together.

For 1 serving, put 3 tbsp. (50 mL) dry mix into mug. Add boiling water. Stir. Garnish with whipped topping and chocolate. Makes 2 cups (500 mL) dry mix, enough for 10 servings.

1 serving: 103 Calories; 5 g Protein; 0.7 g Total Fat; 20 g Carbohydrate; 71 mg Sodium

Pictured above.

Minted Hot Chocolate

Multiply this recipe by the number of guests. Very simple but extraordinary. ☺ *Keep grated chocolate in the refrigerator for any occasion.*

Chocolate milk, heated	¾ cup	175 mL
Peppermint schnapps (or ⅛ tsp., 0.5 mL, peppermint flavoring)	1 tbsp.	15 mL
Frozen whipped topping (in a tub), thawed, (or whipped cream)	2 tbsp.	30 mL
Grated chocolate, sprinkle		
Fresh mint, for garnish		

Heat milk in small saucepan until scalding hot but not boiling. Add schnapps. Use heavy medium saucepan or double boiler when making several drinks. Pour into serving mug.

Garnish with whipped topping. Sprinkle with grated chocolate. Garnish with mint. Serves 1.

1 serving: 223 Calories; 6 g Protein; 6.3 g Total Fat; 28 g Carbohydrate; 120 mg Sodium

Pictured above.

Frappé

Cool and refreshing.Very smooth. Pronounced frap-AY.
☺ This can be made ahead and frozen. Simply thaw
and process in blender when ready to serve.

Cold prepared coffee	1½ cups	375 mL
Chocolate syrup	¼ cup	60 mL
Vanilla ice cream	1½ cups	375 mL
Crushed ice	½ cup	125 mL

Put all 4 ingredients into blender. Process until smooth. Makes 4 servings, ⅔ cup (150 mL) each.

1 serving: 126 Calories; 2 g Protein; 4.9 g Total Fat; 20 g Carbohydrate; 93 mg Sodium

Pictured on page 55.

Crabapple Liqueur

Glistening clear. ☺ Make at least five weeks ahead.
Store on the shelf in an airtight container.

Crabapples, cut in half	4 qts.	4 L
Granulated sugar	4 cups	1 L
Vodka	26 oz.	810 mL

Fill 4 quart (4 L) container ¾ full with crab apples. Pour sugar over top. Add vodka. Add remaining ¼ of crabapples to fill. Put lid on. Let stand on counter or in cupboard. Turn jar upside down then right side up, once a day, for 7 days. Let stand 1 month. Strain through sieve, discarding crabapples. Strain liqueur through 4 layers of cheesecloth. Makes 6 cups (1.5 L) liqueur.

2 tbsp. (30 mL) liqueur: 114 Calories; trace Protein; 0.1 g Total Fat; 20 g Carbohydrate; 1 mg Sodium

Pictured below.

Variation: Gin may be used in place of vodka.

Raspberry Liqueur

Crabapple Liqueur

Apricot Liqueur

Serve as a beverage or over ice cream or custard.
Adds color and flavor. ☺ Make at least two months ahead.
Store on the shelf in an airtight container.

Dried apricots, quartered	1 lb.	454 g
Vodka	4⅓ cups	1.1 L
Granulated sugar	4 cups	1 L

Combine all 3 ingredients in glass container. Cover and let stand for 6 to 8 weeks. Shake jar lightly once a week. Strain through double cheesecloth. Discard apricots. Makes 5 cups (1.25 L) liqueur.

2 tbsp. (30 mL) liqueur: 138 Calories; trace Protein; trace Total Fat; 21 g Carbohydrate; 1 mg Sodium

Pictured on page 57.

Cranberry Liqueur

Clear and red. Use leftover cranberries in muffins.
☺ Make at least six weeks ahead. Store on
the shelf in an airtight container.

Cranberries, fresh or frozen, coarsely chopped	4 cups	1 L
Granulated sugar	3 cups	750 mL
Gin	2 cups	500 mL
Vanilla	1 tsp.	5 mL

Combine all 4 ingredients in jar. Put lid on. Let stand at room temperature for 6 weeks. Shake bottle well once a week. After 6 weeks, strain twice through 4 layers of cheesecloth. Makes 3⅓ cups (825 mL) liqueur.

2 tbsp. (30 mL) liqueur: 131 Calories; trace Protein; trace Total Fat; 24 g Carbohydrate; 1 mg Sodium

Pictured on page 57.

Raspberry Liqueur

Vibrant red color. ☺ Make at least three weeks ahead.
Store on the shelf in an airtight container.

Raspberries, fresh or frozen (unsweetened)	4 cups	1 L
Granulated sugar	3¼ cups	810 mL
Vodka	3⅓ cups	825 mL

Measure all 3 ingredients into 2 quart (2 L) bottle. Put lid on bottle. Let stand on counter or in cupboard. Gently turn jar upside down then right side up, once a day, for 3 weeks. Strain through double cheesecloth. Makes 7 cups (1.75 L) liqueur.

2 tbsp. (30 mL) liqueur: 78 Calories; trace Protein; trace Total Fat; 12 g Carbohydrate; trace Sodium

Pictured on this page.

Left: Cherry Brandy, below   Center: Apricot Liqueur, page 56   Bottom Right: Mint Liqueur, below   Top Right: Cranberry Liqueur, page 56

Cherry Brandy

Beautiful deep red color. Very clear. ☺ *Make at least three months ahead. Store on the shelf in an airtight container.*

Ripe, dark fresh cherries (about 6 cups, 1.5 L)	2 lbs.	900 g
Granulated sugar	3¹/₂ cups	875 mL
Brandy	3¹/₃ cups	825 mL

Poke cherries in several places with skewer or wooden pick. Layer cherries, with sugar, in large jar. Pour brandy over top. Put lid on bottle and store in cool, dark place. Shake bottle once a week for 2 to 3 months. Strain through double cheesecloth. Discard cherries. Makes 6¹/₂ cups (1.6 L) brandy.

¹/₄ cup (60 mL) brandy: 193 Calories; trace Protein; 0.2 g Total Fat; 31 g Carbohydrate; 1 mg Sodium

Pictured above.

Cherry Liqueur

Use vodka or gin rather than brandy.

Mint Liqueur

Just the right color and clarity. ☺ *Make at least one month ahead. Store on the shelf in an airtight container.*

Granulated sugar	1¹/₂ cups	375 mL
Water	³/₄ cup	175 mL
Vodka	1¹/₂ cups	375 mL
Lime juice	1 tbsp.	15 mL
Vanilla	1¹/₂ tsp.	7 mL
Peppermint flavoring	¹/₄ tsp.	1 mL
Green food coloring drops	5	5

Combine sugar and water in saucepan. Bring to a boil, stirring often. Simmer, covered, for 5 minutes. Cool.

Add remaining 5 ingredients. Stir. Let stand for 1 month before serving. Makes 3 cups (750 mL) liqueur.

2 tbsp. (30 mL) liqueur: 82 Calories; 0 g Protein; 0 g Total Fat; 13 g Carbohydrate; trace Sodium

Pictured above.

Breads & Quick Breads

Nothing is more welcome than the opportunity to enjoy a wonderfully warm, fresh piece of homemade bread—a real treat that your guests are certain to appreciate. There is a myth that homemade bread takes a lot of work, which means visitors to your home feel extra special that you went to so much trouble! In fact, breads and quick breads are simple to make and can be frozen after baking, ready to be pulled from the freezer at a moment's notice. Whether you are entertaining for brunch, dinner or just coffee, homemade bread is gladly received.

G' Morning Muffins

Perfect in the morning with a cup of coffee. ☺ Have the dry ingredients combined the night before. These freeze well.

Large egg	1	1
Canned crushed pineapple, drained, 6 tbsp. (100 mL) juice reserved	14 oz.	398 mL
Grated carrot	½ cup	125 mL
Cooking oil	¼ cup	60 mL
Reserved pineapple juice		
All-purpose flour	1½ cups	375 mL
Quick-cooking rolled oats (not instant)	¾ cup	175 mL
Brown sugar, packed	½ cup	125 mL
Baking powder	1 tbsp.	15 mL
Baking soda	1 tsp.	5 mL
Ground cinnamon	1 tsp.	5 mL
Salt	¼ tsp.	1 mL
Raisins	1/3 cup	75 mL

Stir first 5 ingredients together in medium bowl.

Combine remaining 8 ingredients in large bowl. Stir to distribute. Make a well in center. Pour carrot mixture into well. Stir just to moisten. Fill greased muffin cups almost full. Bake in 400°F (205°C) oven for 18 to 20 minutes until golden brown. Wooden pick inserted in center should come out clean. Let stand for 5 minutes. Remove from pan to rack to cool. Makes 12 muffins.

1 muffin: 175 Calories; 3 g Protein; 5 g Total Fat; 30 g Carbohydrate; 160 mg Sodium

Pictured on this page.

Rhubarb Muffins

Golden brown with chunks of red. Use either fresh or frozen rhubarb. ☺ These freeze well.

Cooking oil	⅓ cup	75 mL
Brown sugar, packed	1 cup	250 mL
Large egg	1	1
Vanilla	1¼ tsp.	6 mL
Sour milk (1 tbsp., 15 mL, lemon juice plus milk)	⅔ cup	150 mL
Rhubarb, cut into ¼ inch (6 mm) cubes (see Note)	1⅓ cups	325 mL
Chopped walnuts	⅓ cup	75 mL
All-purpose flour	1⅔ cups	400 mL
Baking powder	¾ tsp.	4 mL
Baking soda	¾ tsp.	4 mL
Salt	¼ tsp.	1 mL

Beat cooking oil and brown sugar together in bowl. Beat in egg. Add vanilla and sour milk. Mix.

Add rhubarb and walnuts. Stir.

Stir next 4 ingredients together in separate bowl. Add all at once to wet mixture. Stir just to moisten. Fill greased muffin cups almost full. Bake in 400°F (205°C) oven for 20 to 25 minutes until wooden pick inserted in center comes out clean. Let stand for 5 minutes. Remove from pan to rack to cool. Makes 1 dozen muffins.

1 muffin: 238 Calories; 3 g Protein; 9.6 g Total Fat; 35 g Carbohydrate; 171 mg Sodium

Note: If using frozen rhubarb, thaw completely and drain.

Pictured on page 59.

G' Morning Muffins

Rhubarb Muffins, page 58   Batter Ready Ginger Muffins, below   Batter Ready Bran Muffins, below

Batter Ready Ginger Muffins

Quick to make. ⏱ *Batter can be prepared three weeks ahead of time and kept in the refrigerator. These freeze well too.*

Hard margarine (or butter), softened	1½ cups	375 mL
Granulated sugar	1 cup	250 mL
Large eggs	4	4
Fancy (or cooking) molasses	1½ cups	375 mL
Buttermilk, fresh or reconstituted from powder	1 cup	250 mL
Vanilla	1½ tsp.	7 mL
All-purpose flour	5¼ cups	1.3 L
Ground cinnamon	1½ tsp.	7 mL
Ground ginger	1½ tsp.	7 mL
Ground nutmeg	½ tsp.	2 mL
Ground cloves	¼ tsp.	1 mL
Salt	¾ tsp.	4 mL
Baking soda	1 tbsp.	15 mL
Raisins	1½ cups	375 mL

Cream margarine and sugar together well in large bowl. Beat in eggs, 1 at a time. Add molasses. Beat to mix. Add buttermilk and vanilla. Mix.

Stir next 8 ingredients together well in separate bowl. Add to molasses mixture. Stir just to moisten. Store in covered container in refrigerator for up to 3 weeks. Fill greased muffin cups almost full. Bake in 400°F (205°C) oven for 15 to 20 minutes until wooden pick inserted in center comes out clean. Let stand for 5 minutes. Remove from pan to rack to cool. Makes 3 dozen muffins.

1 muffin: 233 Calories; 3 g Protein; 9.0 g Total Fat; 36 g Carbohydrate; 269 mg Sodium

Pictured above.

Batter Ready Bran Muffins

Breakfast, brunch or morning coffee becomes easier with this batter on hand. ⏱ *Bake them as you need, or bake the batch and freeze.*

All-bran cereal (not bran flakes)	6 cups	1.5 L
Boiling water	2 cups	500 mL
Hard margarine (or butter), softened	1 cup	250 mL
Granulated sugar	2 cups	500 mL
Brown sugar, packed	1 cup	250 mL
Large eggs	4	4
Buttermilk, fresh or reconstituted from powder	4 cups	1 L
All-purpose flour	5 cups	1.25 L
Baking soda	2 tbsp.	30 mL
Salt	1 tsp.	5 mL
Raisins (or chopped dates) optional	2 cups	500 mL

Combine cereal and boiling water in large bowl. Let stand.

Cream margarine and both sugars. Beat in eggs, 1 at a time. Add buttermilk. Mix.

Stir flour, baking soda and salt together in separate bowl. Add to batter. Add raisins. Stir just to moisten. Store in covered container in refrigerator for up to 6 weeks. Fill greased muffin cups almost full. Bake in 400°F (205°C) oven for 15 to 20 minutes until wooden pick inserted in center comes out clean. Let stand for 5 minutes. Remove from pan to rack to cool. Makes about 6 dozen muffins.

1 muffin: 129 Calories; 3 g Protein; 3.4 g Total Fat; 24 g Carbohydrate; 242 mg Sodium

Pictured above.

Zucchini Muffinettes

Moist and light in texture. A nice breakfast or brunch muffin. ⏱ Make ahead and freeze for unexpected coffee guests.

Large eggs	5	5
Cooking oil	1/4 cup	60 mL
Finely chopped onion	1 1/2 cups	375 mL
Grated sharp Cheddar cheese	3/4 cup	175 mL
Bacon slices, cooked crisp and crumbled	4	4
Grated zucchini, with peel, packed	2 3/4 cups	675 mL
All-purpose flour	1 cup	250 mL
Baking powder	1 1/2 tsp.	7 mL
Salt	1/2 tsp.	2 mL

Beat eggs together in bowl. Add next 5 ingredients. Stir together well.

Add flour, baking powder and salt. Fill greased mini-muffin pans almost full. Bake in 350°F (175°C) oven for about 30 minutes. Let stand for 5 minutes. Remove from pan to rack to cool. Makes 3 1/2 dozen mini-muffins.

1 mini-muffin: 48 Calories; 2 g Protein; 3.0 g Total Fat; 3 g Carbohydrate; 64 mg Sodium

Pictured on page 63.

Zucchini Squares

Leave cheese out of batter. Spread batter in greased 9 x 9 inch (22 x 22 cm) pan. Sprinkle with cheese. Bake in 350°F (175°C) oven for 30 to 40 minutes.

Flaky Biscuits

Great served with Freezer Marmalade, page 73. ⏱ Have dry ingredients ready the night before or make ahead and freeze.

All-purpose flour	2 cups	500 mL
Baking powder	1 tbsp.	15 mL
Baking soda	1/4 tsp.	1 mL
Salt	1/2 tsp.	2 mL
Hard margarine (or butter)	1/4 cup	60 mL
Plain yogurt	3/4 cup	175 mL
Milk	1/4 cup	60 mL

Measure first 5 ingredients into bowl. Cut in margarine until crumbly.

Add yogurt and milk. Stir to form a soft ball. Knead 6 times on lightly floured surface. Pat or roll out 3/4 inch (2 cm) thick. Cut into 2 1/2 inch (6.3 cm) rounds. Arrange on ungreased baking sheet. Bake in 375°F (190°C) oven for 10 to 12 minutes. Makes 12 biscuits.

1 biscuit: 131 Calories; 3 g Protein; 4.6 g Total Fat; 19 g Carbohydrate; 208 mg Sodium

Pictured on page 61.

Remember to make room in the front closet for guests' coats. If you are going to use a bed to pile extra coats onto, be sure to tidy the bedroom. Place a small arrangement of fresh flowers on the dresser or nightstand.

Ham Biscuits

Serve hot right from the oven! Small bits of ham throughout. ⏱ These freeze well.

All-purpose flour	2 cups	500 mL
Baking powder	1 tbsp.	15 mL
Baking soda	1/2 tsp.	2 mL
Salt	1/2 tsp.	2 mL
Hard margarine (or butter)	1/4 cup	60 mL
Canned flakes of ham, drained, liquid reserved	6 1/2 oz.	184 g
Reserved liquid, plus milk to make	3/4 cup	175 mL

Mix first 5 ingredients in bowl until crumbly.

Add ham. Stir together lightly.

Add reserved liquid plus milk to ham mixture. Stir to form a soft ball. Knead 6 to 8 times on lightly floured surface. Pat or roll out 3/4 inch (2 cm) thick. Cut into 2 inch (5 cm) rounds. Arrange on ungreased baking sheet. Bake in 425°F (220°C) oven for 12 to 15 minutes. Makes 16 biscuits.

1 biscuit: 121 Calories; 4 g Protein; 5.5 g Total Fat; 13 g Carbohydrate; 329 mg Sodium

Pictured on page 61.

1. Cranberry Iced Tea, page 53
2. Ham Biscuits, page 60
3. Flaky Biscuits, page 60
4. Whole Wheat Loaf, page 63
5. Freezer Marmalade, page 73

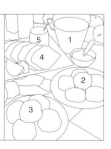

Herb Biscuits

Definite dill flavor with a hint of onion. Traditional "layered" look. ☺ Combine the dry ingredients in the morning or night before, or make ahead and freeze.

All-purpose flour	2 cups	500 mL
Granulated sugar	2 tsp.	10 mL
Baking powder	1 tbsp.	15 mL
Salt	½ tsp.	2 mL
Parsley flakes	½ tsp.	2 mL
Chopped chives	1 tsp.	5 mL
Dill weed	½ tsp.	2 mL
Cooking oil	3 tbsp.	50 mL
Milk	⅔ cup	150 mL

Measure first 7 ingredients into bowl. Stir. Make a well.

Add cooking oil and milk. Stir just to moisten. Knead 6 to 8 times on lightly floured surface. Pat or roll out ¾ inch (2 cm) thick. Cut into 2 inch (5 cm) rounds. Arrange on ungreased baking sheet. Bake in 400°F (205°C) oven for about 15 minutes. Makes 12 biscuits.

1 biscuit: 121 Calories; 3 g Protein; 3.8 g Total Fat; 19 g Carbohydrate; 125 mg Sodium

Pictured on page 63.

Whole Meal Biscuits

More like a crispy cracker than a biscuit. Sweet, but with the wheat and oat flavors coming through. ☺ These freeze well.

Whole wheat flour	1⅓ cups	325 mL
Quick-cooking rolled oats (not instant)	⅓ cup	75 mL
Brown sugar, packed	⅓ cup	75 mL
Baking powder	1 tsp.	5 mL
Salt	½ tsp.	2 mL
Hard margarine (or butter), softened	6 tbsp.	100 mL
Milk	¼ cup	60 mL

Combine first 6 ingredients in bowl. Cut in margarine until crumbly.

Add milk. Mix well. Add a bit more, if needed, to hold together to roll. Roll out to ¼ inch (6 mm) thickness on lightly floured surface. Cut into 3 inch (7.5 cm) rounds. Arrange on greased baking sheet. Bake in 350°F (175°C) oven for 20 to 25 minutes until lightly browned. Makes 12 biscuits.

1 biscuit: 136 Calories; 3 g Protein; 6.3 g Total Fat; 18 g Carbohydrate; 189 mg Sodium

Pictured on page 153.

Raisin Orange Biscuits

A great accompaniment with tea. ☺ Combine and cover the orange peel and raisins in the morning. Raisins will help keep peel soft. Or, make ahead and freeze.

All-purpose flour	2 cups	500 mL
Granulated sugar	2 tbsp.	30 mL
Baking powder	4 tsp.	20 mL
Salt	½ tsp.	2 mL
Hard margarine (or butter)	¼ cup	60 mL
Grated orange peel	1 tbsp.	15 mL
Raisins	½ cup	125 mL
Large egg, fork-beaten	1	1
Milk	½ cup	125 mL

Measure first 5 ingredients into bowl. Cut in margarine until crumbly.

Add orange peel and raisins. Stir together.

Add egg and milk. Stir to form a soft ball. Knead 6 times on lightly floured surface. Pat or roll out ¾ inch (2 cm) thick. Cut into 2 inch (5 cm) rounds. Arrange on ungreased baking sheet. Bake in 425°F (220°C) oven for about 12 minutes. Makes 16 biscuits.

1 biscuit: 120 Calories; 3 g Protein; 3.8 g Total Fat; 19 g Carbohydrate; 141 mg Sodium

Pictured on page 64.

Hot Biscuits

Light, fluffy texture. Serve these with any main course. ☺ These freeze well.

All-purpose flour	2 cups	500 mL
Baking powder	4 tsp.	20 mL
Cream of tartar	½ tsp.	2 mL
Salt	½ tsp.	2 mL
Granulated sugar	2 tsp.	10 mL
Hard margarine (or butter)	¼ cup	60 mL
Milk	¾ cup	175 mL
Milk, for brushing tops (optional)	1 tbsp.	15 mL

Measure first 6 ingredients into bowl. Cut in margarine until crumbly.

Add first amount of milk. Stir to form a soft ball. Pat or roll out ¾ inch (2 cm) thick on lightly floured surface. Cut into 2 inch (5 cm) rounds. Arrange on ungreased baking sheet.

Brush tops with second amount of milk. Bake in 450°F (230°C) oven for 12 to 15 minutes until risen and browned. Makes 12 biscuits.

1 biscuit: 129 Calories; 3 g Protein; 4.5 g Total Fat; 19 g Carbohydrate; 191 mg Sodium

Pictured on page 125.

Top: Prune Loaf, page 64
Center: Herb Biscuits, page 62
Bottom: Zucchini Muffinettes, page 60

Blueberry Loaf

Delicious blueberries throughout.
🕐 *Make ahead, with the glaze, and freeze.*

Hard margarine (or butter), softened	½ cup	125 mL
Granulated sugar	1 cup	250 mL
Large eggs	2	2
Buttermilk, fresh or reconstituted from powder	⅔ cup	150 mL
Grated peel of 1 medium lemon		
All-purpose flour	2 cups	500 mL
Baking powder	2 tsp.	10 mL
Salt	½ tsp.	2 mL
Blueberries, fresh or frozen	1½ cups	375 mL
All-purpose flour	1 tbsp.	15 mL
Glaze:		
Lemon juice	3 tbsp.	50 mL
Granulated sugar	¼ cup	60 mL

Cream margarine and sugar together well. Beat in eggs, 1 at a time. Add buttermilk and lemon peel. Mix.

Measure first amount of flour, baking powder and salt into separate bowl. Stir together well. Add to batter. Stir just to moisten.

Toss blueberries with second amount of flour in separate bowl. Add to batter, stirring gently and quickly. Turn into greased 9 x 5 x 3 inch (22 x 12.5 x 7.5 cm) loaf pan. Bake in 350°F (175°C) oven for about 1½ hours until wooden pick inserted in center comes out clean.

Glaze: Heat and stir lemon juice and second amount of sugar together in small saucepan until sugar is dissolved. Spoon evenly over top of hot loaf before removing from pan. Cool in pan for 10 minutes. Remove from pan to rack to cool. Wrap to store. Cuts into 18 slices.

1 slice: 192 Calories; 3 g Protein; 6.3 g Total Fat; 32 g Carbohydrate; 159 mg Sodium

Pictured below.

Whole Wheat Loaf

Does not contain yeast. Quick to prepare.
🕐 *Freezes well.*

Whole wheat flour	2 cups	500 mL
All-purpose flour	1 cup	250 mL
Granulated sugar	⅓ cup	75 mL
Baking soda	1 tsp.	5 mL
Salt	1 tsp.	5 mL
Buttermilk, fresh or reconstituted from powder	2 cups	500 mL

Measure first 5 ingredients into bowl. Mix.

Add buttermilk. Stir just to moisten. Turn into greased 9 x 5 x 3 inch (22 x 12.5 x 7.5 cm) loaf pan. Bake in 375°F (190°C) oven for 55 to 65 minutes until wooden pick inserted in center comes out clean. Let stand for 2 to 3 minutes. Remove from pan to rack to cool. Cuts into 16 slices.

1 slice: 114 Calories; 4 g Protein; 0.7 g Total Fat; 24 g Carbohydrate; 290 mg Sodium

Pictured on page 61.

Blueberry Loaf

Raisin Orange Biscuits, page 62   Hovis-Like Bread, page 65   Chocolate Orange Bread, page 65

Prune Loaf

A nice mild taste of spices. Firm but moist texture. ☉ Freezes well.

Hard margarine (or butter), softened	½ cup	125 mL
Granulated sugar	1 cup	250 mL
Large eggs	2	2
Puréed prunes (baby food)	½ cup	125 mL
All-purpose flour	1½ cups	375 mL
Baking soda	1 tsp.	5 mL
Salt	½ tsp.	2 mL
Ground cinnamon	½ tsp.	2 mL
Ground nutmeg	¼ tsp.	1 mL
Ground cloves	¼ tsp.	1 mL
Finely chopped pitted dried prunes	1 cup	250 mL
Chopped pecans (or walnuts)	½ cup	125 mL

Cream margarine and sugar together in bowl. Beat in eggs, 1 at a time. Add puréed prunes. Beat together to make a smooth mixture.

Stir next 6 ingredients together in separate bowl. Add to batter. Stir just to moisten.

Mix in prunes and pecans. Turn into greased 9 x 5 x 3 inch (22 x 12.5 x 7.5 cm) loaf pan. Bake in 350°F (175°C) oven for about 1 hour until wooden pick inserted in center comes out clean. Let stand for 10 minutes. Remove from pan to rack to cool. Cuts into 18 slices.

1 slice: 190 Calories; 2 g Protein; 8.5 g Total Fat; 27 g Carbohydrate; 224 mg Sodium

Pictured on page 63.

Apple Cherry Bread

Excellent cherry and nut flavor with just a hint of almond. ☉ Prepare walnuts and cherries in the morning. Freezes well.

Hard margarine (or butter)	½ cup	125 mL
Granulated sugar	¾ cup	175 mL
Large eggs	2	2
Almond flavoring	½ tsp.	2 mL
Applesauce	1 cup	250 mL
Reserved maraschino cherry juice	2 tbsp.	30 mL
All-purpose flour	2 cups	500 mL
Baking powder	2 tsp.	10 mL
Baking soda	½ tsp.	2 mL
Salt	½ tsp.	2 mL
Chopped walnuts	½ cup	125 mL
Chopped maraschino cherries, blotted dry, juice reserved	¾ cup	175 mL

Cream margarine and sugar together in medium bowl. Beat in eggs, 1 at a time. Mix in almond flavoring.

Add applesauce and cherry juice. Stir.

Stir flour, baking powder, baking soda and salt together in separate bowl. Add to applesauce mixture. Stir just to moisten.

Stir in walnuts and cherries. Turn into greased 9 x 5 x 3 inch (22 x 12.5 x 7.5 cm) loaf pan. Bake in 350°F (175°C) oven for about 55 minutes until an inserted wooden pick comes out clean. Let stand for 20 minutes. Remove from pan to rack to cool. Cuts into 18 slices.

1 slice: 181 Calories; 3 g Protein; 8.4 g Total Fat; 24 g Carbohydrate; 187 mg Sodium

Pictured on page 68.

Peanut Butter Loaf

A light peanut butter flavor. Not over-powering.
🕑 *Freezes well.*

Large egg	1	1
Granulated sugar	½ cup	125 mL
Smooth peanut butter	½ cup	125 mL
Milk	1¼ cups	300 mL
All-purpose flour	2 cups	500 mL
Baking powder	4 tsp.	20 mL
Salt	1 tsp.	5 mL

Beat egg in bowl. Add sugar and peanut butter. Beat together. Slowly mix in milk.

In separate bowl, stir flour, baking powder and salt together. Add to peanut butter mixture. Stir just to moisten. Turn into greased 9 x 5 x 3 inch (22 x 12.5 x 7.5 cm) loaf pan, being sure to push into corners. Bake in 350°F (175°C) oven for about 1 hour until wooden pick inserted in center comes out clean. Let stand for 10 minutes. Remove from pan to rack to cool. Cuts into 18 slices.

1 slice: 133 Calories; 4 g Protein; 4.4 g Total Fat; 20 g Carbohydrate; 203 mg Sodium

Pictured on this page.

Hovis-Like Bread

A heavy bread. No added fat is required.
🕑 *Combine dry ingredients early in the day, or make ahead and freeze.*

Whole wheat (or graham) flour	2 cups	500 mL
All-purpose flour	½ cup	125 mL
Wheat germ	½ cup	125 mL
Brown sugar, packed	2 tbsp.	30 mL
Baking soda	½ tsp.	2 mL
Baking powder	¼ tsp.	1 mL
Salt	½ tsp.	2 mL
Milk	1¾ cups	425 mL

Measure first 7 ingredients into bowl. Stir together.

Add milk. Mix. Turn into greased 8 x 4 x 3 inch (20 x 10 x 7.5 cm) glass loaf pan. Bake in 350°F (175°C) oven for about 1½ hours. Cuts into about 18 slices.

1 slice: 84 Calories; 4 g Protein; 0.9 g Total Fat; 16 g Carbohydrate; 127 mg Sodium

Pictured on page 64.

Chocolate Orange Bread

Rich golden brown loaf with chocolate chips well distributed. Not too sweet. 🕑 *Make ahead, without glaze, and freeze. Glaze on day of serving.*

Large egg	1	1
Cooking oil	⅓ cup	75 mL
Granulated sugar	⅔ cup	150 mL
Prepared orange juice	1 cup	250 mL
Grated peel of 1 medium orange		
All-purpose flour	2 cups	500 mL
Baking powder	1 tbsp.	15 mL
Salt	½ tsp.	2 mL
Semisweet chocolate chips	⅔ cup	150 mL
Orange Glaze:		
Icing (confectioner's) sugar	1 cup	250 mL
Prepared orange juice	2 tbsp.	30 mL

Beat egg, cooking oil and sugar together well in bowl. Add orange juice and orange peel. Mix.

Sift flour, baking powder and salt over top. Stir just to moisten.

Add chocolate chips. Stir. Turn into greased 9 x 5 x 3 inch (22 x 12.5 x 7.5 cm) loaf pan. Bake in 350°F (175°C) oven for about 1 hour until wooden pick inserted in center comes out clean. Let stand for 15 minutes. Remove from pan to rack to cool.

Orange Glaze: Mix icing sugar with orange juice, adding more or less juice to make proper consistency. Drizzle over loaf. Cuts into 18 slices.

1 slice: 194 Calories; 2 g Protein; 7.1 g Total Fat; 32 g Carbohydrate; 83 mg Sodium

Pictured on page 64.

Peanut Butter Loaf

Butterscotch Rolls

Cinnamon Pull-Aparts

Lots of gooey syrup. Be sure and have paper napkins for everyone's sticky fingers. ☺ *Make the night before and bake in the morning to serve warm for breakfast. Or bake and freeze.*

Frozen dough buns	20	20
Brown sugar, packed	1 cup	250 mL
Ground cinnamon	1 tbsp.	15 mL
Vanilla pudding powder (not instant), 6 serving size (measure about 7½ tbsp., 125 mL)	½	½
Raisins	½ cup	125 mL
Chopped pecans (or walnuts)	⅓ cup	75 mL
Hard margarine (or butter)	⅓ cup	75 mL
Golden corn syrup	2 tbsp.	30 mL

Arrange frozen buns in greased 12 cup (2.7 L) bundt pan.

Mix brown sugar, cinnamon, pudding powder, raisins and pecans. Sprinkle over buns.

Heat and stir margarine and corn syrup together in small saucepan until melted. Drizzle over sugar mixture on buns. Cover with wet tea towel. Let stand on counter for 7 to 8 hours or overnight, until doubled in size. Bake in 350°F (175°C) oven for about 25 minutes. Let stand for 5 minutes. Turn out onto plate. Makes 20 buns.

1 bun: 274 Calories; 5 g Protein; 7.5 g Total Fat; 48 g Carbohydrate; 329 mg Sodium

Pictured below.

Butterscotch Rolls

Holds shape nicely. A delicious pull-apart bun. ☺ *Prepare late at night as they need only seven hours to rise, or make mid-morning to have ready for the evening meal. These freeze well.*

Frozen dough buns	20	20
Butterscotch pudding powder (not instant), 6 serving size (measure about 7½ tbsp., 125 mL)	½	½
Brown sugar, packed	¾ cup	175 mL
Ground cinnamon	1 tsp.	5 mL
Chopped pecans	¾ cup	175 mL
Hard margarine (or butter), melted	½ cup	125 mL

Arrange frozen buns in greased 12 cup (2.7 L) bundt pan.

Mix pudding powder, brown sugar, cinnamon and pecans in bowl. Sprinkle over buns.

Drizzle melted margarine over top. Cover with foil. Let stand on counter overnight for about 8 hours. Bake in 350°F (175°C) oven for 25 to 30 minutes. Let stand for 5 minutes. Turn out onto plate. Makes 20 rolls.

1 roll: 274 Calories; 5 g Protein; 10.9 g Total Fat; 40 g Carbohydrate; 343 mg Sodium

Pictured above.

Cinnamon Pull-Aparts

Blueberry Buns

A cinnamon bun that has blueberries in place of raisins. Delicious change. ☺ Allow two and one half hours to make these if you want to serve them warm from the oven. These freeze well.

Granulated sugar	2 tsp.	10 mL
Warm water	1 cup	250 mL
Envelopes active dry yeast (or scant 2 tbsp., 30 mL)	2 x ¼ oz.	2 x 8 g
Large eggs	2	2
Cooking oil	⅓ cup	75 mL
Granulated sugar	½ cup	125 mL
Warm milk	1 cup	250 mL
All-purpose flour	2 cups	500 mL
All-purpose flour, approximately	4½ cups	1.1 L
Filling:		
Hard margarine (or butter), softened	½ cup	125 mL
Brown sugar, packed	¾ cup	175 mL
Ground cinnamon	2½ tsp.	12 mL
Blueberries (or saskatoon berries)	3 cups	750 mL
Icing:		
Icing (confectioner's) sugar	1½ cups	375 mL
Hard margarine (or butter), softened	¼ cup	60 mL
Milk or water	3 tbsp.	50 mL
Vanilla	½ tsp.	2 mL

Stir first amount of sugar into warm water in large bowl. Sprinkle yeast over top. Let stand for 10 minutes. Stir to dissolve yeast.

Mix in eggs, cooking oil, second amount of sugar, milk and first amount of flour. Beat together well.

Work in enough of the second amount of flour until dough pulls away from sides of bowl. Turn out onto lightly floured surface. Knead for 8 to 10 minutes until smooth and elastic. Place in greased bowl, turning once to grease top. Cover with tea towel. Let stand in oven with light on and door closed for about 60 minutes until doubled in size. Divide dough into 3 equal portions. Roll each into 9 x 12 inch (22 x 30 cm) rectangle, ¼ inch (6 mm) thick.

Filling: Spread each rectangle with ⅓ of margarine, ⅓ of brown sugar and sprinkle with ⅓ of cinnamon. Scatter ⅓ of blueberries over top of each. Roll up tightly from long side. Cut each roll into 9 even slices. Place cut side down in greased 9 x 9 inch (22 x 22 cm) pans. Cover with tea towel. Let stand in oven with light on and door closed for about 1 hour until doubled in size. Bake in 375°F (190°C) oven for about 20 minutes. Turn out onto rack.

Icing: Beat all 4 ingredients together in bowl adding more icing sugar or milk to make a thin glaze. Drizzle icing over each bun. Makes 27 buns.

1 bun: 278 Calories; 5 g Protein; 9.2 g Total Fat; 45 g Carbohydrate; 78 mg Sodium

Pictured below.

Variation: You may want to make 1 pan with raspberries instead of blueberries. Use 1 cup (250 mL) raspberries to replace 1 cup (250 mL) blueberries.

Blueberry Buns

Breakfasts & Brunches

Can you think of a better way to

begin your day than sharing breakfast with

friends and loved ones? Sometimes it seems like

everyone has different eating habits when it comes to

breakfast, which can make your job as host a tricky one.

This exceptional variety of recipe suggestions has been

compiled so that you can satisfy everyone's early

morning appetite. Try preparing the initial stages

of these recipes ahead of time; you are then

ready to put together a delicious meal

in practically no time.

Denver Bake

A Denver sandwich baked in the oven—how convenient! Has a soufflé-like texture. ☺ Chop the ham, onion and green pepper in the morning, or even the night before.

Biscuit mix	2 cups	500 mL
Milk	½ cup	125 mL
Egg whites (large), room temperature	3	3
Large egg	1	1
Egg yolks (large)	3	3
Cream cheese, softened	4 oz.	125 g
Grated medium Cheddar cheese	1 cup	250 mL
Chopped cooked ham	½ cup	125 mL
Finely chopped onion	⅓ cup	75 mL
Chopped green pepper	¼ cup	60 mL
Prepared mustard	1 tbsp.	15 mL
Prepared horseradish	1 tsp.	5 mL

Stir biscuit mix and milk together to form a soft ball. Press dough in bottom of ungreased 8 × 8 inch (20 × 20 cm) pan.

Beat egg whites until stiff. Set aside.

Beat egg, egg yolks and cream cheese together until smooth. Stir in remaining 6 ingredients. Fold in egg whites. Pour over crust in pan. Bake in 350°F (175°C) oven for 35 to 40 minutes until knife inserted near center comes out clean. Cuts into 6 pieces.

1 piece: 433 Calories; 17 g Protein; 24.6 g Total Fat; 35 g Carbohydrate; 1023 mg Sodium

Pictured on page 68.

1. Denver Bake, page 70
2. Apple Cherry Bread, page 64
3. Eggs Over Toast, page 73
4. Chili Broil, page 70
5. French Onion Quiche, page 70

French Onion Quiche

This appetizing-looking quiche will be devoured at your next luncheon. ☺ Have pie shell prepared the day before. Refrigerate. Make filling in the morning and refrigerate. Stir just before pouring into shell. Bake and serve immediately. Can be baked, then frozen and reheated.

Canned french-fried onions	2¾ oz.	79 g
Grated sharp Cheddar cheese	½ cup	125 mL
Unbaked 9 inch (22 cm) pie shell	1	1
Large eggs	4	4
Seasoning salt	½ tsp.	2 mL
Cayenne pepper	1/16 tsp.	0.5 mL
Worcestershire sauce	1 tsp.	5 mL
Milk	1¼ cups	300 mL
Grated sharp Cheddar cheese	½ cup	125 mL

Measure out ½ cup (125 mL) onions and reserve. Sprinkle remaining onions and first amount of cheese into pie shell.

Beat eggs together in bowl. Add seasoning salt, cayenne pepper, Worcestershire sauce and milk. Beat. Pour over cheese in pie plate.

Scatter second amount of cheese over top. Sprinkle with reserved onions. Bake on bottom rack in 350°F (175°C) oven for about 35 minutes until knife inserted near center comes out clean. Serves 6.

1 serving: 350 Calories; 13 g Protein; 23.2 g Total Fat; 22 g Carbohydrate; 573 mg Sodium

Pictured on page 69.

Chili Broil

So simple. ☺ Assemble on baking sheet and refrigerate up to two hours ahead of time. Broil when ready to serve.

Hamburger buns, split and toasted (buttered, optional)	4	4
Chili con carne (your own or 14 oz., 398 mL can), heated	2 cups	500 mL
Creamed cottage cheese	1 cup	250 mL
Grated medium or sharp Cheddar cheese	1 cup	250 mL

Arrange bun halves on baking sheet.

Spread hot chili over bun halves. Divide cottage cheese among bun halves over chili. Sprinkle with cheese. Broil for about 3 minutes until cheese is bubbly and showing signs of browning. Serves 4.

1 serving: 488 Calories; 29 g Protein; 23.2 g Total Fat; 40 g Carbohydrate; 1255 mg Sodium; excellent source of Dietary Fiber

Pictured on page 68.

Top (on plate): Breakfast Strata, this page
Bottom (on plate): Mac 'N' Cheese Surprise, below

Mac 'N' Cheese Surprise

The eggs and soup turn this into a company dish.
☺ Very quick to prepare. Assembles in one bowl;
bakes in one dish.

Condensed cream of mushroom soup	2 × 10 oz.	2 × 284 mL
Milk	2 cups	500 mL
Uncooked elbow macaroni	2 cups	500 mL
Grated sharp Cheddar cheese	1 cup	250 mL
Hard-boiled eggs, chopped	3	3
Onion flakes	1 tbsp.	15 mL

Blend soup and milk in large bowl.

Stir in remaining 4 ingredients. Pour into ungreased 9 x 13 inch (22 x 33 cm) pan. Bake in 350°F (175°C) oven for about 1¼ hours until macaroni is tender. Serves 6.

1 serving: 399 Calories; 17 g Protein; 18.4 g Total Fat; 41 g Carbohydrate; 1014 mg Sodium

Pictured above.

Breakfast Strata

Great for company. Serve on Christmas Day,
Boxing Day or any day for breakfast.
A cook's delight. ☺ This is mostly assembled
the night before.

Bread slices, crusts removed	8	8
Grated medium Cheddar cheese	2 cups	500 mL
Small sausages, browned and cut into 4 or 5 pieces each	1½ lbs.	680 g
Large eggs	4	4
Milk	2¼ cups	560 mL
Dry mustard	½ tsp.	2 mL
Onion salt	¼ tsp.	1 mL
Pepper	⅛ tsp.	0.5 mL
Condensed cream of mushroom soup	10 oz.	284 mL
Milk	½ cup	125 mL
Hard margarine (or butter)	2 tbsp.	30 mL
Fine dry bread crumbs	¼ cup	60 mL

Line a greased 9 x 13 inch (22 x 33 cm) pan with bread, trimming to fit.

Sprinkle cheese over top. Scatter sausage over cheese.

Beat eggs together well. Add first amount of milk, mustard, onion salt and pepper. Mix. Pour over cheese-sausage mixture. Chill overnight.

About 1¾ hours before serving, mix mushroom soup with second amount of milk. Pour over all.

Melt margarine. Stir in crumbs. Sprinkle over soup mixture. Bake, uncovered, in 350°F (175°C) oven for about 1½ hours. Makes 8 generous servings.

1 serving: 501 Calories; 22 g Protein; 34.7 g Total Fat; 24 g Carbohydrate; 1121 mg Sodium

Pictured on this page.

Do a walk-through of your party, imagining you are the guest. Hang up your coat, get a drink, have some nibblies, use the washroom. Are there any potential bottlenecks or awkward spots? If so, arrange beverages and trays of food in various locations to help smooth out the traffic flow.

Oven Omelet

Almost a soufflé. The most easy and convenient way to make an omelet. ☺ Fry bacon and onion the day before.

Bacon slices, cut into ½ inch (12 mm) pieces	1 lb.	454 g
Chopped onion	¾ cup	175 mL
Large eggs	12	12
Milk	1 cup	250 mL
Worcestershire sauce	¼ tsp.	1 mL
Salt	½ tsp.	2 mL
Pepper	⅛ tsp.	0.5 mL
Grated Swiss cheese	2 cups	500 mL

Fry bacon pieces and onion in non-stick frying pan until bacon is cooked and onion is soft. Drain well.

Beat eggs together in bowl. Add milk, Worcestershire sauce, salt and pepper. Stir together well.

Stir in cheese and bacon mixture. Pour into greased 2 quart (2 L) casserole dish. Bake in 350°F (175°C) oven for about 50 minutes until set. Serves 8.

1 serving: 330 Calories; 24 g Protein; 23.5 g Total Fat; 5 g Carbohydrate; 609 mg Sodium

Pictured on page 73.

Cheesy Bacon And Eggs

Easy to double recipe for several people or to make only half for fewer. ☺ Cook the bacon and grate the cheese the day before.

Croutons	4 cups	1 L
Grated sharp Cheddar cheese	1 cup	250 mL
Finely chopped onion	½ cup	125 mL
Bacon slices, cooked crisp and crumbled	12	12
Large eggs	10	10
Milk	3½ cups	875 mL
Prepared mustard	2 tsp.	10 mL
Worcestershire sauce	1 tsp.	5 mL
Salt	¼ tsp.	1 mL
Pepper	⅛ tsp.	0.5 mL

Spread croutons in greased 9 x 13 inch (22 x 33 cm) pan. Add cheese, onion and bacon in layers.

Beat eggs together in bowl until frothy. Add remaining 5 ingredients. Beat until blended. Pour slowly over bacon. Bake in 325°F (160°C) oven for about 1 hour until set. Serves 10.

1 serving: 272 Calories; 17 g Protein; 14.5 g Total Fat; 18 g Carbohydrate; 512 mg Sodium

Pictured on page 73.

Baked Bacon And Eggs

This one-dish breakfast helps save time on busy mornings. ☺ No chopping required. Have the bacon sliced at the meat counter, or buy pre-sliced.

Canadian back bacon slices, trimmed of fat	10	10
Large eggs	6	6
Milk	2 cups	500 mL
All-purpose flour	2 cups	500 mL
Baking powder	1 tbsp.	15 mL
Salt	1 tsp.	5 mL
Pepper	¼ tsp.	1 mL

Cover bottom of greased 9 x 13 inch (22 x 33 cm) pan with bacon slices.

Beat eggs together in bowl. Stir in milk.

Add flour, baking powder, salt and pepper. Stir. Pour over bacon. Bake in a 425°F (220°C) oven for about 35 minutes until brown and crusty. Serves 6.

1 serving: 346 Calories; 23 g Protein; 9.6 g Total Fat; 40 g Carbohydrate; 1167 mg Sodium

Pictured on page 73.

Baked Breakfast

Serve with pancake syrup for a lip-smacking dish. ☺ Cook and slice sausages the day before. Cover and refrigerate. Finish the quick assembly in the morning and bake.

Pork sausages (link)	9	9
Pancake mix	1 cup	250 mL
Large egg	1	1
Cooking oil	1 tbsp.	15 mL
Milk	1 cup	250 mL

Poke sausages in several spots. Broil or pan-fry until cooked. Drain well. Cut into ¼ inch (6 mm) coins.

Measure pancake mix, egg, cooking oil and milk into bowl. Stir together until smooth. Pour into greased 9 x 9 inch (22 x 22 cm) pan. Scatter sausage slices over top. Bake in 450°F (230°C) oven for about 20 minutes until wooden pick inserted in center comes out clean. Serves 4.

1 serving: 849 Calories; 44 g Protein; 58.7 g Total Fat; 34 g Carbohydrate; 3049 mg Sodium

Pictured on page 73.

Cheesy Bacon And Eggs, page 72   Baked Breakfast, page 72   Oven Omelet, page 72   Baked Bacon And Eggs, page 72

Eggs Over Toast

Pretty pale yellow sauce with flecks of green and brown.
⊙ Only 20 minutes from start to finish. Or make and
refrigerate the night before. Reheats well.

Condensed cream of mushroom soup	10 oz.	284 mL
All-purpose flour	⅓ cup	75 mL
Milk	⅔ cup	150 mL
Grated sharp Cheddar cheese	1 cup	250 mL
Prepared mustard	2 tsp.	10 mL
Salt	¼ tsp.	1 mL
Pepper	¹⁄₁₆ tsp.	0.5 mL
Onion flakes	1 tbsp.	15 mL
Parsley flakes	½ tsp.	2 mL
Hard-boiled eggs, sliced or chopped	8	8
Bacon slices, cooked crisp and crumbled	4	4
Bread slices, toasted and buttered (optional)	8	8

Stir soup and flour together in saucepan.

Add next 7 ingredients. Heat and stir together until boiling.

Stir in eggs and bacon pieces. Heat through. Makes 2 cups
(500 mL) sauce.

Spoon about 3 tbsp. (50 mL) sauce over each toast slice.
Serves 4.

1 serving: 455 Calories; 26 g Protein; 30 g Total Fat; 19 g Carbohydrate; 1383 mg Sodium

Pictured on page 68 and 69.

Freezer Marmalade

Golden yellow in color. ⊙ The food processor makes this so
much easier. Ideal to freeze in small plastic containers or
baby food jars for gifts. If breakfast company comments
on this, give them one to take home.

Peeled and grated zucchini	8 cups	2 L
Medium oranges, with peel, ground or finely chopped in food processor	6	6
Medium lemons, with peel, ground or finely chopped in food processor	2	2
Canned crushed pineapple, with juice	19 oz.	540 mL
Granulated sugar	6 cups	1.5 L
Packages orange-flavored gelatin (jelly powder)	2 × 3 oz.	2 × 85 g
Package lemon-flavored gelatin (jelly powder)	1 × 3 oz.	1 × 85 g

Combine first 5 ingredients in large Dutch oven. Bring to a
boil, stirring often. Boil for 15 minutes.

Add orange and lemon gelatins. Stir to dissolve. Cool. Pour
into containers. Cover. Freeze. Makes 16 cups (4 L)
marmalade.

2 tbsp. (30 mL) marmalade: 51 Calories; trace Protein; 0.1 g Total Fat; 13 g Carbohydrate;
6 mg Sodium

Pictured on page 61.

Chicken Bunwiches

*For a larger crowd, double the chicken filling and use a
French loaf instead of hamburger buns. Wrap in foil.
Bake for 30 minutes. ☺ These can be prepared
in the morning and baked just before serving.*

Canned flakes of chicken, with liquid	2 x 6½ oz.	2 x 184 g
Grated sharp Cheddar cheese	½ cup	125 mL
Finely chopped celery	⅔ cup	150 mL
Low-fat salad dressing (or mayonnaise)	3 tbsp.	50 mL
Sweet pickle relish	2 tbsp.	30 mL
White vinegar	1 tsp.	5 mL
Dill weed	¼ tsp.	1 mL
Pepper	⅛ tsp.	0.5 mL
Hamburger buns, split	8	8

Mix chicken with liquid in bowl. Add next 7 ingredients. Stir together well.

Remove about ¼ inch (6 mm) from inside centers of tops and bottoms of buns, leaving about a ½ inch (12 mm) edge. Divide filling among them, spreading to fill cavities. Place buns together. Wrap each bun in foil or place, unwrapped, in covered roaster. Heat in 400°F (205°C) oven for about 10 minutes. Makes 8.

1 bunwich: 295 Calories; 13 g Protein; 15.1 g Total Fat; 26 g Carbohydrate; 970 mg Sodium

Pictured below.

Tuna Bunwiches

Substitute two 6½ oz. (184 g) cans drained tuna for the chicken.

Biscuit Snack

*Try this with coffee when friends drop in.
It looks so pretty and appetizing. ☺ Bake ahead
and freeze if desired.*

Filling:

Hard margarine (or butter)	1 tbsp.	15 mL
Chopped onion	½ cup	125 mL
Cooked peas	1 cup	250 mL
Grated medium or sharp Cheddar cheese	1 cup	250 mL
Canned flaked tuna, drained	2 x 6.5 oz.	2 x 184 g
Salad dressing (or mayonnaise)	⅓ cup	75 mL

Biscuit Dough:

All-purpose flour	2 cups	500 mL
Granulated sugar	2 tsp.	10 mL
Baking powder	2 tsp.	10 mL
Salt	1 tsp.	5 mL
Hard margarine (or butter)	6 tbsp.	100 mL
Milk	⅔ cup	150 mL

Filling: Melt margarine in frying pan. Add onion. Sauté until soft. Remove from heat.

Add peas, cheese, tuna and salad dressing. Stir together. Set aside.

Biscuit Dough: Measure next 5 ingredients into bowl. Cut in margarine until mixture is crumbly.

Add milk. Stir to form a soft ball. Turn out onto lightly floured surface. Knead about 8 times. Roll out to 12 x 15 inch (30 x 38 cm) rectangle on ungreased baking sheet. Spoon tuna mixture down center lengthwise. Spread to make about 4 inches (10 cm) wide. Working crosswise, starting 1 inch (2.5 cm) on either side of filling, make a series of slits, 1 inch (2.5 cm) apart, to outside edge of dough. Fold each strip back over filling in overlapping downward angle, pinching ends to seal. Bake in 425°F (220°C) oven for about 20 minutes until browned. Cuts into 10 slices.

1 slice: 319 Calories; 18 g Protein; 15.0 g Total Fat; 27 g Carbohydrate; 650 mg Sodium

Pictured on this page.

Biscuit Snack Chicken Bunwiches

Cakes

We often think of cake as an important part of celebrating birthdays, anniversaries, and weddings—and they bring out a sense of excitement in all of us. But we don't need a special occasion to offer this kind of dessert—it serves equally well as part of a brunch, lunch, dinner or late night get-together.

For your convenience, all of these recipes can be made ahead and frozen until needed. Keep a cake handy just in case company unexpectedly appears at your door, or take one over to a friend's house as a thoughtful homemade gift. After all, everyone appreciates the sweet flavor of a luscious cake.

Devil's Food Cake

Dark and delicious. ☺ *Bake cake ahead and freeze. Ice thawed cake the same day as serving.*

Granulated sugar	1 cup	250 mL
Cocoa	½ cup	125 mL
Water	¼ cup	60 mL
Large eggs	3	3
Sour cream	1 cup	250 mL
Vanilla	1 tsp.	5 mL
All-purpose flour	1½ cups	375 mL
Baking soda	1 tsp.	5 mL
Salt	¼ tsp.	1 mL

Seven-Minute Icing, page 82
Chocolate curls, for garnish

Combine sugar, cocoa and water in small bowl. Stir just to moisten.

Beat eggs in medium bowl until frothy. Add sour cream and vanilla. Mix. Gradually beat in cocoa mixture.

Add flour, baking soda and salt. Beat together on low to moisten. Spread in 2 greased 8 inch (20 cm) round cake pans. Bake in 350°F (175°C) oven for about 30 minutes until wooden pick inserted in center comes out clean. Cool.

Fill and ice cake with Seven-Minute Icing. Garnish with chocolate curls. Cuts into 16 pieces.

1 piece (with icing): 215 Calories; 4 g Protein; 3.4 g Total Fat; 44 g Carbohydrate; 161 mg Sodium

Pictured on front cover.

Pistachio Cake

Cake and icing are both a light green. More like a sponge cake in texture. ☺ *Make ahead and freeze—icing and all!*

White cake mix, 2 layer size	1	1
Instant pistachio pudding powder, 4 serving size	1	1
Large eggs	4	4
Cooking oil	½ cup	125 mL
Club soda	1 cup	250 mL
Pistachio Icing:		
Envelope dessert topping, not prepared	1	1
Milk	½ cup	125 mL
Instant pistachio pudding powder, 4 serving size	1	1
Milk	½ cup	125 mL

Combine first 5 ingredients in bowl. Beat until smooth. Turn into greased 10 inch (25 cm) angel food tube pan. Bake in 350°F (175°C) oven for about 50 minutes until wooden pick inserted in center comes out clean. Let stand for 15 minutes. Turn out onto rack to cool. Cool completely before making icing.

Pistachio Icing: Beat dessert topping and first amount of milk in bowl until stiff.

Add pudding powder and second amount of milk. Beat smooth. Ice top and sides of cake quickly as this icing sets up fast. Cuts into 16 pieces.

1 piece (with icing): 278 Calories; 3 g Protein; 13.1 g Total Fat; 38 g Carbohydrate; 176 mg Sodium

Pictured below.

Pistachio Cake

Chocolate Hot Milk Cake

Light crumb texture. ☺ *Having this uniced cake in the freezer enables you to make a quick Black Forest cake. Just garnish with whipped topping and cherry pie filling, or combine cut up cake with topping and pie filling in a trifle bowl.*

Large eggs	2	2
Granulated sugar	1 cup	250 mL
Vanilla	1 tsp.	5 mL
All-purpose flour	¾ cup	175 mL
Baking powder	1 tsp.	5 mL
Salt	¼ tsp.	1 mL
Cocoa	¼ cup	60 mL
Milk	½ cup	125 mL
Hard margarine (or butter)	1 tbsp.	15 mL

Beat eggs, sugar and vanilla together in bowl for 5 minutes.

Sift in flour, baking powder, salt and cocoa. Stir.

Heat milk and margarine in saucepan until boiling. Stir into batter. Turn into greased 9 x 9 inch (22 x 22 cm) pan. Bake in 350°F (175°C) oven for 25 to 30 minutes until wooden pick inserted in center comes out clean. Cuts into 12 pieces.

1 piece: 129 Calories; 3 g Protein; 2.2 g Total Fat; 26 g Carbohydrate; 86 mg Sodium

Left: Delicious Dessert Cake, below

Pictured on page 77.

In winter, if you run out of fridge or freezer space, put food into a cardboard box or cooler and place outside.

Delicious Dessert Cake

For those with a real sweet tooth. ☺ *Have this in the freezer. Thaw and serve immediately, or refrigerate overnight.*

Chocolate cake mix, 2 layer size	1	1
Sweetened condensed milk (see Note)	11 oz.	300 mL
Caramel sundae topping	1 cup	250 mL
Frozen whipped topping (in a tub), thawed	2 cups	500 mL
Shaved semisweet (or sweet) chocolate	3 tbsp.	50 mL

Prepare cake mix as directed on package. Turn into greased 9 x 13 inch (22 x 33 cm) pan. Bake as directed. Cool. Punch shallow holes in cake with handle of wooden spoon.

Drizzle condensed milk over top. Spread with rubber spatula making sure some gets into holes.

Spread with caramel topping. Spread whipped topping over top. Sprinkle with chocolate. Cuts into 18 pieces.

1 piece: 245 Calories; 3 g Protein; 7.4 g Total Fat; 43 g Carbohydrate; 169 mg Sodium

Note: A 14 oz. (398 mL) can sweetened condensed milk may be used instead.

Pictured above.

Top Center: Sweet Nectar Cake, below   Bottom Center: Chocolate Hot Milk Cake, page 76   Right: Sherry Cake, below

Sweet Nectar Cake

Orange flavor with a hint of apricot. Smells wonderful too. ☺ Make cake ahead of time and freeze. Glaze just before serving.

Orange cake mix, 2 layer size	1	1
Cooking oil	½ cup	125 mL
Large eggs	4	4
Instant vanilla pudding powder, 4 serving size	1	1
Apricot nectar	1 cup	250 mL
Sweet Nectar Glaze:		
Icing (confectioner's) sugar	½ cup	125 mL
Apricot nectar	1 tbsp.	15 mL

Beat first 5 ingredients together in bowl until smooth. Turn into greased and floured 12 cup (2.7 L) bundt pan. Bake in 350°F (175°C) oven for about 50 minutes until wooden pick inserted in center comes out clean. Let stand for 15 minutes. Turn out of pan onto rack to cool.

Sweet Nectar Glaze: Mix icing sugar and nectar well, adding more icing sugar or nectar to make a barely pourable glaze. Spoon onto cake, allowing some to run down sides. Cuts into 16 pieces.

1 piece (with glaze): 256 Calories; 3 g Protein; 12.1 g Total Fat; 35 g Carbohydrate; 151 mg Sodium

Pictured above.

Sherry Cake

This cake stands on its own. Needs no frosting. ☺ Freezes well.

Yellow cake mix, 2 layer size	1	1
Instant vanilla pudding powder, 4 serving size	1	1
Large eggs	4	4
Cooking oil	½ cup	125 mL
Sherry (or alcohol-free sherry)	1 cup	250 mL
Ground cinnamon	1 tbsp.	15 mL
Granulated sugar	1 tbsp.	15 mL

Put first 5 ingredients into bowl. Beat on low to moisten. Beat on medium for about 2 minutes until smooth.

Mix cinnamon and sugar in small bowl. Grease 12 cup (2.7 L) bundt pan well. Coat with cinnamon mixture. Turn batter into pan. Bake in 350°F (175°C) oven for about 45 minutes until wooden pick inserted in center comes out clean. Let stand for 15 minutes. Turn out onto rack to cool. Cuts into 16 pieces.

1 piece: 246 Calories; 3 g Protein; 12.1 g Total Fat; 30 g Carbohydrate; 151 mg Sodium

Pictured above.

Pineapple Cake

Little bits of pineapple throughout the cake. Nice contrast between darker cake and cream-colored icing. ☺ Make cake ahead only and freeze. Ice once cake is thawed.

All-purpose flour	2 cups	500 mL
Granulated sugar	2 cups	500 mL
Large eggs	2	2
Baking soda	1 tsp.	5 mL
Reserved pineapple juice		
Chopped pecans (or walnuts)	1 cup	250 mL
Canned crushed pineapple, drained, juice reserved	19 oz.	540 mL

Vanilla Icing:

Cream cheese, softened	8 oz.	250 g
Hard margarine (or butter)	½ cup	125 mL
Icing (confectioner's) sugar	2 cups	500 mL
Vanilla	1 tsp.	5 mL

Measure first 5 ingredients into medium bowl. Beat together until smooth.

Add pecans and pineapple. Stir. Pour into greased 9 × 13 inch (22 × 33 cm) pan. Bake in 350°F (175°C) oven for about 40 minutes until wooden pick inserted in center comes out clean. Cool.

Vanilla Icing: Beat all 4 ingredients together in bowl until smooth. Ice cake. Cuts into 18 pieces.

1 piece (with icing): 363 Calories; 4 g Protein; 15.2 g Total Fat; 55 g Carbohydrate; 183 mg Sodium

Pictured on page 79.

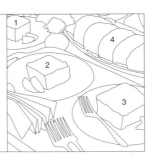

Choosy Cake

A hint of chocolate. Moist, clingy crumb. ☺ Freezes well.

Hard margarine (or butter)	1 cup	250 mL
Water	1 cup	250 mL
Cocoa	2 tbsp.	30 mL
Large eggs	2	2
Vanilla	1 tsp.	5 mL
Baking soda	1 tsp.	5 mL
Milk	½ cup	125 mL
White vinegar	1½ tsp.	7 mL
All-purpose flour	2 cups	500 mL
Granulated sugar	2 cups	500 mL
Salt	½ tsp.	2 mL

Cut margarine into chunks in medium saucepan. Add water and cocoa. Heat, stirring often, until mixture comes to a boil. Remove from heat.

Beat eggs together in medium bowl until frothy. Add vanilla and baking soda. Mix.

Stir milk and vinegar together in small cup. Let stand for 5 minutes to sour. Add to egg mixture. Mix. Add butter mixture and beat on low.

Add flour, sugar and salt. Beat on low to mix. Batter will be thin. Turn into 2 greased 8 inch (20 cm) round cake pans. Bake in 350°F (175°C) oven for about 20 minutes until wooden pick inserted in center comes out clean. Cool. Fill and ice with Quick Chocolate Icing, page 82, or Caramel Icing, page 81. Cuts into 16 pieces.

1 uniced piece: 285 Calories; 3 g Protein; 13.2 g Total Fat; 40 g Carbohydrate; 326 mg Sodium

Pictured below.

Variation: Works well as a slab cake. Pour batter into greased 9 x 13 inch (22 x 33 cm) pan. Bake at 350°F (175°C) for about 30 minutes.

Choosy Cake, above, with
Quick Chocolate Icing,
page 82

Apple Spice Cake

Mildly spicy. Perfect, moist cake texture.
☺ Uniced cake freezes well. Spread topping
over thawed cake and broil.

Hard margarine (or butter), softened	½ cup	125 mL
Granulated sugar	1¼ cups	275 mL
Large eggs	2	2
Canned applesauce (about)	14 oz.	398 mL
All-purpose flour	2½ cups	575 mL
Baking soda	1½ tsp.	7 mL
Baking powder	¼ tsp.	1 mL
Ground cinnamon	1½ tsp.	7 mL
Ground cloves	½ tsp.	2 mL
Salt	½ tsp.	2 mL
Raisins	1 cup	250 mL
Praline Topping:		
Hard margarine (or butter)	6 tbsp.	100 mL
Brown sugar, packed	⅔ cup	150 mL
Milk	2 tbsp.	30 mL
Chopped pecans	½ cup	125 mL
Medium coconut	½ cup	125 mL

Cream margarine and sugar in bowl. Beat in eggs, 1 at a time. Add applesauce. Beat.

Add next 6 ingredients. Beat until smooth.

Stir in raisins. Turn into greased 9 x 13 inch (22 x 33 cm) pan. Bake in 350°F (175°C) oven for 30 to 35 minutes until wooden pick inserted in center comes out clean.

Praline Topping: Combine all 5 ingredients in saucepan. Heat and stir just to dissolve brown sugar. Spread over cake. Broil just until bubbly. Cuts into 16 pieces.

1 piece (with topping): 357 Calories; 4 g Protein; 15.1 g Total Fat; 54 g Carbohydrate; 341 mg Sodium

Pictured on page 78/79.

Hermit Cake

All the good cookie taste is captured in this cake.
☺ Best to freeze without the icing.

Hard margarine (or butter), softened	½ cup	125 mL
Brown sugar, packed	1 cup	250 mL
Large eggs	2	2
Vanilla	1 tsp.	5 mL
Chopped dates	1½ cups	375 mL
Chopped pecans (or walnuts)	1 cup	250 mL
All-purpose flour	1½ cups	375 mL
Baking powder	2 tsp.	10 mL
Ground cinnamon	1 tsp.	5 mL
Salt	½ tsp.	2 mL
Milk	1 cup	250 mL
Caramel Icing:		
Hard margarine (or butter)	3 tbsp.	50 mL
Milk	¼ cup	60 mL
Brown sugar, packed	½ cup	125 mL
Icing (confectioner's) sugar	1½ cups	375 mL

Cream margarine and brown sugar together. Beat in eggs, 1 at a time, until well mixed. Stir in vanilla, dates and pecans.

Combine flour, baking powder, cinnamon and salt in large bowl.

Add milk alternately with flour mixture to butter mixture, beginning and ending with flour mixture. Spread in greased 9 x 9 inch (22 x 22 cm) pan. Bake in 350°F (175°C) oven for 35 to 40 minutes until wooden pick inserted in center comes out clean.

Caramel Icing: Combine first 3 ingredients in saucepan. Heat and stir until boiling. Boil 2 minutes. Cool.

Beat in icing sugar until smooth, adding more milk or icing sugar as needed for spreading consistency. Makes about 1⅓ cups (325 mL) icing. Spread over cooled cake. Cuts into 12 pieces.

1 piece (with icing): 467 Calories; 5 g Protein; 18.6 g Total Fat; 74 g Carbohydrate; 270 mg Sodium; good source of Dietary Fiber

Pictured on page 78.

Serve uniced cake slices on a bed of chocolate or raspberry sauce on dessert plates. Decorative swirls of white chocolate create a visual touch that says, "you're special!"

Angel Roll

Perfect for entertaining for a shower or a farewell.
☺ The cakes, without the filling, can be made ahead of time, rolled in towels and frozen. Simply thaw on counter, prepare the filling, then re-roll! They can be iced with whipped cream if desired.

Angel food cake mix	1	1
Filling:		
Frozen sliced strawberries in syrup, or raspberries, drained berries and syrup reserved	2 x 15 oz.	2 x 425 g
Cornstarch	2 tbsp.	30 mL
Envelopes dessert topping, or whip 2 cups (500 mL) whipping cream	2	2
Milk	1 cup	250 mL
Vanilla	1 tsp.	5 mL

Line bottom of two, 11 x 17 inch (28 x 43 cm) baking pans with waxed paper. Prepare cake mix as directed on package. Turn into prepared pans. Bake in 375°F (190°C) oven for 10 to 12 minutes. Let stand in pans until completely cool. Sprinkle 2 tea towels with icing sugar. Turn cakes out onto towels. Remove waxed paper. Roll up, starting at short end, with towel.

Filling: Mix syrup and cornstarch in saucepan. Heat and stir until boiling and thickened. Cool thoroughly. Add berries. Stir together.

Beat topping, milk and vanilla together according to instructions on envelope. Unroll cakes. Spread each cake with ½ of berry mixture. Spread ½ of whipped topping over each. Roll up, without towel, from short end. Makes 2 uniced filled rolls. Each roll cuts into 10 slices.

1 slice: 160 Calories; 3 g Protein; 1.9 g Total Fat; 34 g Carbohydrate; 56 mg Sodium

Pictured on page 79.

Quick Cake

The batter is quite stiff, but it produces a moist cake.
⊙ Freeze without icing. Ice once thawed.

Hard margarine (or butter)	1 cup	250 mL
Granulated sugar	2 cups	500 mL
Large eggs	5	5
All-purpose flour	2 cups	500 mL
Vanilla	1 tsp.	5 mL
Salt	1 tsp.	5 mL
Glaze:		
Icing (confectioner's) sugar	1 cup	250 mL
Water	1 tbsp.	15 mL
Vanilla	¼ tsp.	1 mL

Cream margarine and sugar together in bowl. Beat in eggs, 1 at a time. Stir in flour, vanilla and salt. Turn into greased 12 cup (2.7 L) bundt pan. Smooth batter. Bake in 325°F (160°C) oven for about 1 hour. Wooden pick inserted in center should come out clean. Let stand for 20 minutes before removing from pan. Cool.

Glaze: Mix icing sugar, water and vanilla. Add more water or icing sugar to make a barely pourable glaze. Makes ⅔ cup (150 mL) glaze. Spread over top of cooled cake, allowing some to run down sides. Cuts into 16 pieces.

1 piece (with glaze): 324 Calories; 4 g Protein; 14 g Total Fat; 47 g Carbohydrate; 333 mg Sodium

Pictured below.

Quick Cake

Quick Chocolate Icing

Makes a soft toffee-like topping. Try with Choosy Cake, page 80. ⊙ Quick and easy using ingredients readily on hand in your kitchen.

Granulated sugar	1 cup	250 mL
Hard margarine (or butter)	¼ cup	60 mL
Cocoa	2 tbsp.	30 mL
Corn syrup	2 tbsp.	30 mL
Milk	⅓ cup	75 mL

Measure all 5 ingredients into small saucepan. Heat and stir until mixture comes to a boil. Boil for 1 minute. Remove from heat. Pour into small bowl. Beat on high until just cool. Bowl will still feel warm when finished. To see if it has thickened enough, push some icing up the inside edge to top of bowl. It should almost stay there. Ice cake or squares immediately while it is still spreadable. Makes 1 cup (250 mL) icing.

1 tbsp. (15 mL) icing: 86 Calories; trace Protein; 3.1 g Total Fat; 15 g Carbohydrate; 39 mg Sodium

Pictured on page 80.

Seven-Minute Icing

Use to ice Devil's Food Cake, page 75.
⊙ This icing can be made ahead and frozen.

Granulated sugar	1½ cups	375 mL
Water	⅓ cup	75 mL
Egg whites (large), room temperature	2	2
Salt, just a pinch		

Combine all 4 ingredients in top of double boiler. Beat well. Place over rapidly boiling water. Beat on high constantly for 7 minutes until soft peaks form when beater is raised. Makes 4 cups (1 L) icing, enough to fill and frost double layer cake.

6 tbsp. (100 mL) icing: 112 Calories; 1 g Protein; 0 g Total Fat; 28 g Carbohydrate; 10 mg Sodium

Pictured on front cover.

Pink Cloud Icing

Add ½ package (about 3 tbsp., 50 mL) raspberry-flavored gelatin (jelly powder) along with the other 4 ingredients.

Candied Nuts

A well-placed dish of candied nuts by the sofa or

on the coffee table is your silent invitation for guests

to help themselves to as little or as much as they want.

And you can be certain that with these delectable treats

within arm's reach they will, indeed, indulge.

As an added convenience, these enchanting

confections can be made in advance of any occasion,

kept frozen and pulled at a moment's notice when

company graces your front door. Your guests will feel as

though you put so much effort into their visit!

Caramelized Nuts

Strong caramel flavor and dark color. ☉ Make ahead and store in covered container for up to one month, or freeze for longer storage.

Granulated sugar	1 cup	250 mL
Water	½ cup	125 mL
Nuts, your choice	2 cups	500 mL

Heat sugar in heavy frying pan until melted and caramel in color.

Stir in water. It will spatter furiously so be careful. Stir constantly until caramel melts and mixes with water. Sugar may lump, but continue stirring and heating until smooth.

Add nuts. Stir to coat. Spread on greased baking sheet with sides. Bake in 300°F (150°C) oven for about 30 minutes. Cool. Makes 2 cups (500 mL) nuts.

¼ cup (60 mL) nuts: 251 Calories; 3 g Protein; 14.8 g Total Fat; 29 g Carbohydrate; 3 mg Sodium

Pictured on this page.

Sugar-Coated Nuts

Great for gift giving. ☉ Make ahead and freeze, or store in covered container.

Mixture of pecan halves, walnut halves, or whole blanched almonds	4 cups	1 L
Egg whites (large), room temperature	2	2
Granulated sugar	1 cup	250 mL
Salt	¹/₁₆ tsp.	0.5 mL
Hard margarine (or butter), melted	2 tbsp.	30 mL

Scatter nuts on ungreased baking sheet. Bake in 350°F (175°C) oven for about 12 minutes, stirring every 5 minutes, until toasted. Cool. Reduce heat to 325°F (160°C).

Beat egg whites in bowl until soft peak stage. Beat in sugar and salt gradually until stiff. Fold in cooled pecans.

Grease baking sheet with sides with margarine. Spread nut mixture in pan. Bake for about 30 minutes, stirring every 8 to 10 minutes, until toasted. Makes about 5½ cups (1.4 L) nuts.

¼ cup (60 mL) nuts: 177 Calories; 2 g Protein; 14.4 g Total Fat; 13 g Carbohydrate; 23 mg Sodium

Pictured below.

Bottom Left: Caramelized Nuts

Top Right: Sugar-Coated Nuts

Caramel Popcorn

Cereal Party Mix

Cereal Party Mix

Perfect for any occasion. Takes only ten minutes to mix and coat—but you have to work fast once you start! Freezes well.

Small pretzels	**1 cup**	**250 mL**
Rice squares cereal (such as Crispix)	**6 cups**	**1.5 L**
Salted peanuts (or pecan halves)	**1 cup**	**250 mL**
Brown sugar, packed	**3/4 cup**	**175 mL**
Hard margarine (or butter)	**1/3 cup**	**75 mL**
Liquid honey	**1/4 cup**	**60 mL**
Vanilla	**1 tsp.**	**5 mL**

Measure first 3 ingredients into large greased roaster or other large oven-proof container.

Combine brown sugar, margarine and honey in saucepan. Heat and stir until sugar dissolves and mixture starts to boil. Boil gently, without stirring, for 5 minutes. Remove from heat.

Stir in vanilla. Pour over cereal mixture. Stir well to coat. Bake in 250°F (120°C) oven for 1 hour, stirring well every 15 minutes. Immediately turn out onto greased baking sheet. Cool, stirring occasionally. Makes 8 cups (2 L) mix.

1/2 cup (125 mL) mix: 208 Calories; 4 g Protein; 9.1 g Total Fat; 30 g Carbohydrate; 283 mg Sodium

Pictured above.

Caramel Popcorn

Be prepared to make this often. It will disappear quickly! Can be made well ahead. Can even be frozen. Unwrap to thaw to retain crispiness.

Popcorn (pop about 2/3 cup, 150 mL)	**6 qts.**	**6 L**
Hard margarine (or butter)	**1 cup**	**250 mL**
Brown sugar, packed	**1 1/2 cups**	**375 mL**
White corn syrup	**1/2 cup**	**125 mL**
Baking soda	**1 tsp.**	**5 mL**

Prepare popcorn and put into large greased roaster.

Melt margarine in large saucepan. Add sugar and syrup. Heat, stirring occasionally, until boiling. Boil, without stirring, for 3 minutes.

Quickly stir in baking soda. Immediately pour over popcorn. Stir well to coat. Bake, uncovered, in 250°F (120°C) oven for 45 minutes, stirring every 15 minutes. When cool enough to handle, break apart. Store in airtight container. Makes 24 cups (6 L) popcorn.

1 cup (250 mL) popcorn: 190 Calories; 1 g Protein; 8.7 g Total Fat; 28 g Carbohydrate; 162 mg Sodium

Pictured on this page.

Toasted Pecans

These will disappear by the handful. Make anytime. Only seven minutes preparation time. Freezes well.

Hard margarine (or butter)	**2 tbsp.**	**30 mL**
Salt	**1/2 tsp.**	**2 mL**
Pecan halves	**3 cups**	**750 mL**

Melt margarine in medium saucepan. Stir in salt. Add pecans. Stir well. Spread on ungreased baking sheet with sides. Bake in 350°F (175°C) oven for 10 to 15 minutes until lightly toasted. Cool. Makes 3 cups (750 mL) pecans.

1/4 cup (60 mL) pecans: 202 Calories; 2 g Protein; 20.7 g Total Fat; 5 g Carbohydrate; 131 mg Sodium

Pictured on page 85.

Glazed Munchies

Nice, shiny glaze. ⏱ *Make whenever time permits. Freezes well.*

Rice squares cereal (such as Crispix)	5 cups	1.25 L
Whole wheat squares cereal (such as Shreddies)	3 cups	750 mL
Small pretzels	3 cups	750 mL
Pecan halves	2 cups	500 mL
Hard margarine (or butter)	⅔ cup	150 mL
Liquid honey	½ cup	125 mL
Maple flavoring	½ tsp.	2 mL

Measure first 4 ingredients into large bowl or roaster.

Melt margarine in saucepan. Stir in honey and flavoring. Heat and stir to blend. Pour over cereal. Stir well to coat. Spread on ungreased baking sheets with sides or in large roaster. Bake in 350°F (175°C) oven, stirring every 4 minutes. This will take 12 to 15 minutes. Spread over countertop or in flat pans to cool. Store airtight. Makes 12 cups (3 L) munchies.

½ cup (125 mL) munchies: 209 Calories; 3 g Protein; 12.3 g Total Fat; 24 g Carbohydrate; 278 mg Sodium

Pictured below.

Sugared Peanuts

⏱ *These are so delicious, you'll have to hide them in the freezer until you are ready to serve to guests.*

Granulated sugar	2 cups	500 mL
Water	1 cup	250 mL
Peanuts (unsalted is best for flavor)	4 cups	1 L

Put all 3 ingredients into Dutch oven. Heat, stirring often with a wooden spoon, until boiling. Boil on medium, stirring continually, for about 10 minutes until mixture just crystallizes. Remove immediately and quickly spread in single layer on ungreased baking sheet with sides. Bake in 300°F (150°C) oven for 15 minutes. Shake or stir. Bake for 15 minutes. Loosen peanuts with the back of pancake lifter. Cool. Store in airtight container. Makes 8 cups (2 L).

¼ cup (60 mL) peanuts: 158 Calories; 4 g Protein; 9.3 g Total Fat; 17 g Carbohydrate; 1 mg Sodium

Pictured below.

Top Left: Glazed Munchies, this page
Bottom Left: Toasted Pecans, page 84
Right: Sugared Peanuts, above

Cookies

We fill our jars with them, offer them to

children as treats and deliver them as gifts to family

and friends, but we don't always consider cookies

as something to serve our adult guests. Cookies

bring out the child in each of us, and everyone

appreciates their sweet tempting flavors.

When offering a plate of dessert treats to your

guests, or when preparing a buffet dessert table, don't

forget to include a selection of these delicious cookies.

Leave a container full in the freezer for unexpected

visitors...they will be impressed.

Soft Spiced Cookies

A mild spice drop cookie. Soaking the raisins in boiling water enhances the flavor and makes them plump. ☺ Can be frozen.

Water	½ cup	125 mL
Raisins	1 cup	250 mL
Hard margarine (or butter), softened	½ cup	125 mL
Granulated sugar	1 cup	250 mL
Large egg	1	1
Vanilla	1 tsp.	5 mL
All-purpose flour	2 cups	500 mL
Baking soda	¾ tsp.	4 mL
Baking powder	½ tsp.	2 mL
Ground cinnamon	¾ tsp.	4 mL
Ground nutmeg	¼ tsp.	1 mL
Ground allspice	¼ tsp.	1 mL
Salt	1/16 tsp.	0.5 mL
Chopped walnuts	½ cup	125 mL

Pour water over raisins in small saucepan. Heat until boiling. Remove from heat. Let stand for 5 minutes.

Cream margarine and sugar together in bowl. Beat in egg and vanilla. Add raisins with water. Stir.

Stir in remaining 8 ingredients. Drop by rounded tablespoonfuls onto ungreased baking sheet. Bake in 375°F (190°C) oven for 10 to 15 minutes until soft. Makes 4 dozen cookies.

1 cookie: 76 Calories; 1 g Protein; 3.1 g Total Fat; 11 g Carbohydrate; 51 mg Sodium

Pictured below.

Soft Spiced Cookies, this page

Nutty Refrigerator Cookies, page 87

Boiled Butterscotch Cookies

A good one for young cooks to make.
☺ No baking required. Can be frozen.

Hard margarine (or butter)	½ cup	125 mL
Skim evaporated milk (small can)	⅔ cup	150 mL
Granulated sugar	1½ cups	375 mL
Butterscotch chips	1 cup	250 mL
Quick-cooking rolled oats (not instant)	3½ cups	875 mL
Medium coconut	½ cup	125 mL

Put margarine, evaporated milk and sugar into saucepan. Heat and stir until boiling. Boil for 1 minute, stirring constantly. Remove from heat.

Add butterscotch chips. Stir until melted.

Add rolled oats and coconut. Stir well. Cool for 5 to 10 minutes. Drop by tablespoonfuls onto waxed paper. Chill until firm. Store in airtight container. Makes about 3 dozen cookies.

1 cookie: 128 Calories; 2 g Protein; 4.3 g Total Fat; 21 g Carbohydrate; 43 mg Sodium

Pictured on this page.

Bottom Left:
Almond Refrigerator Cookies

Top Right:
Boiled Butterscotch Cookies

Almond Refrigerator Cookies

Grandma called these "icebox" cookies. ☺ Dough keeps in refrigerator for up to one week or can be frozen. Cookies freeze well too.

Hard margarine (or butter)	1 cup	250 mL
Brown sugar, packed	¾ cup	175 mL
Almond flavoring	½ tsp.	2 mL
All-purpose flour	2 cups	500 mL
Ground cinnamon	¾ tsp.	4 mL
Ground nutmeg	¼ tsp.	1 mL
Sour cream	¼ cup	60 mL
Baking soda	¼ tsp.	1 mL
Flaked almonds	½ cup	125 mL

Cream margarine, brown sugar and flavoring together in bowl.

Mix in flour, cinnamon and nutmeg.

Stir sour cream and baking soda together. Add to creamed mixture and stir.

Mix in almonds. Shape into 2 rolls, 2 inches (5 cm) in diameter. Wrap in waxed paper. Refrigerate for 6 to 8 hours or overnight. Cut into ⅛ inch (3 mm) thick slices. Arrange on ungreased baking sheet. Bake in 325°F (160°C) oven for about 10 minutes. Makes about 6 dozen cookies.

1 cookie: 53 Calories; 1 g Protein; 3.3 g Total Fat; 5 g Carbohydrate; 38 mg Sodium

Pictured on this page.

Nutty Refrigerator Cookies

Spicy "icebox" cookies. ☺ Prepare and refrigerate dough up to one week. Slice and bake as needed. The dough can also be frozen.

Hard margarine (or butter), softened	1 cup	250 mL
Brown sugar, packed	1 cup	250 mL
Granulated sugar	1 cup	250 mL
Large eggs	2	2
Vanilla	1¼ tsp.	6 mL
All-purpose flour	3½ cups	875 mL
Ground cinnamon	2 tsp.	10 mL
Ground nutmeg	1 tsp.	5 mL
Baking soda	1 tsp.	5 mL
Finely chopped pecans (or walnuts)	1½ cups	375 mL

Cream margarine and both sugars together in bowl. Beat in eggs, 1 at a time. Mix in vanilla.

Measure remaining 5 ingredients into separate bowl. Stir well. Add to batter. Mix well. Shape into 3 rolls, about 2 inches (5 cm) in diameter. Wrap in waxed paper. Refrigerate overnight. Slice thinly. Arrange on ungreased baking sheet. Bake in 375°F (190°C) oven for 10 to 12 minutes. Makes about 76 cookies.

1 cookie: 86 Calories; 1 g Protein; 4.4 g Total Fat; 11 g Carbohydrate; 51 mg Sodium

Pictured on page 86.

Chocolate Chippers

Plump, soft, chewy drop cookie. ☺ Can be frozen. Thaw while wrapped to keep from drying.

Hard margarine (or butter), softened	1 cup	250 mL
Brown sugar, packed	1 cup	250 mL
Large eggs	2	2
Vanilla	1 tsp.	5 mL
All-purpose flour	2¼ cups	560 mL
Baking soda	1 tsp.	5 mL
Instant vanilla pudding powder, 4 serving size	1	1
Semisweet chocolate chips	2 cups	500 mL
Chopped walnuts (optional)	¾ cup	175 mL

Cream margarine and brown sugar together in bowl. Beat in eggs, 1 at a time. Add vanilla. Mix.

Add flour, baking soda and pudding powder. Mix.

Add chocolate chips and walnuts. Mix into dough. Drop by heaping teaspoonfuls onto ungreased baking sheet. Bake in 350°F (175°C) oven for 10 to 12 minutes. Do not overbake. Store in airtight container. Makes 5 dozen cookies.

1 cookie: 101 Calories; 1 g Protein; 5.6 g Total Fat; 13 g Carbohydrate; 70 mg Sodium

Pictured below.

Chocolate Chippers

Brown-Eyed Susans

Chocolate flavor with pretty yellow filling. ☺ Can be made ahead and frozen. Fill when needed.

Large eggs	2	2
Granulated sugar	1 cup	250 mL
Hard margarine (or butter), melted	½ cup	125 mL
Vanilla	½ tsp.	2 mL
All-purpose flour	2¼ cups	560 mL
Cocoa	6 tbsp.	100 mL
Cream of tartar	1 tsp.	5 mL
Baking soda	½ tsp.	2 mL
Salt	¼ tsp.	1 mL
Filling:		
Hard margarine (or butter), softened	¼ cup	60 mL
Icing (confectioner's) sugar	1¼ cups	300 mL
Skim evaporated milk	2 tbsp.	30 mL
Vanilla	¼ tsp.	1 mL
Almond flavoring	⅛ tsp.	0.5 mL
Salt	1/16 tsp.	0.5 mL
Yellow food coloring, as desired		

Beat first 4 ingredients together well in bowl.

Add flour, cocoa, cream of tartar, baking soda and salt. Mix until moistened. Roll into 1½ inch (3.8 cm) balls. Arrange on greased baking sheet. Flatten with bottom of glass. Bake in 375°F (190°C) oven for about 10 minutes. Cool.

Filling: Beat all 7 ingredients together, adding more icing sugar or milk for thick spreading consistency, and enough color to make a pleasing yellow. Spread on cookies to sandwich together. Makes 1 cup (250 mL) filling. Makes about 20 filled cookies or 40 single cookies.

1 filled cookie: 203 Calories; 3 g Protein; 8.1 g Total Fat; 31 g Carbohydrate; 190 mg Sodium

Pictured on page 89.

Brown-Eyed Susans, page 88

Pastry Strips, below

Pastry Strips

These yummy cookies are best eaten the same day as they tend to lose their buttery flavor. ☺ Make these in the morning as they take about an hour to assemble and an hour to bake.

Strips:

Hard margarine (or butter), softened	½ cup	125 mL
All-purpose flour	1 cup	250 mL
Water	2 tbsp.	30 mL

Topping:

Hard margarine (or butter)	½ cup	125 mL
Water	1 cup	250 mL
Almond flavoring	1 tsp.	5 mL
All-purpose flour	1 cup	250 mL
Large eggs	3	3

Glaze:

Icing (confectioner's) sugar	1½ cups	375 mL
Hard margarine (or butter), softened	2 tbsp.	30 mL
Vanilla	1 tsp.	5 mL
Warm water	1-2 tbsp.	15-30 mL

Finely chopped pecans (or walnuts), optional

Strips: Cut margarine into flour in medium bowl until crumbly.

Add water. Mix into a ball. Refrigerate for 10 minutes. Divide dough into 2 equal parts. Divide each part into 3 equal portions, making 6 portions. Press each portion into 3 x 12 inch (7.5 x 30 cm) strips on 2 ungreased baking sheets. Allow about a 3 inch (7.5 cm) space between strips.

Topping: Place margarine, water and almond flavoring in saucepan. Heat until boiling.

Add flour all at once. Stir briskly until batter pulls away from sides of saucepan and forms a ball. Remove from heat.

Beat in eggs, 1 at a time, until smooth. Divide into 6 portions. Spread over full length of each strip. Bake in 350°F (175°C) oven for about 60 minutes until dried and crisp. Cool.

Glaze: Mix all 4 ingredients in bowl, adding more icing sugar or water to make spreading consistency. Drizzle over top.

Sprinkle with pecans. Cut each strip crosswise into 10 pieces. Makes 60 small strips.

1 strip: 65 Calories; 1 g Protein; 4 g Total Fat; 7 g Carbohydrate; 46 mg Sodium

Pictured above.

Desserts

Like the last note in an opera or the closing line of a film, a spectacular dessert at the end of dinner can leave an exquisite lasting impression with your guests. And it isn't as fussy or time-consuming as you might think to prepare a mouthwatering creation everyone will rave about. In fact, some of the most elaborate and eye-catching desserts are actually very simple to prepare. A well-placed chocolate curl, a piece of fresh fruit, or a dollop of whipped topping, can instantly create a magnificent dessert presentation that your guests will not soon forget!

Classic Cheesecake

Great topped with Cherry Sauce, page 96. ☺ Bake this ahead without any topping, and keep in the freezer for when friends and family visit.

Crust:		
Hard margarine (or butter)	6 tbsp.	100 mL
Graham cracker crumbs	1½ cups	375 mL
Granulated sugar	1 tbsp.	15 mL

Filling:		
Creamed cottage cheese, smoothed in blender	2½ cups	625 mL
Granulated sugar	1 cup	250 mL
All-purpose flour	¼ cup	60 mL
Light cream cheese, softened	4 oz.	125 g
Large eggs	2	2
Skim evaporated milk	½ cup	125 mL
Milk	¼ cup	60 mL
Lemon juice	1½ tbsp.	25 mL
Vanilla	1 tsp.	5 mL

Crust: Melt margarine in saucepan. Stir in graham crumbs and sugar. Press in bottom of ungreased 9 inch (22 cm) spring-form pan. Bake in 350°F (175°) oven for about 10 minutes.

Filling: Purée cottage cheese in blender. Turn into bowl. Add sugar and flour. Stir together well.

Beat in cream cheese. Beat in eggs, 1 at a time. Add both milks, lemon juice and vanilla. Mix. Pour over crust. Bake in 350°F (175°C) oven for about 60 to 70 minutes until set around outside. Center will be a bit wobbly when shaken. Run a sharp knife around edge to allow cheesecake to settle evenly. Chill thoroughly. Serves 16.

1 serving: 205 Calories; 8 g Protein; 7.8 g Total Fat; 26 g Carbohydrate; 374 mg Sodium

Pictured on this page.

Classic Cheesecake, above, with Cherry Sauce, page 96

Boston Cream Pie

Not a pie at all! Make cake and custard ahead. ☺ Assemble and glaze the day you want to serve. Keep refrigerated.

Cake:

Hard margarine (or butter), softened	½ cup	125 mL
Granulated sugar	1 cup	250 mL
Large eggs	2	2
Vanilla	1 tsp.	5 mL
All-purpose flour	1¾ cups	425 mL
Baking powder	2 tsp.	10 mL
Salt	¼ tsp.	1 mL
Milk	¾ cup	175 mL

Filling:

Granulated sugar	¼ cup	60 mL
All-purpose flour	1 tbsp.	15 mL
Cornstarch	1 tbsp.	15 mL
Milk	1 cup	250 mL
Large egg	1	1
Vanilla	½ tsp.	2 mL

Glaze:

Icing (confectioner's) sugar	1¼ cups	300 mL
Cocoa	2½ tbsp.	37 mL
Hard margarine (or butter), melted	1 tbsp.	15 mL
Milk	2½ tbsp.	37 mL

Cake: Cream margarine and sugar together well in bowl. Add eggs, 1 at a time, beating well after each addition. Add vanilla. Mix in.

Stir flour, baking powder and salt together in separate bowl.

Add flour mixture in 3 parts alternately with milk in 2 parts, beginning and ending with flour mixture. Divide between 2 greased 8 inch (20 cm) round cake pans. Bake in 350°F (175°C) oven for about 25 minutes until wooden pick inserted in center comes out clean. Cool.

Filling: Mix sugar, flour and cornstarch in saucepan. Gradually whisk in milk. Heat until boiling and slightly thickened. Remove from heat.

Beat in egg and vanilla. Return to heat. Heat on low for 1 minute until thickened. Cool.

Glaze: Beat all 4 ingredients together, adding more milk or icing sugar to make a barely pourable glaze.

To assemble, place 1 cake layer on plate. Spread with filling. Top with second cake layer. Spoon glaze on top. Spread to edge allowing some to drizzle down sides. Chill for at least 1 hour before serving. Cuts into 12 wedges.

1 wedge: 330 Calories; 5 g Protein; 11 g Total Fat; 54 g Carbohydrate; 202 mg Sodium

Pictured on page 93.

Cracker Dessert

Looks and tastes just like French pastry. Very impressive. Smaller pieces are quite in order. ☺ Plan ahead for this as it needs to stand at least 24 hours. Delicious even on the third day.

Instant vanilla pudding powders, 4 serving size each	2	2
Milk	4 cups	1 L
Unsalted soda crackers, approximately	84	84
Frozen whipped topping (in a tub), thawed	4 cups	1 L

Fruit Sauce:

Sliced fresh strawberries (or blueberries or saskatoons), see Note	2 cups	500 mL
Water	1 cup	250 mL
Granulated sugar	½ cup	125 mL
Cornstarch	2 tbsp.	30 mL

Beat pudding powder and milk together in bowl until smooth.

Line ungreased 9 x 13 inch (22 x 33 cm) pan with crackers. Spread ⅓ of pudding over top. Spread with ⅓ of whipped topping. Repeat layers twice more. Refrigerate for 24 hours, or even longer for good results.

Fruit Sauce: Mix all 4 ingredients in saucepan. Heat and stir until boiling and thickened. Cool. Drizzle sauce over individual servings. Cuts into 24 pieces.

1 piece: 163 Calories; 3 g Protein; 5.3 g Total Fat; 27 g Carbohydrate; 170 mg Sodium

Pictured on page 92 and 93.

Note: Frozen fruit, thawed, may be equally substituted.

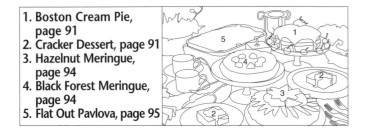

Hazelnut Meringue

A very showy torte-like dessert. ☺ The meringues can be made days ahead. Assemble just before serving

Egg whites (large), room temperature	3	3
Cream of tartar	¼ tsp.	1 mL
Granulated sugar	¾ cup	175 mL
Toasted sliced filberts (hazelnuts), finely chopped	¾ cup	175 mL
Filling:		
Envelopes dessert topping, prepared according to package directions	2	2
Mango, peeled and sliced	1	1
Papaya, peeled and sliced	1	1
Sliced fresh strawberries	1 cup	250 mL
Granulated sugar (optional)	2 tbsp.	30 mL

Place 8 inch (20 cm) round cake pan on top of foil. Draw around it marking circle. Repeat, making a second circle beside the first. Grease circles. Beat egg whites and cream of tartar together in bowl until soft peaks form. Add first amount of sugar gradually while beating until stiff.

Fold in filberts. Divide and spread in circles on foil. Bake in 275°F (140°C) oven for 1 hour. Turn oven off. Let meringue remain in oven for 2 hours to dry. Cool thoroughly before removing from foil. Place 1 meringue on flat serving plate.

Filling: Spread ½ of dessert topping over meringue on plate.

Arrange ½ of mango slices around outside edge. Place ½ of papaya slices inside, close to mango. Fill center with ½ of strawberries. Sprinkle with 1 tbsp. (15 mL) sugar. Cover with second meringue. Spread with remaining ½ of topping. Repeat fruit arrangement with second half of fruit and sugar. Cuts into 12 wedges.

1 wedge: 169 Calories; 3 g Protein; 7.7 g Total Fat; 24 g Carbohydrate; 31 mg Sodium

Pictured on page 93.

Black Forest Meringue

So pretty and so easy to assemble. ☺ The meringues can be made days ahead. Complete the topping a few hours before serving.

Egg whites (large), room temperature	2	2
Cream of tartar	⅛ tsp.	0.5 mL
Granulated sugar	½ cup	125 mL
Icing (confectioner's) sugar	¾ cup	175 mL
Cocoa	1½ tbsp.	25 mL
Hard margarine (or butter), softened	1½ tbsp.	25 mL
Prepared coffee (or water)	2½ tsp.	12 mL
Vanilla	¼ tsp.	1 mL
Canned cherry pie filling	½ × 19 oz.	½ × 540 mL
Frozen whipped topping (in a tub), thawed	½ cup	125 mL

Beat egg whites and cream of tartar together in bowl until soft peaks form. Gradually beat in sugar, beating until very stiff and glossy. Lay foil on baking sheet. Place 8 inch (20 cm) round cake pan on top of foil. Draw around it marking circle. Grease circle. Spread stiff egg whites to cover, making center lower than outside rim. Bake in 275°F (140°C) oven for 1 hour. Turn oven off. Let meringue remain in oven for 2 hours to dry. Cool thoroughly before removing from foil. Place on flat serving plate.

Beat next 5 ingredients together well in small bowl. Add more icing sugar or coffee if needed to make good consistency for piping or holding shape. Pipe or spoon around top of outer edge of meringue, forming a rim.

Spoon cherry filling in center. Spread to cover area up to rim.

Spoon little dabs of whipped topping here and there over top. Cuts into 8 wedges.

1 wedge: 182 Calories; 1 g Protein; 3.9 g Total Fat; 37 g Carbohydrate; 50 mg Sodium

Pictured on page 92/93.

Flat Out Pavlova

Pretty as a picture. Pronounced pav-LOH-vah. ☺ This cuts even nicer if made the day before. Meringue can be made two days ahead, then filling can be added one day ahead or in the morning of your entertaining.

Egg whites (large), room temperature	6	6
Vanilla	1 tsp.	5 mL
Cream of tartar	½ tsp.	2 mL
Granulated sugar	1½ cups	375 mL
Filling:		
Light cream cheese, softened	8 oz.	250 g
Granulated sugar	1 cup	250 mL
Envelopes dessert topping, prepared according to package directions	2	2
Miniature marshmallows	2 cups	500 mL
Topping:		
Canned cherry pie filling	19 oz.	540 mL
Sliced fresh strawberries	2 cups	500 mL
Lemon juice	1 tsp.	5 mL

Beat egg whites, vanilla and cream of tartar together in bowl until frothy.

Gradually beat in sugar. Beat until stiff. Spread in greased 9 x 13 inch (22 x 33 cm) pan. Bake in 275°F (140°C) oven for 1 hour. Turn oven off. Leave meringue in oven for 6 hours or overnight to dry.

Filling: Beat cream cheese and sugar together well in bowl. Add dessert topping. Beat to mix. Stir in marshmallows. Spread over meringue. Cover. Chill in refrigerator for 5 hours or overnight.

Topping: Stir pie filling, strawberries and lemon juice together in bowl. Spread over filling. Cuts into 15 pieces.

1 piece: 282 Calories; 4 g Protein; 5.2 g Total Fat; 57 g Carbohydrate; 206 mg Sodium

Pictured on page 92.

Rhubarb Dessert

Rhubarb Dessert

Very showy red color with a creamy topping. Not too sweet. ☺ Bake one day, serve the next.

Bottom Layer:		
Hard margarine (or butter), melted	½ cup	125 mL
All-purpose flour	1 cup	250 mL
Granulated sugar	2 tbsp.	30 mL
Filling:		
Sliced rhubarb (red is best)	4 cups	1 L
Granulated sugar	1 cup	250 mL
Prepared orange juice	⅓ cup	75 mL
Envelope unflavored gelatin	1 × ¼ oz.	1 × 7 g
Water	¼ cup	60 mL
Topping:		
Frozen whipped topping,(in a tub), thawed	2 cups	500 mL

Bottom Layer: Melt margarine in saucepan. Add flour and sugar. Mix well. Pack in ungreased 9 x 9 inch (22 x 22 cm) pan. Bake in 350°F (175°C) oven for 12 to 15 minutes until lightly browned.

Filling: Combine rhubarb, sugar and orange juice in saucepan. Simmer for about 10 minutes until rhubarb is tender. Remove from heat.

Sprinkle gelatin over water in small dish. Let stand for 1 minute. Stir into hot mixture to dissolve. Cool. Pour over bottom layer. Refrigerate overnight or until firm.

Topping: Spread whipped topping over all. Cuts into 12 pieces.

1 piece: 239 Calories; 2 g Protein; 11 g Total Fat; 34 g Carbohydrate; 93 mg Sodium

Pictured above.

Crème Caramel

A traditional custard base with caramel "hat." Very showy.
☺ Can be made the night before or the morning of.

Caramel:

Granulated sugar	1 cup	250 mL
Hot water	¼ cup	60 mL

Custard:

Large eggs	4	4
All-purpose flour	1 tbsp.	15 mL
Granulated sugar	⅓ cup	75 mL
Milk	2½ cups	625 mL
Vanilla	1½ tsp.	7 mL
Salt	¼ tsp.	1 mL
Hot water		

Caramel: Heat sugar in heavy saucepan until melted and medium brown. Remove from heat.

Add hot water very slowly. It will spatter furiously. Stir until blended, returning to heat, if needed, to blend completely. Pour into ungreased round casserole dish, about 8 inches (20 cm) in diameter. Let sit for 1 minute to thicken slightly. Tilt dish to coat bottom completely and up sides at least 1½ inches (3.8 cm).

Custard: Beat eggs lightly in bowl. Add flour. Beat on low until mixed. Add sugar, milk, vanilla and salt. Mix. Pour carefully into dish. Set dish into roaster. Add hot water to depth of 1 inch (2.5 cm). Bake in 350°F (175°C) oven for about 50 to 60 minutes until a knife inserted halfway between center and edge comes out clean. Remove dish to rack. Cool at room temperature for 1 hour. Refrigerate for 4 hours or overnight. Run knife around sides. Invert onto plate. Serves 8.

1 serving: 212 Calories; 6 g Protein; 3.4 g Total Fat; 40 g Carbohydrate; 157 mg Sodium

Pictured on page 100.

To clean silk flowers, place them in a large paper bag and pour in 1 cup (250 mL) salt. Shake vigorously. Remove and shake off any remaining salt.

Cherry Sauce

Great over pound cake slices, ice cream or bananas. Really good with Classic Cheesecake, page 90. Even good over ham. ☺ Sauce reheats well, so make it ahead of time.

Fresh or frozen pitted cherries, quartered	1 cup	250 mL
Water	1 cup	250 mL
Granulated sugar	1 cup	250 mL
Almond flavoring	½ tsp.	2 mL
Cornstarch	2 tsp.	10 mL
Water	1 tbsp.	15 mL

Heat first 4 ingredients in saucepan for about 7 minutes, stirring often, until cherries are cooked.

Mix cornstarch and second amount of water in small cup. Add to hot cherry mixture, stirring until boiling and thickened. Makes 1⅓ cups (325 mL) sauce.

⅓ cup (75 mL) sauce: 236 Calories; trace Protein; 0.4 g Total Fat; 60 g Carbohydrate; 1 mg Sodium

Pictured on page 90.

Chilled Dessert, page 97

Chilled Dessert

A light chocolate and nutty flavor. ☺ *For easier cutting, make this a day ahead and keep chilled until ready to serve.*

Bottom Layer:

Hard margarine (or butter)	½ cup	125 mL
All-purpose flour	1 cup	250 mL
Granulated sugar	2 tbsp.	30 mL
Finely chopped walnuts (or pecans)	½ cup	125 mL

Second Layer:

Light cream cheese, softened	8 oz.	250 g
Icing (confectioner's) sugar	1 cup	250 mL
Envelope dessert topping, prepared according to package directions	1	1

Third Layer:

Instant vanilla pudding powder, 6 serving size	1	1
Instant chocolate pudding powder, 6 serving size	1	1
Milk	4½ cups	1.1 L

Topping:

Envelopes dessert topping, prepared according to package directions	2	2

Bottom Layer: Melt margarine in saucepan. Stir in flour, sugar and walnuts. Pack in ungreased 9 x 13 inch (22 x 33 cm) pan. Bake in 325°F (160°C) oven for 15 minutes until golden. Cool.

Second Layer: Beat cream cheese and icing sugar together in bowl until smooth.

Fold dessert topping into cheese mixture. Spread over cooled bottom layer.

Third Layer: Pour vanilla and chocolate pudding powders into bowl. Add milk. Beat until smooth. Pour over second layer. Smooth top.

Topping: Spread or pipe dessert topping over third layer. Chill. Cuts into 18 pieces.

1 piece: 293 Calories; 5 g Protein; 13.7 g Total Fat; 39 g Carbohydrate; 414 mg Sodium

Pictured on page 96.

Saucy Bananas

Saucy Bananas

Smooth-as-satin sauce. ☺ *Prepare the sauce ahead and reheat just before serving.*

Sweet Chocolate Sauce:

Milk chocolate chips	1 cup	250 mL
Brown sugar, packed	½ cup	125 mL
Hard margarine (or butter)	2 tbsp.	30 mL
Milk	¼ cup	60 mL
Corn syrup	2 tbsp.	30 mL
Vanilla	½ tsp.	2 mL
Bananas	4	4
Rounded scoops of vanilla ice cream	6	6

Sweet Chocolate Sauce: Combine first 6 ingredients in heavy medium saucepan. Heat and stir on medium until chocolate is melted and sugar is dissolved. Bring to a boil. Remove from heat. Add a bit more milk if too thick. Makes 1 cup (250 mL) sauce.

Slice bananas into 6 sherbet dishes. Place 1 scoop of ice cream in each dish over bananas. Divide sauce over top. Serves 6.

1 serving: 501 Calories; 6 g Protein; 21.6 g Total Fat; 76 g Carbohydrate; 148 mg Sodium

Pictured above.

Fudgy Sauce

Use semisweet chocolate chips instead of milk chocolate to give a deep fudge flavor and an entirely different sauce.

Lemon Dessert

Warn your family not to touch this ready-and-waiting refrigerator dessert. ☺ *Can be made up to two days ahead.*

Bottom Layer:		
All-purpose flour	1½ cups	375 mL
Hard margarine (or butter), softened	¾ cup	175 mL
Brown sugar, packed	¼ cup	60 mL
Second Layer:		
Cream cheese, softened	8 oz.	250 g
Icing (confectioner's) sugar	1 cup	250 mL
Frozen whipped topping, (in a tub), thawed	1 cup	250 mL
Third Layer:		
Instant lemon pudding powder, 4 serving size each	2	2
Milk	3 cups	750 mL
Lemon juice	1 tsp.	5 mL
Topping:		
Frozen whipped topping, (in a tub), thawed	2 cups	500 mL
Finely chopped walnuts	3 tbsp.	50 mL

Bottom Layer: Mix flour, margarine and brown sugar in bowl until crumbly. Press into ungreased 9 × 13 inch (22 × 33 cm) pan. Bake in 350°F (175°C) oven for 10 minutes until golden. Cool.

Second Layer: Beat cream cheese and icing sugar together in bowl until smooth.

Fold in whipped topping. Spread over bottom layer.

Third Layer: Pour pudding powder into bowl. Add milk and lemon juice. Beat until smooth. Pour over second layer. Chill.

Topping: Spread whipped topping over lemon layer. Sprinkle with walnuts. Chill. Cuts into 18 pieces.

1 piece: 314 Calories; 4 g Protein; 17.8 g Total Fat; 36 g Carbohydrate; 198 mg Sodium

Pictured on page 101.

When guests arrive, make time for introductions. If there is something that might be a common bond between guests, initiate the topic, then politely excuse yourself to greet new guests or to attend to a last-minute appetizer.

Dessert Special

Crunchy bottom layer. ☺ *A convenient make-ahead refrigerator dessert.*

Crust:		
Hard margarine (or butter)	½ cup	125 mL
Vanilla wafer crumbs	2 cups	500 mL
Second Layer:		
Hard margarine (or butter) softened	½ cup	125 mL
Light cream cheese	8 oz.	250 g
Icing (confectioner's) sugar	1½ cups	375 mL
Third Layer:		
Canned crushed pineapple, drained well	14 oz.	398 mL
Frozen sliced strawberries in syrup, drained well	15 oz.	425 g
Topping:		
Frozen whipped topping, (in a tub), thawed	4 cups	1 L
Sliced almonds, toasted	½ cup	125 mL

Crust: Melt margarine in saucepan. Stir in wafer crumbs. Press in ungreased 9 × 13 inch (22 × 33 cm) pan. Bake in 350°F (175°C) oven for 8 to 10 minutes. Cool.

Second Layer: Cream margarine, cream cheese and icing sugar together well in bowl. Spread over crust.

Third Layer: Mix pineapple and strawberries in bowl. Scatter over second layer.

Topping: Spread with whipped topping. Sprinkle with almonds. Chill. Cuts into 18 pieces.

1 piece: 311 Calories; 3 g Protein; 20.6 g Total Fat; 31 g Carbohydrate; 289 mg Sodium

Pictured on page 100/101.

Almond Dessert

Lovely presentation even without the top layer.
Not too sweet. ☺ This can be made ahead and
frozen without the top layer.

Bottom Layer:		
All-purpose flour	1½ cups	375 mL
Granulated sugar	¼ cup	60 mL
Hard margarine (or butter), softened	½ cup	125 mL
Egg yolk (large)	1	1
Filling:		
Almond paste, softened	8 oz.	225 g
Rice flour	½ cup	125 mL
Large eggs	2	2
Egg white (large)	1	1
Almond flavoring	½ tsp.	2 mL
Salt	¼ tsp.	1 mL
Top Layer:		
Icing (confectioner's) sugar	1 cup	250 mL
Milk	2 tbsp.	30 mL
Toasted sliced almonds	½ cup	125 mL

Bottom Layer: Mix flour, sugar and margarine until crumbly.

Add egg yolk. Mix. Press in bottom and ½ inch (12 mm) up sides of ungreased 10 inch (25 cm) springform pan.

Filling: Combine all 6 ingredients in blender. Process until smooth. Pour into prepared pan. Bake in 325°F (160°C) oven for 45 to 50 minutes until browned.

Top Layer: Beat icing sugar and milk together in small bowl until smooth. Spread over warm dessert.

Sprinkle with almonds. Cool. Cuts into 12 wedges.

1 wedge: 343 Calories; 7 g Protein; 16.9 g Total Fat; 42 g Carbohydrate; 172 mg Sodium; good source of Dietary Fiber

Pictured on this page.

Pumpkin Dessert

Almost like pumpkin pie—but without the crust.
☺ A cake mix makes this very easy. Only 20 minutes
to assemble. Make the day before. Serve
cold, or reheat and serve warm.

Large eggs	4	4
Granulated sugar	1¼ cups	300 mL
Canned pumpkin	2 × 14 oz.	2 × 398 mL
Ground cinnamon	1½ tsp.	7 mL
Ground ginger	1 tsp.	5 mL
Ground nutmeg	½ tsp.	2 mL
Ground cloves	½ tsp.	2 mL
Salt	1 tsp.	5 mL
Evaporated milk	1½ cups	375 mL
Topping:		
Yellow cake mix, 2 layer size	1	1
Hard margarine (or butter)	½ cup	125 mL
Ice cream (or whipped cream), optional		

Beat eggs on high in medium bowl until frothy. Beat in sugar.

Add next 6 ingredients. Beat until well mixed.

Add evaporated milk. Beat on low to blend. Pour into greased 9 x 13 inch (22 x 33 cm) pan.

Topping: Put next 2 ingredients into bowl, cut in margarine until crumbly. Sprinkle over pumpkin mixture. Bake in 350°F (175°C) oven for 1½ hours until knife inserted near center comes out fairly clean.

Serve hot with ice cream or cold with whipped cream. Serves 18.

1 serving: 266 Calories; 5 g Protein; 10 g Total Fat; 41 g Carbohydrate; 360 mg Sodium

Pictured on page 100.

Almond Dessert

Orange Trifle

More marmalade can be used if desired.
🕐 *A definite make-ahead. Cake can be
frozen long before it's needed.*

Prepared orange juice	2 cups	500 mL
Grated orange peel	1 tbsp.	15 mL
Milk	1½ cups	375 mL
Vanilla	¼ tsp.	1 mL
Granulated sugar	¾ cup	175 mL
Cornstarch	2½ tbsp.	37 mL
Salt	½ tsp.	2 mL
Large eggs, fork-beaten	2	2
Yellow cake mix, 2 layer size	1	1
Orange marmalade (or red jam)	½ cup	125 mL
Frozen whipped topping, (in a tub), thawed	2 cups	500 mL
Maraschino cherries (or orange slices), for garnish		

Heat first 4 ingredients in saucepan until boiling.

Mix sugar, cornstarch and salt in bowl. Stir in eggs. Mix well. Stir into boiling liquid until mixture returns to a boil and thickens. Cool. Makes 4 cups (1 L) sauce.

Prepare cake mix as directed on package. Bake in greased 9 x 13 inch (22 x 33 cm) pan as directed. Cool. Cut into 1 inch (2.5 cm) slices.

Spread cake slices with marmalade. Cut into cubes. Place ⅓ of cubes in trifle bowl. Spoon on ⅓ of sauce. Repeat 2 more times. Chill.

Spread with whipped topping. Garnish with cherries. Serves 18.

1 serving: 231 Calories; 3 g Protein; 6.3 g Total Fat; 42 g Carbohydrate; 200 mg Sodium

Pictured on page 100.

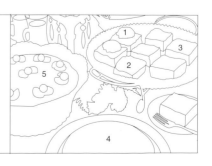

Lemon Angel Dessert

Cuts beautifully. 🕐 *Can be made the day before.*

Sweetened condensed milk (see Note)	11 oz.	300 mL
Lemon juice	⅔ cup	150 mL
Envelope dessert topping, prepared according to package directions	1	1
Baked large angel food cake, broken up into bite-size pieces	1	1
Maraschino cherries	12	12

Stir condensed milk and lemon juice together in medium bowl. Reserve ¼ of mixture.

Reserve ¼ of prepared dessert topping. Fold remaining ¾ of topping into ¾ of milk mixture.

Add cake. Fold together until combined. Spread in ungreased 9 x 9 inch (22 x 22 cm) pan. Spread with reserved ¼ of milk mixture. Top with reserved ¼ of topping. Chill.

Top individual pieces with cherry. Cuts into 12 pieces.

1 piece: 239 Calories; 6 g Protein; 4.3 g Total Fat; 46 g Carbohydrate; 157 mg Sodium

Pictured below.

Note: A 14 oz. (398 mL) can may be substituted with no changes to the other ingredients.

Kahlua Dessert

Very rich. Very smooth. Very good.
🕐 *A frozen dessert to keep handy in the freezer.*

Crust:		
Hard margarine (or butter)	¼ cup	60 mL
Graham cracker crumbs	1 cup	250 mL
Cocoa	2 tbsp.	30 mL
Granulated sugar	2 tbsp.	30 mL
Filling:		
Large marshmallows	32	32
Milk	½ cup	125 mL
Kahlua	6 tbsp.	100 mL
Frozen whipped topping, (in a tub), thawed	2 cups	500 mL

Crust: Melt margarine in saucepan. Stir in graham crumbs, cocoa and sugar. Reserve 3 tbsp. (50 mL). Pack remaining crumbs in ungreased 8 x 8 inch (20 x 20 cm) pan.

Filling: Combine marshmallows and milk in large saucepan. Heat, stirring often, until marshmallows are melted and mixture is smooth. Cool.

Add Kahlua to cooled mixture. Pour over crust. Chill until set.

Spread with whipped topping. Sprinkle with reserved crumbs. Cover. Freeze. Serves 12.

1 serving: 218 Calories; 2 g Protein; 8.6 g Total Fat; 32 g Carbohydrate; 139 mg Sodium

Pictured below.

Top Left: Lemon Angel Dessert, above   Bottom Left: Kahlua Dessert, above   Center Right: Cool Fruit Delight, page 103

Chipped Dumplings

Saucy-rich with chocolate chips. ☺ The sauce can be made ahead and simply reheated when ready to make the dumplings.

Sauce:		
Brown sugar, packed	½ cup	125 mL
Granulated sugar	½ cup	125 mL
Cocoa	2 tbsp.	30 mL
All-purpose flour	2 tbsp.	30 mL
Hard margarine (or butter)	1 tbsp.	15 mL
Vanilla	1 tsp.	5 mL
Salt	¼ tsp.	1 mL
Water	1¾ cups	425 mL
Dumplings:		
All-purpose flour	1 cup	250 mL
Granulated sugar	3 tbsp.	50 mL
Baking powder	1½ tsp.	7 mL
Salt	½ tsp.	2 mL
Semisweet chocolate chips	½ cup	125 mL
Milk	½ cup	125 mL
Cooking oil	2 tbsp.	30 mL

Sauce: Measure first 4 ingredients into saucepan. Mix well.

Add margarine, vanilla, salt and water. Heat, stirring often, until mixture comes to a boil. Pour into ungreased 3 quart (3 L) casserole dish.

Dumplings: Stir first 5 ingredients together in medium bowl.

Add milk and cooking oil. Stir to make soft dough. Drop by tablespoonfuls into syrup in dish. Should make about 12 dumplings. Bake, uncovered, in 350°F (175°C) oven for about 30 minutes. Wooden pick inserted in center of dumpling should come out clean. Serves 8.

1 serving: 303 Calories; 3 g Protein; 9.4 g Total Fat; 54 g Carbohydrate; 289 mg Sodium

Pictured on this page.

Chipped Dumplings

Cool Fruit Delight

Very showy. Light taste with just a touch of sweetness. ☺ Can be made the day before or frozen.

Crust:		
Hard margarine (or butter)	6 tbsp.	100 mL
Graham cracker crumbs	1½ cups	375 mL
Brown sugar, packed	1 tbsp.	15 mL
Filling:		
Reserved fruit cocktail juice	½ cup	125 mL
Miniature marshmallows	10 oz.	250 g
Light sour cream	1 cup	250 mL
Canned fruit cocktail, drained, juice reserved	2 × 14 oz.	2 × 398 mL
Maraschino cherries, for garnish	18	18

Crust: Melt margarine in saucepan. Stir in graham crumbs and brown sugar. Reserve 2 tbsp. (30 mL) for topping. Pack remainder in ungreased 9 inch (22 cm) springform pan. Bake in 350°F (175°C) oven for 10 minutes. Cool.

Filling: Heat juice in saucepan. Add marshmallows. Stir often as marshmallows melt. Cool to room temperature.

Stir in sour cream and fruit cocktail. Chill in refrigerator, stirring often and scraping down sides, until mixture shows signs of thickening. Pour over crust. Sprinkle with reserved crumbs.

Garnish with cherries. Chill. Cuts into 12 wedges.

1 wedge: 228 Calories; 3 g Protein; 8.6 g Total Fat; 38 g Carbohydrate; 195 mg Sodium

Pictured on page 102.

Fish & Seafood

When your evening of entertaining includes serving dinner, consider one or more of these fabulous fish and seafood recipes. Refreshing, exotic flavors of the sea come shining through in such impressive dishes as Coulibiac or Shrimp Casserole. This is a wonderful collection of elegant yet simple-to-prepare recipes, suitable for any occasion.

Whole Salmon

Dark brown sauce with bits of onion. Easy recipe.
Sauce can be made ahead and reheated before serving.

Whole salmon, pan ready, head and tail removed	4 lbs.	1.8 kg
Water, to cover		
Seasoning salt	1 tsp.	5 mL
Cornstarch	1 tbsp.	15 mL
Water	1 cup	250 mL
Chopped green onion	¾ cup	175 mL
Soy sauce	¼ cup	60 mL
Brown sugar, packed	2 tbsp.	30 mL
Ground ginger	½ tsp.	2 mL

Poach salmon in first amount of water with seasoning salt for about 20 minutes until it flakes when tested with fork. Drain. Carefully remove skin just before serving.

Stir cornstarch into second amount of water in small saucepan. Heat and stir until boiling and thickened.

Add green onion, soy sauce, brown sugar and ginger. Stir. Heat through. Spoon over fish or serve separately. Makes 1½ cups (375 mL) sauce. Serves 8.

1 serving: 139 Calories; 17 g Protein; 5.3 g Total Fat; 6 g Carbohydrate; 774 mg Sodium

Pictured on page 105.

Cold Party Salmon

A fantastic method to precook a whole salmon.
Prepare salmon ahead, wrap well and refrigerate for up to 24 hours.

Whole dressed salmon (4-5 lbs., 1.8-2.3 kg), head and tail removed if desired	1	1
Sprigs of parsley (or ½ tsp., 2 mL, flakes)	2	2
Bay leaf	1	1
White wine	½ cup	125 mL
Salt	1 tsp.	5 mL
Peppercorns	3	3
Cold water, to cover		

Garnishes:
Cucumber slices, shrimp, lemon wedges, crab sticks, parsley, lettuce, salad dressing (or mayonnaise), smoked salmon strips

Place salmon on rack in fish kettle or large roaster with rack. If using a rack without handles, use cheesecloth under salmon with enough cheesecloth over edge of roaster to enable you to lift salmon out and onto separate rack to cool.

Add parsley, bay leaf, wine, salt and peppercorns. Cover with enough water to just cover salmon. Cover. Place kettle or roaster on 2 burners. Bring to a gentle boil. Boil for 2 minutes. Internal temperature should read 140°F (60°C) on meat thermometer. Turn off heat if stove is electric and let stand, covered, on burners for 1 hour. If using a gas stove, turn burners to lowest heat for 15 minutes. Turn burners off. Let kettle or roaster stand for 45 minutes. Lift out rack. Drain salmon well. Remove skin. Transfer to long, large platter. Cool completely.

Garnishes: Decorate salmon as desired. Serves about 20.

1 serving: 49 Calories; 6 g Protein; 2.1 g Total Fat; trace Carbohydrate; 157 mg Sodium

Pictured on page 105.

Because fish and shellfish deteriorate quickly, be sure to buy the freshest possible. Order ahead of your event and pick it up within 24 hours of serving. Do not freeze. Refrigerate in a bowl or bag, packed with ice cubes or crushed ice.

Left: Coulibiac, below　　　　　Center: Whole Salmon, page 104　　　　　Right: Cold Party Salmon, page 104

Coulibiac

Pronounced koo-lee-BYAHK. This is time consuming
but fun and easy to make. A real show stopper.
☺ Prepare everything up to the baking stage
and refrigerate for up to one hour before company arrives.
Pop in the oven when ready.

Frozen puff pastry sheets, thawed at room temperature for 20 minutes	14¼ oz.	397 g
Salmon fillet (tail end, about 1½ lbs., 680 g), poached, drained and cooled	1	1
Filling:		
Hard margarine (or butter)	1 tbsp.	15 mL
Chopped onion	1½ cups	375 mL
Sliced fresh mushrooms	2 cups	500 mL
Cooked white rice	1½ cups	375 mL
Non-fat sour cream	1 cup	250 mL
Dill weed	1 tsp.	5 mL
Chopped chives	2 tsp.	10 mL
Salt, sprinkle		
Pepper, sprinkle		
Hard-boiled eggs, coarsely chopped	3	3
Egg Wash:		
Large egg	1	1
Water	1 tbsp.	15 mL

Roll 1 pastry sheet 4 inches (10 cm) longer and 2 inches (5 cm) wider than salmon fillet, following the shape of the fillet, on lightly floured baking sheet with sides.

Filling: Melt margarine in frying pan. Add onion and mushrooms. Sauté for about 5 minutes until soft and liquid is evaporated. Cool.

Stir rice, sour cream, dill weed and chives together in bowl. Add cooled onion mixture. Spread ½ of rice mixture over rolled pastry to within 1 inch (2.5 cm) of edge.

Arrange salmon fillet over top. Tuck rice mixture under fillet where necessary. Sprinkle with salt and pepper.

Sprinkle egg over fillet. Cover with second ½ of rice mixture. Dampen edges. Roll out second piece of pastry. Lay over top. Cut top pastry even with bottom pastry. Crimp edges with fork to seal. Use trimmed pieces of pastry to form a head and fins.

Egg Wash: Beat egg and water together in small bowl. Brush over pastry. Make slits on top of pastry with scissors to make scales for steam to escape. Bake in 425°F (220°C) oven for about 10 minutes. Reduce heat to 350°F (175°C). Bake for about 20 minutes until browned. Serve hot. Serves 6 to 8.

⅙ recipe: 640 Calories; 35 g Protein; 33.9 g Total Fat; 49 g Carbohydrate; 538 mg Sodium

Pictured above.

Surprise Company Dish

The surprise is that this dish is like a tuna sandwich.
⏰ Must be made the night before.

White sandwich bread slices, to cover, crusts removed	6-8	6-8
Canned flaked tuna, drained	2 × 6½ oz.	2 × 184 g
Light salad dressing (or mayonnaise)	¼ cup	60 mL
Sweet pickle relish	2 tbsp.	30 mL
Lemon juice	1 tbsp.	15 mL
Prepared mustard	1 tbsp.	15 mL
Grated medium or sharp Cheddar cheese	1 cup	250 mL
Seasoning salt	¼ tsp.	1 mL
White sandwich bread slices, to cover, crusts removed	6-8	6-8
Large eggs	8	8
Milk	3 cups	750 mL
Salt	¾ tsp.	4 mL
Pepper	¼ tsp.	1 mL
Seasoning salt	½ tsp.	2 mL
Cayenne pepper	¼-½ tsp.	1-2 mL

Cover bottom of greased 9 × 13 inch (22 × 33 cm) pan with first amount of bread slices.

Stir next 7 ingredients in bowl. Spread over top.

Cover with remaining bread slices.

Beat eggs in bowl. Beat in remaining 5 ingredients. Pour over all. Cover. Refrigerate overnight. Bake, uncovered, in 350°F (175°C) oven for about 1 hour until browned and knife inserted near center comes out clean. Serves 8.

1 serving: 365 Calories; 30 g Protein; 14.5 g Total Fat; 27 g Carbohydrate; 1044 mg Sodium

Pictured below.

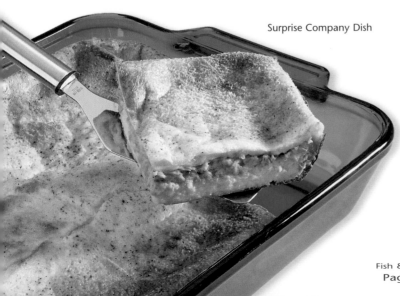

Surprise Company Dish

Crab Enchiladas

"Heat" up this Mexican-style dish by using canned jalepeño peppers instead of the chilies. ⏰ The sauce can be prepared ahead and reheated when ready to assemble.

Hard margarine (or butter)	1 tbsp.	15 mL
Chopped onion	1 cup	250 mL
Canned tomatoes, broken up	14 oz.	398 mL
Tomato sauce	7½ oz.	213 mL
Canned chopped green chilies, drained	4 oz.	114 mL
Granulated sugar	1 tsp.	5 mL
Dried whole oregano	½ tsp.	2 mL
Dried sweet basil	¼ tsp.	1 mL
Salt	¼ tsp.	1 mL
Seasoning salt	⅛ tsp.	0.5 mL
Crabmeat, cartilage removed (or imitation crabmeat)	1 lb.	454 g
Grated Monterey Jack cheese	½ cup	125 mL
Canned pitted ripe olives, chopped	4.5 oz.	125 mL
Corn tortillas	12	12
Grated Monterey Jack cheese	1 cup	250 mL

Melt margarine in frying pan. Add onion. Sauté until soft.

Combine next 8 ingredients in saucepan. Mix well. Add onions. Bring to a boil, stirring often. Simmer, uncovered, for 10 minutes. Cover bottom of ungreased 9 × 13 inch (22 × 33 cm) pan with ¼ cup (60 mL) sauce. Set aside. Reserve ½ cup (125 mL) sauce.

Stir crabmeat, first amount of cheese, reserved ½ cup (125 mL) sauce and olives together in separate bowl.

Dip tortillas quickly, 1 at a time, into remaining sauce. Place ¼ cup (60 mL) crab mixture at 1 end of tortilla. Roll up. Place seam side down in prepared pan. Spoon remaining sauce over rolls.

Scatter second amount of cheese over all. Bake, uncovered, in 350°F (175°C) oven for about 25 minutes until heated through. Makes 12 enchiladas.

1 enchilada: 205 Calories; 14 g Protein; 7.4 g Total Fat; 22 g Carbohydrate; 636 mg Sodium

Pictured on page 107.

Crab Special, below

Crab Enchiladas, page 106

Crab Special

Bright orange cheese covers red tomato slices, resting on a creamy pasta base. ⊙ Can be assembled in the morning and baked shortly before serving.

Elbow macaroni	1½ cups	375 mL
Boiling water	2 qts.	2 L
Cooking oil (optional)	2 tsp.	10 mL
Salt	1 tsp.	5 mL
Hard margarine (or butter)	2 tsp.	10 mL
Chopped onion	½ cup	125 mL
Light cream cheese, cut up	8 oz.	250 g
Light sour cream	1 cup	250 mL
Creamed cottage cheese	½ cup	125 mL
Canned crabmeat, drained and cartilage removed	2 × 4.2 oz.	2 × 120 g
Seasoning salt	½ tsp.	2 mL
Medium tomatoes, thinly sliced, to cover surface	1-2	1-2
Grated sharp Cheddar cheese	1 cup	250 mL

Cook macaroni in boiling water, cooking oil and salt in large, uncovered, saucepan for 5 to 7 minutes until tender but firm. Drain.

Melt margarine in frying pan. Add onion. Sauté until soft.

Add cream cheese, sour cream and cottage cheese. Stir together until cream cheese is melted.

Add crabmeat and seasoning salt. Stir. Add macaroni. Stir. Turn into ungreased 2 quart (2 L) casserole dish.

Cover with tomato slices and cheese. Bake, uncovered, in 350°F (175°C) oven for about 30 minutes. Serves 6.

1 serving: 368 Calories; 22 g Protein; 18.7 g Total Fat; 27 g Carbohydrate; 1013 mg Sodium

Pictured above.

Crab Extraordinaire

Serve in puff pastry shells for an elegant dinner. ⊙ Very good the next day served cold as a dip or spread.

Hard margarine (or butter)	1 tbsp.	15 mL
Sliced or chopped fresh mushrooms	1 cup	250 mL
Chopped onion	½ cup	125 mL
All-purpose flour	2 tbsp.	30 mL
Salt	½ tsp.	2 mL
Pepper	⅛ tsp.	0.5 mL
Skim evaporated milk	1½ cups	375 mL
Milk	1 cup	250 mL
Chopped pimiento	1 tbsp.	15 mL
Cayenne pepper	¹⁄₁₆ tsp.	0.5 mL
Canned crabmeat, drained and cartilage removed	2 × 4.2 oz.	2 × 120 g

Melt margarine in frying pan. Add mushrooms and onion. Sauté until soft.

Sprinkle with flour, salt and pepper. Mix in.

Stir in both milks until boiling and thickened.

Add pimiento, cayenne pepper and crabmeat. Heat through. Makes 3 cups (750 mL) sauce.

¾ cup (175 mL) sauce: 200 Calories; 19 g Protein; 4.4 g Total Fat; 21 g Carbohydrate; 912 mg Sodium

Pictured on front cover.

Shrimp Casserole

Very picturesque. ☺ Assemble in the morning and refrigerate until ready to bake.

Fresh asparagus, cut into 1 inch (2.5 cm) pieces (about 4½ cups, 1.1 L)	1½ lbs.	680 g
Boiling water, 1 inch (2.5 cm) deep	1 cup	250 mL
Large eggs, fork-beaten	6	6
Finely chopped onion	⅓ cup	75 mL
Finely chopped green pepper	½ cup	125 mL
Garlic powder	¼ tsp.	1 mL
Salt	½ tsp.	2 mL
Pepper	¼ tsp.	1 mL
Ground thyme, just a pinch		
Cooked fresh shrimp (or 2 cans 4 oz., 113 g, each, rinsed and drained)	2 cups	500 mL
Grated sharp Cheddar cheese	1 cup	250 mL

Cook asparagus in boiling water for 3 to 5 minutes until tender-crisp. Drain.

Combine next 8 ingredients in bowl. Add asparagus. Stir. Turn into greased 2 quart (2 L) casserole dish. Bake, uncovered, in 350°F (175°C) oven for 1¼ hours.

Sprinkle with cheese. Bake for 5 to 10 minutes until set. Serves 6.

1 serving: 242 Calories; 25 g Protein; 12.6 g Total Fat; 9 g Carbohydrate; 520 mg Sodium

Pictured on page 109.

Baked Cod

Quite colorful. ☺ Using condensed soup is the key to this quick recipe. Only ten minutes preparation time.

Cod fillets (or other)	1¾ lbs.	795 g
Salt, sprinkle		
Pepper, sprinkle		
Condensed cream of mushroom soup	10 oz.	284 mL
Green onions, chopped	6-8	6-8
Canned sliced mushrooms, drained	10 oz.	284 mL
Milk	¼ cup	60 mL

Arrange fish fillets in single layer in greased 9 × 13 inch (22 × 33 cm) pan. Sprinkle with salt and pepper.

Stir soup, green onion, mushrooms and milk together in bowl. Spoon over fillets. Bake, uncovered, in 350°F (175°C) oven for about 20 minutes until fish flakes when tested with a fork. Serves 8.

1 serving: 130 Calories; 19 g Protein; 3.7 g Total Fat; 4 g Carbohydrate; 445 mg Sodium

Pictured on page 109.

Crab Imperial

Very creamy, but not runny. ☺ This can be made in the morning, refrigerated and baked when ready.

All-purpose flour	¼ cup	60 mL
Salt	1 tsp.	5 mL
Pepper	¼ tsp.	1 mL
Milk	2 cups	500 mL
Grated Parmesan cheese	1½ tbsp.	25 mL
Light salad dressing (or mayonnaise)	¼ cup	60 mL
Dry mustard	¼ tsp.	1 mL
Chopped pimiento	2 tbsp.	30 mL
Hot pepper sauce	⅛ tsp.	0.5 mL
Worcestershire sauce	⅛ tsp.	0.5 mL
Crabmeat, cartilage removed, (or imitation crabmeat), 6 pieces reserved for garnish	1 lb.	454 g
Grated Parmesan cheese, sprinkle		
Paprika, sprinkle		

Stir flour, salt and pepper in saucepan. Whisk in milk, a little at a time, until no lumps remain. Add first amount of cheese. Heat and stir until boiling.

Stir in next 6 ingredients in order given. Divide among 6 scallop shells or ramekins. Place shells on baking sheet.

Sprinkle with second amount of cheese. Sprinkle with paprika. Bake, uncovered, in 375°F (190°C) oven for 15 to 20 minutes until bubbly hot. Serves 6.

1 serving: 165 Calories; 18 g Protein; 5.2 g Total Fat; 10 g Carbohydrate; 999 mg Sodium

Pictured on page 109.

1. Crab Imperial, page 108
2. Smoky Pasta, page 110
3. Baked Cod, page 108
4. Shrimp Casserole, page 108

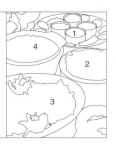

Smoky Pasta

The sauce can be made ahead and refrigerated.
When ready to serve, reheat and add pasta.

Penne pasta	3½ cups	875 mL
Boiling water	3 qts.	3 L
Cooking oil (optional)	1 tbsp.	15 mL
Salt	2 tsp.	10 mL
Sauce:		
Skim evaporated milk	1 cup	250 mL
Cooked fresh or frozen shrimp	¼ lb.	113 g
(or 1 can 4 oz., 113 g, rinsed and drained)		
Prepared horseradish	½ tbsp.	7 mL
Dill weed	½ tsp.	2 mL
Salt, just a pinch		
Pepper, sprinkle		
Smoked fish fillet, cut bite size	8 oz.	225 g
Chopped green onion	½ cup	125 mL
Cornstarch	2 tsp.	10 mL
Water	1 tbsp.	15 mL

Cook penne pasta in boiling water, cooking oil and salt in large, uncovered pot for 10 to 12 minutes until tender but firm. Drain. Return to pot. Keep warm.

Sauce: Combine next 8 ingredients in large saucepan. Heat through.

Combine cornstarch and water. Stir into shrimp mixture. Bring to a boil to thicken. Add pasta and fish chunks. Makes 7 cups (1.75 L) pasta.

1 cup (250 mL) pasta: 259 Calories; 16 g Protein; 2.4 g Total Fat; 42 g Carbohydrate; 293 mg Sodium

Pictured on page 109.

Clearly label fish before freezing, indicating what type of fish and the date they were frozen. White fish (such as cod and halibut) keeps for 12 months; oily fish (such as trout and herring) keeps for six months; cooked fish will last for three months.

Baked Fish

Baked Fish

Assemble in the morning and refrigerate.
Bake when ready.

Fresh fillets (such as cod or sole)	2¼ lbs.	1 kg
Lemon juice	3 tbsp.	50 mL
Minced onion flakes	1 tbsp.	15 mL
Salt	½ tsp.	2 mL
Pepper, sprinkle		
Chopped chives	2 tsp.	10 mL
Paprika, sprinkle		
Toasted sliced almonds	1½ tbsp.	25 mL
Sauce:		
Cornstarch	½ tbsp.	7 mL
Water	1 tbsp.	15 mL

Sprinkle fish fillets with lemon juice. Lay ½ of fillets in greased 8 x 8 inch (20 x 20 cm) pan.

Sprinkle with next 4 ingredients. Lay second ½ of fillets over top.

Sprinkle with paprika and almonds. Bake in 400°F (205°C) oven for about 25 minutes until fish flakes when tested with fork.

Sauce: Using turkey baster, remove liquid from pan to small saucepan. Combine cornstarch and water in small cup. Add to liquid. Heat, stirring constantly, until boiling and thickened. Makes about 1 cup (250 mL) sauce. Serve over fish. Serves 6 to 8.

⅙ recipe: 154 Calories; 30 g Protein; 2 g Total Fat; 3 g Carbohydrate; 328 mg Sodium

Pictured above.

Baked Halibut

A firm, white fish with a mild flavor.
☉ Marinate, assemble and refrigerate in
the morning until ready to bake.

Fish steaks, serving-size portions	2 lbs.	900 g
Marinade:		
Lemon juice	2 tbsp.	30 mL
Cooking oil	1/4 cup	60 mL
White vinegar	1 1/2 tbsp.	25 mL
Granulated sugar	1/2 tsp.	2 mL
Paprika	1/2 tsp.	2 mL
Salt	1/2 tsp.	2 mL
Pepper	1/16 tsp.	0.5 mL
Canned french-fried onions	2 3/4 oz.	79 g
Grated Parmesan cheese	2 1/2 tbsp.	37 mL

Place fish in ungreased shallow pan.

Marinade: Stir next 7 ingredients in bowl. Spoon over fish. Marinate for 30 minutes, turning fish over after 15 minutes. Remove fish, discarding the marinade, to greased baking dish, large enough to hold in single layer.

Crush onions into separate bowl. Add cheese. Stir. Sprinkle over fish. Bake, uncovered, in 350°F (175°C) oven for 25 to 30 minutes until fish flakes when tested with fork. Serves 6.

1 serving: 261 Calories; 33 g Protein; 11.2 g Total Fat; 6 g Carbohydrate; 302 mg Sodium

Pictured below.

Coddled Cod

Bright orange and yellow atop bright red.
Unique appearance. ☉ Prepare up to one hour
ahead and pop in oven when ready.

Fine dry bread crumbs	1/4 cup	60 mL
Cod (or sole) fillets	2 lbs.	900 g
Fine dry bread crumbs	1/4 cup	60 mL
Canned tomatoes, broken up	14 oz.	398 mL
Dried whole oregano	2 tsp.	10 mL
Dried sweet basil	2 tsp.	10 mL
Salt, sprinkle		
Pepper, sprinkle		
Light salad dressing (or mayonnaise)	2/3 cup	150 mL
Grated medium or sharp Cheddar cheese	2/3 cup	150 mL
Lemon juice	1/2 tsp.	2 mL
Prepared mustard	1/2 tsp.	2 mL

Sprinkle first amount of bread crumbs in single layer in ungreased baking sheet with sides. Lay cod over top. Sprinkle with second amount of bread crumbs.

Mix tomatoes, oregano, basil, salt and pepper in bowl. Pour carefully over fish.

Stir salad dressing, cheese, lemon juice and mustard together in small bowl. Spoon over tomato mixture. Bake, uncovered, in 400°F (205°C) oven for about 20 minutes until fish flakes when tested with fork. Serves 6 to 8.

1/6 recipe: 310 Calories; 32 g Protein; 13.2 g Total Fat; 15 g Carbohydrate; 470 mg Sodium

Pictured below.

Baked Halibut

Coddled Cod

Meat & Poultry

Dinner entertaining may take a little more effort than a simple afternoon tea, but it can still remain a congenial, relaxed event that allows everyone gathered around your table to feel both welcome and important.

When choosing a meat or poultry dish for the main course, keep in mind that it will be the focus of the meal. This section offers a wonderful variety of beef, chicken, turkey and pork recipes to choose from. In addition, take advantage of the many tips on how to prepare these dishes well in advance of guests arriving at your door. After all, entertaining should be easy, and these recipes were developed with that in mind.

Simple Stroganoff

Serve over rice or broad noodles. ☾ *Steak can be sliced earlier, leaving the actual stir-frying to be done when ready. Slicing steak is easier when partially frozen.*

Hard margarine (butter browns too fast)	1 tbsp.	15 mL
Sirloin steak, cut across grain into ⅛ inch (3 mm) thick slices	1 lb.	454 g
Light sour cream	1¼ cups	300 mL
Envelope dry onion soup mix, stirred before dividing	½ × 1½ oz.	½ × 42 g
Paprika	¼ tsp.	1 mL
Sherry (or alcohol-free sherry)	1 tbsp.	15 mL

Melt margarine in non-stick frying pan. Stir-fry steak until no pink remains.

Add remaining 4 ingredients. Heat on low, stirring often, until heated through. Do not boil. Serves 4.

1 serving: 246 Calories; 25 g Protein; 12.7 g Total Fat; 6 g Carbohydrate; 586 mg Sodium

Pictured on page 115.

Swiss Steak Supreme

The gravy mix really adds to the beefy flavor. Steak is easier to cut thinly if partially frozen. ☾ *Make ahead and freeze, or at least do all the chopping in the morning.*

Sirloin steak, cut into thin strips	2 lbs.	900 g
Sliced or chopped onion	2½ cups	625 mL
Chopped celery	1½ cups	375 mL
Large green pepper, cut into strips	1	1
Envelope mushroom beef gravy mix	1 × ¾ oz.	1 × 21 g
Envelope dry onion soup mix	1 × 1½ oz.	1 × 42 g
Canned mushroom pieces, with liquid	10 oz.	284 mL
Canned tomatoes, broken up	14 oz.	398 mL
Steak sauce	1 tbsp.	15 mL
Garlic powder (or 2 cloves garlic, minced)	½ tsp.	2 mL

Place steak strips in small roaster.

Scatter onion, celery and green pepper over top.

Stir remaining 6 ingredients together in bowl. Pour over top. Stir lightly. Cover. Bake in 325°F (160°C) oven for 1½ to 2 hours until beef is very tender. Makes 8 cups (2 L). Serves 8.

1 serving: 199 Calories; 25 g Protein; 4.9 g Total Fat; 14 g Carbohydrate; 871 mg Sodium

Pictured below.

Swiss Steak Supreme

Apricot Beef Bake

Casual Casserole

You may serve this meal-in-one from the roaster as is, or if you would like to fancy it up, set roaster on large piece of colored foil (from a florist) and gather sides upward. Tie foil in place with a wide ribbon. ☉ Do all the vegetable preparation in the morning. There's a lot to do.

Extra lean ground beef	2 lbs.	900 g
Thinly sliced celery	2½ cups	625 mL
Thinly sliced onion, in rings	3 cups	750 mL
Thinly sliced carrot	2 cups	500 mL
Thinly sliced fresh mushrooms (or 10 oz., 284 mL, drained)	2 cups	500 mL
Thinly sliced zucchini, with peel	4 cups	1 L
Large baking potatoes, thinly sliced	3	3
Condensed tomato soup	2 × 10 oz.	2 × 284 mL
Dried sweet basil	2 tsp.	10 mL
Dried tarragon	¼ tsp.	1 mL
Salt	1½ tsp.	7 mL
Pepper	¼ tsp.	1 mL

Place ground beef in medium ungreased roaster. Pat down to cover bottom evenly. Layer celery, onion, carrot, mushrooms, zucchini and potato in order over beef. Roaster will be very full but will settle during cooking.

Combine soup, basil, tarragon, salt and pepper in small bowl. Stir well. Spoon over all. Bake, covered, in 350°F (175°C) oven for 1 hour. Remove cover. Bake for 1¼ to 1½ hours, basting every 30 minutes, until vegetables are tender. Serves 8.

1 serving: 410 Calories; 33 g Protein; 17.7 g Total Fat; 31 g Carbohydrate; 1163 mg Sodium; excellent source of Dietary Fiber

Pictured below.

Casual Casserole

Apricot Beef Bake

The apricot flavor is mild but noticeable. An easy one-dish stew. ☉ Can be made ahead and frozen.

Beef stew meat, large cubes	2 lbs.	900 g
Finely chopped onion	1½ cups	375 mL
Canned apricots, with juice, processed in blender	14 oz.	398 mL
Tomato sauce	¼ cup	60 mL
White vinegar	2 tsp.	10 mL
Worcestershire sauce	2 tsp.	10 mL
Brown sugar, packed	2 tsp.	10 mL
Ground ginger	¼ tsp.	1 mL
Ground allspice	¼ tsp.	1 mL
Salt	1 tsp.	5 mL
Pepper	¼ tsp.	1 mL

Place stew meat in 3 quart (3 L) casserole dish. Sprinkle onion over top. Bake, uncovered, in 400°F (205°C) oven for 10 minutes. Stir. Bake for 10 minutes.

Reduce oven temperature to 325°F (160°C). Add remaining 9 ingredients. Stir. Cover. Bake for 2½ to 3 hours until very tender. Serves 8.

1 serving: 151 Calories; 19 g Protein; 3.5 g Total Fat; 11 g Carbohydrate; 443 mg Sodium

Pictured above.

Corned Beef Patties

Serve in hamburger buns or as patties with potato and vegetable. ☺ *Make patties ahead and refrigerate until ready to bake.*

Canned corned beef hash	14 oz.	398 mL
Large egg	1	1
Onion powder	¼ tsp.	1 mL
Salt	¼ tsp.	1 mL
Pepper	⅛ tsp.	0.5 mL
Sweet pickle relish	4 tsp.	20 mL
Process cheese slices	4	4
Tomato slices	4	4

Mix first 5 ingredients in bowl. Divide into 4 portions. Shape into patties. Place on greased baking sheet with sides. Broil each side of patties for about 5 minutes until brown.

Spread 1 tsp. (5 mL) relish over each patty. Top with cheese slice then tomato slice. Broil until cheese starts to melt. Serves 4.

1 serving: 393 Calories; 36 g Protein; 26 g Total Fat; 3 g Carbohydrate; 1656 mg Sodium

Pictured on page 115.

Reubens

Shape portions into square patties. Brown both sides. Place on 4 slices of rye bread. Cover each patty with ⅓ cup (75 mL) hot sauerkraut and 1 slice process Swiss cheese. Top each with slice of rye bread. Makes 4 sandwiches.

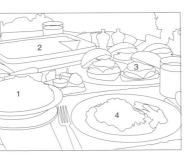

Beef With Ginger

Pleasant nip of ginger with a hint of sweetness from the cookies. Serve over noodles or rice. ⊙ Cut up beef and vegetables in the morning. Cover separately and refrigerate until almost serving time. Cooking time is only about 20 minutes.

Beef sirloin steak	¾ lb.	340 g
All-purpose flour	⅓ cup	75 mL
Ground ginger	½ tsp.	2 mL
Salt	½ tsp.	2 mL
Pepper	⅛ tsp.	0.5 mL
Cooking oil	1 tbsp.	15 mL
Onion, cut in half lengthwise, then sliced	1¼ cups	300 mL
Sliced celery	1⅔ cups	400 mL
Thinly sliced carrot	1⅓ cups	325 mL
Hot water	1½ cups	375 mL
Cider vinegar	⅓ cup	75 mL
Beef bouillon powder	2 tbsp.	30 mL
Medium noodles	8 oz.	250 g
Boiling water	3 qts.	3 L
Cooking oil (optional)	1 tbsp.	15 mL
Salt	2 tsp.	10 mL
Sauce:		
Water	1½ cups	375 mL
Gingersnap cookie crumbs	½ cup	125 mL
Beef bouillon powder	2 tsp.	10 mL

Cut steak across the grain into very thin strips. This is easier to do if you partially freeze steak first.

Put flour, ginger, salt and pepper into bowl. Stir. Add steak strips. Stir to coat.

Heat cooking oil in frying pan on medium-high. Brown steak in oil. Remove to bowl.

Add onion, celery and carrot to hot frying pan. Stir-fry for 5 minutes. Reduce heat.

Add water, vinegar and bouillon powder. Stir well. Cover. Simmer for 5 to 7 minutes until vegetables are tender-crisp.

Cook noodles in boiling water, cooking oil and salt in large, uncovered, saucepan for 5 to 7 minutes until tender but firm. Drain.

Sauce: Stir water, crumbs and bouillon powder together in small bowl. Stir into vegetable mixture. Add beef. Heat until boiling and thickened. Spoon over pasta. Serves 6.

1 serving (with noodles): 362 Calories; 20 g Protein; 6.8 g Total Fat; 55 g Carbohydrate; 1156 mg Sodium; good source of Dietary Fiber

Pictured on page 123.

Almost Lasagne

Super easy to make. Unexpected company is in for a treat. ⊙ A wonderful help-mate to have baked and frozen. Best to cut before freezing.

Lean ground beef	2 lbs.	900 g
Thick, chunky spaghetti sauce	2 cups	500 mL
Chopped onion	1 cup	250 mL
Salt	1 tsp.	5 mL
Pepper	¼ tsp.	1 mL
Medium noodles	8 oz.	250 g
Boiling water	3 qts.	3 L
Cooking oil (optional)	1 tbsp.	15 mL
Salt	2 tsp.	10 mL
Light cream cheese	4 oz.	125 g
Non-fat sour cream	1 cup	250 mL
Creamed cottage cheese	1 cup	250 mL
Grated medium or sharp Cheddar cheese	1 cup	250 mL

Scramble-fry ground beef in non-stick frying pan until no pink remains.

Add spaghetti sauce, onion, first amount of salt and pepper. Stir. Simmer for 10 minutes.

Cook noodles in boiling water, cooking oil and second amount of salt in uncovered Dutch oven for 7 to 8 minutes until tender but firm. Drain.

Mix cream cheese, sour cream and cottage cheese in bowl.

Assemble in ungreased 3 quart (3 L) casserole dish as follows:

1.   ½ of noodles
2.   ½ of beef mixture
3.   ½ of cottage cheese mixture
4.   ½ of noodles
5.   ½ of beef mixture
6.   ½ of cottage cheese mixture
7.   All Cheddar cheese

Bake, uncovered, in 350°F (175°C) oven for 35 to 40 minutes. Let stand for 10 minutes before serving. Serves 8.

1 serving: 535 Calories; 37 g Protein; 25.9 g Total Fat; 37 g Carbohydrate; 1135 mg Sodium

Pictured on page 114/115.

Thai Noodles

Just the right amount of "hot." A nice, colorful dish.
🕐 *Make sauce ahead and add to pasta just before serving.*

Broken-up fettuccine noodles	4 cups	1 L
Boiling water	3 qts.	3 L
Cooking oil (optional)	1 tbsp.	15 mL
Salt	2 tsp.	10 mL
Lean ground beef	1 lb.	454 g
Sesame oil	2 tsp.	10 mL
Red pepper, slivered	1	1
Yellow pepper slivered	1	1
Chopped onion	1 cup	250 mL
Dried crushed chilies	1/4 tsp.	1 mL
Minced fresh ginger	1/2 tbsp.	7 mL
Garlic cloves, minced (or 3/4 tsp., 4 mL, garlic powder)	3	3
Canned tomatoes, broken up	14 oz.	398 mL
Granulated sugar	1 tsp.	5 mL
Red wine vinegar	1 tsp.	5 mL
Ground coriander	1 tsp.	5 mL
Salt	1/2 tsp.	2 mL
Pepper	1/4 tsp.	1 mL
Light soy sauce	3 tbsp.	50 mL
Peanut sauce (available in Asian section in grocery store)	2 tbsp.	30 mL

Cook fettuccine noodles in boiling water, cooking oil and salt in large, uncovered, saucepan for 5 to 7 minutes until tender but firm. Drain. Return pasta to saucepan. Keep warm.

Scramble-fry ground beef in non-stick wok or frying pan until no pink remains. Drain. Remove to bowl. Wipe wok clean with paper towel.

Heat sesame oil in wok or frying pan. Add next 6 ingredients. Stir-fry for 3 to 5 minutes.

Add remaining 8 ingredients and beef. Simmer, uncovered, for 4 to 5 minutes. Add to pasta in saucepan. Toss. Makes 8 cups (2 L) noodles.

1 cup (250 mL) noodles: 215 Calories; 15 g Protein; 7.4 g Total Fat; 22 g Carbohydrate; 678 mg Sodium

Pictured on page 114.

Bean Stew

If stew can be beautiful, this is it. Warm colors and great taste. 🕐 *Can be made ahead and frozen.*

Cooking oil	1 tbsp.	15 mL
Lean ground beef	1 1/2 lbs.	680 g
Chopped onion	2 cups	500 mL
Bacon slices, diced	6	6
Condensed tomato soup	2 × 10 oz.	2 × 284 mL
Canned kidney beans, with liquid	2 × 14 oz.	2 × 398 mL
Medium carrots, thinly sliced	5	5
Medium potatoes, cubed	5	5
Salt	1 tsp.	5 mL
Pepper	1/2 tsp.	2 mL

Heat cooking oil in frying pan. Add ground beef, onion and bacon. Scramble-fry until beef is browned and no pink remains. Drain well.

Put soup, kidney beans with liquid, carrot and potato into large saucepan. Add salt and pepper. Stir. Add beef mixture. Bring to a slow boil. Cover. Simmer for about 1 1/4 hours until vegetables are cooked. Makes 12 cups (3 L) stew.

1 cup (250 mL) stew: 269 Calories; 17 g Protein; 8.6 g Total Fat; 32 g Carbohydrate; 912 mg Sodium; excellent source of Dietary Fiber

Pictured below.

Bean Stew

Beef Crusted Pie

This attractive dish takes extra time to prepare. ☺ *Ground beef can be cooked and cooled ahead. Vegetables can be cut up and cheese can be grated.*

Lean ground beef	1½ lbs.	680 g
Salt	¾ tsp.	4 mL
Pepper	¼ tsp.	1 mL
Biscuit mix	2⅔ cups	650 mL
Water	⅔ cup	150 mL
Filling:		
Tomatoes, thinly sliced	3	3
Thinly sliced zucchini, with peel	1½ cups	375 mL
Small green pepper, chopped	1	1
Grated medium or sharp Cheddar cheese	¾ cup	175 mL
Onion flakes	1 tbsp.	15 mL
Low-fat salad dressing (or mayonnaise)	½ cup	125 mL
Non-fat sour cream	1 cup	250 mL

Scramble-fry ground beef with salt and pepper in non-stick frying pan until no pink remains. Drain well. Cool.

Mix biscuit mix with water in bowl. Press in bottom and 1 inch (2.5 cm) up sides of greased 9 x 13 inch (22 x 33 cm) pan.

Filling: Spread beef over crust. Add layer of tomato, zucchini and green pepper.

Combine cheese, onion flakes, salad dressing and sour cream in bowl. Mix. Spoon over all. Bake, uncovered, in 350°F (175°C) oven for 30 to 35 minutes. Serves 8.

1 serving: 436 Calories; 23 g Protein; 20.6 g Total Fat; 39 g Carbohydrate; 1081 mg Sodium

Pictured on page 119.

Meat 'N' Potato Bake

This tasty dish will remind you of Shepherd's Pie. ☺ *Can be made ahead and frozen.*

Large egg	1	1
Milk	¼ cup	60 mL
Fine dry bread crumbs	½ cup	125 mL
Chopped onion	1 cup	250 mL
Ketchup	⅓ cup	75 mL
Seasoning salt	½ tsp.	2 mL
Salt	½ tsp.	2 mL
Pepper	¼ tsp.	1 mL
Lean ground beef	1½ lbs.	680 g
Topping:		
Medium potatoes, peeled and quartered	4	4
Water, to cover		
Milk	¼ cup	60 mL
Onion salt	½ tsp.	2 mL
Pepper	⅛ tsp.	0.5 mL

Paprika, sprinkle

Beat egg in bowl. Add next 7 ingredients. Stir well.

Add ground beef. Mix. Pack into greased 2 quart (2 L) casserole dish. Bake, uncovered, in 350°F (175°C) oven for 45 minutes. Drain off any fat.

Topping: Cook potato in water until tender. Drain.

Add milk, onion salt and pepper. Mash together well. Spread over meatloaf.

Sprinkle with paprika. Bake for about 20 minutes until potatoes are hot and beef is cooked. Serves 6.

1 serving: 336 Calories; 25 g Protein; 11.1 g Total Fat; 33 g Carbohydrate; 782 mg Sodium

Pictured below.

Tangy-Sauced Patties, page 119

Meat 'N' Potato Bake, above

Beef Crusted Pie, page 118

Tangy-Sauced Patties

More of a nip than a bite. ☺ The patties can be made ahead and frozen.

Large egg	1	1
Milk	⅓ cup	75 mL
Quick-cooking rolled oats (not instant)	1 cup	250 mL
Finely chopped onion	1 cup	250 mL
Salt	1 tsp.	5 mL
Pepper	½ tsp.	2 mL
Lean ground beef	1 lb.	454 g
Tangy Sauce:		
Brown sugar, packed	½ cup	125 mL
Prepared mustard	2 tbsp.	30 mL
Lemon juice	2 tsp.	10 mL
Tomato sauce	14 oz.	398 mL

Beat egg and milk together in bowl. Add rolled oats, onion, salt and pepper. Stir.

Add ground beef. Mix well. Shape into ¼ cup (60 mL) patties. Cook in non-stick frying pan, browning both sides, until no pink remains.

Tangy Sauce: Heat and stir all 4 ingredients in saucepan until hot. Serve over patties. Makes about 12 patties and 2 cups (500 mL) sauce.

1 patty (with sauce): 172 Calories; 10 g Protein; 6.8 g Total Fat; 18 g Carbohydrate; 505 mg Sodium

Pictured on page 118.

Beef Medallions

Beef is very tender and sauce is loaded with mushrooms and onion. Have your butcher slice the beef thinly or slice beef when partially frozen. ☺ Slice the vegetables and have ready in the refrigerator.

Hard margarine (or butter)	1 tbsp.	15 mL
Cooking oil	1 tbsp.	15 mL
Beef tenderloin medallions, cut ¼ inch (6 mm) thick (about 8-12)	1 lb.	454 g
All-purpose flour		
Salt, sprinkle		
Hard margarine (or butter)	1 tsp.	5 mL
Sliced fresh mushrooms	2 cups	500 mL
Sliced green onion	½ cup	125 mL
Milk	1 cup	250 mL
Beef bouillon powder	2 tsp.	10 mL
Cornstarch	1 tbsp.	15 mL
Red (or alcohol-free red) wine	2 tbsp.	30 mL

Heat first amount of margarine and cooking oil in non-stick frying pan.

Coat medallions on both sides with flour. Add to frying pan. Sprinkle with salt. Brown both sides until desired doneness. Remove to platter. Cover. Keep warm.

Heat second amount of margarine in frying pan. Add mushrooms and onion. Sauté until onion is soft and liquid is evaporated.

Mix milk, bouillon powder and cornstarch in bowl. Add to mushroom mixture. Stir until boiling and thickened.

Stir in wine. Divide beef medallions, overlapping one another, on each plate. Spoon sauce over top. Serves 4.

1 serving: 270 Calories; 24 g Protein; 14.8 g Total Fat; 8 g Carbohydrate; 425 mg Sodium

Pictured below.

Beef Medallions

Meatloaf Extraordinaire, below   Beef Stew, page 122   Stir-Fried Supper, page 121

Meatloaf Extraordinaire

Comfort food at its finest.
⏲ *This can be made ahead and frozen.*

Sauce:

Tomato sauce	7½ oz.	213 mL
Brown sugar, packed	⅓ cup	75 mL
White vinegar	⅓ cup	75 mL
Prepared mustard	1 tsp.	5 mL

Loaf:

Large egg	1	1
Finely chopped onion	1 cup	250 mL
Salt	1 tsp.	5 mL
Pepper	¼ tsp.	1 mL
Beef bouillon powder	2 tsp.	10 mL
Worcestershire sauce	1 tsp.	5 mL
Fine dry bread crumbs	½ cup	125 mL
Lean ground beef	2 lbs.	900 g

Sauce: Place all 4 ingredients in bowl. Stir together well. Divide into 2 equal portions.

Loaf: Beat egg in bowl. Add next 6 ingredients. Add ½ of sauce. Stir well.

Add ground beef. Mix very well. Pack firmly into greased 9 x 5 x 3 inch (22 x 12.5 x 7.5 cm) loaf pan. Spread remaining ½ of sauce over top. Bake in 350°F (175°C) oven for 1½ hours. Drain off any fat. Cuts into 8 slices.

1 slice: 264 Calories; 23 g Protein; 10.5 g Total Fat; 19 g Carbohydrate; 779 mg Sodium

Pictured above.

Company Meatloaf

Fairly traditional meatloaf, but with a "crowning" touch.
⏲ *Prepare the meatloaf in the morning and have ready in the pan, or make ahead and freeze, without the the glaze.*

Large eggs	2	2
Milk	⅔ cup	150 mL
Fine dry bread crumbs	1 cup	250 mL
Finely chopped onion	1¼ cups	300 mL
Grated carrot	⅔ cup	150 mL
Grated sharp Cheddar cheese	1 cup	250 mL
Seasoning salt	1 tsp.	5 mL
Worcestershire sauce	1 tsp.	5 mL
Salt	1 tsp.	5 mL
Pepper	¼ tsp.	1 mL
Lean ground beef	1½ lbs.	680 g

Topping:

Ketchup	¼ cup	60 mL
Brown sugar, packed	¼ cup	60 mL
Prepared mustard	2 tsp.	10 mL

Beat eggs together in bowl. Add next 9 ingredients. Stir. Let stand for 5 minutes to moisten bread crumbs.

Add ground beef. Mix well. Turn into greased 9 x 5 x 3 inch (22 x 12.5 x 7.5 cm) loaf pan. Bake in 350°F (175°C) oven for 1 hour. Drain.

Topping: Mix ketchup, brown sugar and mustard in small bowl. Spread over top of meatloaf. Bake in 350°F (175°C) oven for 30 minutes. Drain off any remaining fat. Cuts into 8 slices.

1 slice: 329 Calories; 24 g Protein; 14.3 g Total Fat; 26 g Carbohydrate; 909 mg Sodium

Pictured on page 123.

Stir-Fried Supper

Serve with steamed rice. Lots of sauce. Partially freezing the beef makes cutting easier. ⏱ *If you have all ingredients ready and at hand, you can have a conversation while stir-frying.*

Cooking oil	1 tbsp.	15 mL
Sirloin steak, cut across grain into thin strips	1 lb.	454 g
Large onion, halved lengthwise then thinly sliced	1	1
Grated carrot	1 cup	250 mL
Water	3 tbsp.	50 mL
Packed bok choy (or spinach or chard) leaves, chopped	2 cups	500 mL
Frozen pea pods, thawed	10 oz.	300 g
Sauce:		
Soy sauce	¼ cup	60 mL
Cornstarch	1 tbsp.	15 mL
Ketchup	1 tbsp.	15 mL
Brown sugar, packed	1 tbsp.	15 mL
Worcestershire sauce	¼ tsp.	1 mL

Heat cooking oil in wok or large frying pan until hot. Add beef strips. Stir-fry until desired doneness. Transfer to bowl.

Add onion, carrot and water to pan. Reduce heat. Cover. Simmer for 5 to 6 minutes until tender, adding more water if necessary.

Add bok choy and pea pods. Stir-fry for about 1 minute. Add beef. Stir.

Sauce: Stir soy sauce and cornstarch together in bowl. Add ketchup, brown sugar and Worcestershire sauce. Pour over meat mixture. Stir-fry until boiling and thickened. Makes 6 cups (1.5 L) stir-fry.

1½ cups (375 mL) stir-fry: 261 Calories; 27 g Protein; 7.9 g Total Fat; 20 g Carbohydrate; 1239 mg Sodium; good source of Dietary Fiber

Pictured on page 120.

Beefy Rice Casserole

An all-in-one casserole. ⏱ *Make ahead and freeze without the onion topping. Add when ready to reheat.*

Cooking oil	1 tsp.	5 mL
Lean ground beef	1 lb.	454 g
Chopped onion	2 cups	500 mL
Condensed cream of chicken soup	10 oz.	284 mL
Condensed cream of mushroom soup	10 oz.	284 mL
Water	1½ cups	375 mL
Uncooked long grain white rice	¾ cup	175 mL
Soy sauce	2 tbsp.	30 mL
Pepper	¼ tsp.	1 mL
Garlic powder	⅛ tsp.	0.5 mL
Ground ginger	⅛ tsp.	0.5 mL
Canned french-fried onions (or chow mein noodles)	2¾ oz.	79 g

Heat cooking oil in non-stick frying pan. Add ground beef and onion. Scramble-fry until beef is no longer pink and onion is soft. Drain well. Transfer to large bowl.

Add next 8 ingredients. Mix well. Turn into ungreased 2 quart (2 L) casserole dish. Cover. Bake in 350°F (175°C) oven for about 60 minutes until rice is tender.

Place onions over top. Bake, uncovered, for about 10 minutes to heat. Serves 6.

1 serving: 379 Calories; 19 g Protein; 16.5 g Total Fat; 37 g Carbohydrate; 1250 mg Sodium

Pictured below.

Beefy Rice Casserole

Beef Burgundy

Delicious stew served over noodles. ☺ Can be made ahead and frozen. Save some time by preparing carrots and onion in the morning.

Inside round beef roast, cubed bite size	2 lbs.	900 g
Medium carrots, halved lengthwise then cut crosswise	6-8	6-8
Medium onions, sliced	2	2
Boiling water	1 cup	250 mL
Beef bouillon powder	2 tsp.	10 mL
Burgundy (or other red or alcohol-free) wine	½ cup	125 mL
Bay leaf	1	1
Ground thyme	¼ tsp.	1 mL
Ground cloves, just a pinch		
Salt	½ tsp.	2 mL
Pepper	⅛ tsp.	0.5 mL
Bacon bits	2 tsp.	10 mL
Liquid gravy browner	1 tsp.	5 mL
Cornstarch (optional)	2 tbsp.	30 mL
Water (optional)	2 tbsp.	30 mL

Arrange meat in small roaster. Scatter carrot and onion over top.

Mix first amount of boiling water and bouillon powder in bowl. Stir.

Add next 8 ingredients. Stir. Pour over beef and vegetables. Cover. Bake in 300°F (150°C) oven for 3 to 3½ hours until beef is very tender. Serves 6.

Stir cornstarch into second amount of water. Drain beef, pouring liquid into saucepan. Bring to a boil. Stir cornstarch mixture into boiling liquid until it returns to a boil and thickens. Add water if needed to make 2 cups (500 mL). Pour over beef and vegetables. Stir. Makes 6 cups (1.5 L) stew.

1½ cups (375 mL) stew: 323 Calories; 38 g Protein; 7.5 g Total Fat; 20 g Carbohydrate; 861 mg Sodium; good source of Dietary Fiber

Pictured on page 123.

Beef Stew

Mellow flavors of wine and curry. ☺ This easy one-dish meal can be made ahead and frozen.

Inside round beef roast or beef stew meat, cut bite size	2 lbs.	900 g
Boiling water, to cover		
Chopped onion	1 cup	250 mL
Small green pepper, cut into strips	1	1
Canned tomatoes, with juice, cut up	14 oz.	398 mL
Curry powder	½-1 tsp.	2-5 mL
Garlic powder	⅛ tsp.	0.5 mL
Celery salt	⅛ tsp.	0.5 mL
Granulated sugar	1 tsp.	5 mL
Salt	1 tsp.	5 mL
Pepper	¼ tsp.	1 mL
Liquid gravy browner	1-2 tsp.	5-10 mL
Canned mushroom slices, drained	10 oz.	284 mL
Red wine	3 tbsp.	50 mL
Cornstarch	1½ tbsp.	25 mL

Combine beef and boiling water in Dutch oven. Cover and simmer for 1¼ hours.

Add next 10 ingredients. Cover. Simmer for about 30 minutes until onion is soft and beef is very tender.

Stir in mushrooms.

Stir wine and cornstarch together in small cup. Stir into stew until boiling and thickened. Makes 6 cups (1.5 L) stew.

1½ cups (375 mL) stew: 291 Calories; 38 g Protein; 7.3 g Total Fat; 16 g Carbohydrate; 1149 mg Sodium; good source of Dietary Fiber

Pictured on page 120.

Lasagne

Simple to prepare. Good consistency—neither dry, nor too runny. ⏱ This can be assembled, covered and refrigerated hours ahead. Bake when needed, or bake ahead and reheat. Can be cut and frozen, ready for an event.

Cooking oil	1 tbsp.	15 mL
Chopped onion	1¼ cups	300 mL
Garlic powder (or 1 clove garlic, minced)	¼ tsp.	1 mL
Lean ground beef	2 lbs.	900 g
Tomato sauce	14 oz.	398 mL
Tomato paste	5½ oz.	156 mL
Canned sliced mushrooms, drained	10 oz.	284 mL
Salt	2 tsp.	10 mL
Pepper	¼ tsp.	1 mL
Ground oregano	½ tsp.	2 mL
Granulated sugar	1 tsp.	5 mL
Hot water	2 cups	500 mL
Lasagne noodles	12	12
Boiling water	4 qts.	4 L
Cooking oil (optional)	1 tbsp.	15 mL
Salt	1 tbsp.	15 mL
Creamed cottage cheese	2 cups	500 mL
Grated mozzarella cheese	4 cups	1 L
Grated Parmesan cheese, sprinkle		

Heat cooking oil in frying pan. Add onion, garlic powder and ground beef. Scramble-fry until onion is soft and beef is no longer pink. This is easier to do in 2 batches. Turn into Dutch oven.

Add next 8 ingredients. Heat, stirring often, until mixture begins to simmer. Simmer for 20 minutes. Stir occasionally.

Cook lasagne noodles in boiling water, cooking oil and salt in uncovered Dutch oven for 14 to 16 minutes until tender but firm. Drain. Rinse with cold water. Drain. Assemble in ungreased 9 x 13 inch (22 x 33 cm) pan.

Assemble in layers:

1. Thin layer of meat sauce
2. ½ of noodles
3. All cottage cheese
4. ½ of mozzarella cheese
5. ½ of remaining meat sauce
6. ½ of noodles
7. ½ of meat sauce
8. ½ of mozzarella cheese
9. All Parmesan cheese

Bake, uncovered, in 350°F (175°C) oven for 45 to 55 minutes until golden. Lay foil over top if it browns too quickly. Serves 8.

1 serving: 653 Calories; 47 g Protein; 34.7 g Total Fat; 37 g Carbohydrate; 1651 mg Sodium; good source of Dietary Fiber

Pictured on page 123.

---

1. Hot Biscuits, page 62
2. Sweet And Sour Pork, page 128
3. Pork Tenderloin, page 128
4. Mixed Grill, page 130
5. Spinach Apple Toss, page 148

Beef Brisket

Very tender. Very quick to prepare—only five minutes. ⏱ Prepare brisket first thing in the morning, refrigerate until noon, then bake. Your afternoon is free to visit or do other preparations.

Dry mustard	1½ tsp.	7 mL
Flat beef brisket, trimmed of fat	4 lbs.	1.8 kg
Paprika	½ tsp.	2 mL
Medium onions, sliced	2	2
Paprika	½ tsp.	2 mL
Salt, sprinkle		
Pepper, sprinkle		
Gravy:		
Drippings, plus water to make	3 cups	750 mL
All-purpose flour	6 tbsp.	100 mL
Salt	1 tsp.	5 mL
Pepper	¼ tsp.	1 mL
Water	½ cup	125 mL
Liquid gravy browner (optional)		

Sprinkle dry mustard over bottom of large roaster. Lay beef brisket over top. Sprinkle with first amount paprika. Arrange onion over brisket. Sprinkle with second amount paprika, salt and pepper. Cover. Bake in 250°F (120°C) oven for 4½ hours. Remove meat and onions to a covered dish. Keep warm.

Gravy: Heat drippings plus water in saucepan until boiling.

Stir flour, salt and pepper together in bowl. Whisk in second amount of water until no lumps remain. Stir into boiling liquid until mixture returns to a boil and thickens. Add a bit of gravy browner if needed, to make gravy a better color. Return meat and onions to roaster. Heat through. Serves 10.

1 serving: 395 Calories; 35 g Protein; 24.8 g Total Fat; 6 g Carbohydrate; 354 mg Sodium

Pictured on page 128.

Baked Ham Slices

A delicate spice and sweetness.
🕐 *This only takes five minutes to prepare, and less than an hour to bake.*

Brown sugar, packed	¼ cup	60 mL
Ground allspice	¼ tsp.	1 mL
Ground cloves	⅛ tsp.	0.5 mL
Canned crushed pineapple, with juice	14 oz.	398 mL
Center cut ham steaks, each ½ inch (12 mm) thick, (about 2 lbs., 900 g total weight), trimmed of fat	2	2

Combine first 4 ingredients in bowl. Mix.

Lay ham steaks in single layer on ungreased baking sheet with sides. Spoon pineapple mixture over top. Bake, uncovered, in 400°F (205°C) oven for 30 to 40 minutes. Serves 6.

1 serving: 262 Calories; 30 g Protein; 6.5 g Total Fat; 21 g Carbohydrate; 1907 mg Sodium

Pictured on page 128.

Sauced Pork Balls

This is ideal to serve over rice. 🕐 *The sauce and the meatballs can be made the day before. Simply reheat and serve!*

Canned unsweetened pineapple tidbits, with juice	14 oz.	398 mL
Water	1¼ cups	300 mL
Soy sauce	2 tbsp.	30 mL
White vinegar	¼ cup	60 mL
Brown sugar, packed	6 tbsp.	100 mL
Cornstarch	¼ cup	60 mL
Garlic salt	¼ tsp.	1 mL
Pork Meatballs (large), page 127, cooked	30	30

Combine first 7 ingredients in large saucepan. Heat and stir until boiling and thickened.

Add meatballs. Heat through. Makes 8 servings.

1 serving: 319 Calories; 28 g Protein; 7.6 g Total Fat; 34 g Carbohydrate; 1013 mg Sodium

Pictured on page 128.

Sauced Wieners

Omit meatballs. Slice 1½ lbs. (680 g) wieners into coin-size pieces. Add to sauce. Fat and sodium content will be higher.

Ginger Pork

Nice and tangy. ☺ *The sauce and the pork can be made ahead separately and combined when it's time to reheat. Can also be frozen.*

Ginger Sauce:

Cooking oil	1 tbsp.	15 mL
Finely chopped onion	½ cup	125 mL
Finely chopped green pepper	¼ cup	60 mL
Grated carrot	¼ cup	60 mL
White vinegar	3 tbsp.	50 mL
Brown sugar, packed	¼ cup	60 mL
Soy sauce	1 tbsp.	15 mL
Ketchup	1 tbsp.	15 mL
Ground ginger	¼ tsp.	1 mL
Garlic powder	¼ tsp.	1 mL
Cornstarch	2 tsp.	10 mL
Water	1 tbsp.	15 mL
Cooking oil	1 tbsp.	15 mL
Boneless pork tenderloin or loin pork chops, trimmed of fat, cut into thin strips	1 lb.	454 g

Ginger Sauce: Heat cooking oil in frying pan. Add onion, green pepper and carrot. Stir-fry until soft.

Add next 6 ingredients. Stir.

Mix cornstarch and water in small bowl. Add to sauce. Stir until thickened. Keep warm.

Heat second amount of cooking oil in separate frying pan. Add pork strips. Stir-fry until no longer pink. Add sauce. Stir. Serves 4.

1 serving: 271 Calories; 25 g Protein; 9.8 g Total Fat; 21 g Carbohydrate; 376 mg Sodium

Pictured below.

Ginger Pork

Ham And Pasta Bake, page 129

Spiced Plum Pork Chops

Rich, dark sauce. ☺ *The strained plums are very convenient to use in this recipe. Reheat pork chops in sauce.*

Cooking oil, divided	2 tsp.	10 mL
Pork chops, trimmed of fat	12	12
Cooking apples, cored and sliced (such as McIntosh)	3	3
Jars strained plums (baby food)	3 × 4½ oz.	3 × 128 mL
Ground cinnamon	¼ tsp.	1 mL
Ground cloves	⅛ tsp.	0.5 mL
Salt, just a pinch		
White vinegar	2 tbsp.	30 mL

Heat 1 tsp. (5 mL) cooking oil in deep frying pan. Add 6 pork chops. Brown both sides. Remove to plate. Add second 1 tsp. (5 mL) cooking oil to pan. Add remaining 6 pork chops. Brown both sides.

Place ½ of apple slices over 6 pork chops in frying pan.

Stir next 5 ingredients together in bowl. Spoon ½ of plum mixture over apples on pork chops. Arrange remaining pork chops over top. Cover with second ½ of apples and remaining plum mixture. Cover. Simmer for about 30 minutes. Add a bit of water to sauce if needed. Remove cover. Simmer for about 10 minutes. Remove pork chops and keep warm. Boil sauce in pan until thickened. Serve with pork chops. Serves 8.

1 serving: 321 Calories; 31 g Protein; 14 g Total Fat; 18 g Carbohydrate; 76 mg Sodium

Pictured on page 127.

Spareribs Delish, below

Spiced Plum Pork Chops, page 126

Spareribs Delish

Very pungent aroma. Strong, spicy taste with an "afterburn." ⏲ *This can be prepared ahead and frozen right in the marinade.*

Pork spareribs, cut into 3 rib sections	6 lbs.	2.7 kg
Brown sugar, packed	1 cup	250 mL
Onion flakes (or ¼ cup, 60 mL, finely chopped onion)	2 tbsp.	30 mL
Prepared mustard	6 tbsp.	100 mL
Prepared horseradish	1 tbsp.	15 mL
Worcestershire sauce	2½ tbsp.	37 mL
Soy sauce	6 tbsp.	100 mL
Prepared orange juice	½ cup	125 mL
Garlic powder	⅛ tsp.	0.5 mL

Place ribs in large bowl or sealable plastic bag.

Stir remaining 8 ingredients together in separate bowl. Pour over ribs. Cover or seal. Marinate 6 to 8 hours, or overnight, turning occasionally. Strain marinade through sieve into saucepan. Heat until boiling. Boil for 2 minutes. Remove from heat. Reserve. Place ribs in roaster. Cover. Bake in 350°F (175°C) oven for 1½ to 2 hours until tender. Remove cover. Baste with reserved marinade. Bake for about 10 minutes to glaze. Serves 8.

1 serving: 545 Calories; 33 g Protein; 30.8 g Total Fat; 34 g Carbohydrate; 1109 mg Sodium

Pictured above.

Pork Meatballs

Nicely seasoned. ☺ *Make extra to store in your freezer for easy entertaining. Freeze loosely on trays. Keep frozen meatballs in plastic bags in freezer for two to three months.*

Large eggs, fork-beaten	2	2
Fine dry bread crumbs	1 cup	250 mL
Seasoning salt	1 tbsp.	15 mL
Pepper	½ tsp.	2 mL
Onion powder	½ tsp.	2 mL
Garlic powder	½ tsp.	2 mL
Dried whole oregano	½ tsp.	2 mL
Lean ground pork	2 lbs.	900 g

Combine first 7 ingredients in bowl. Stir well.

Add ground pork. Mix well. Divide pork mixture into 3 equal parts. Divide each ⅓ into 10 large meatballs. For smaller meatballs, divide pork mixture into 4 equal parts. Divide each ¼ into 20 meatballs. Arrange on ungreased baking sheet with sides. Bake larger meatballs in 400°F (205°C) oven for 20 minutes until golden brown. Bake smaller meatballs for 13 to 15 minutes until golden brown. Cool on paper towel to absorb fat. Makes 30 large meatballs or 80 small meatballs.

1 large meatball: 61 Calories; 7 g Protein; 2 g Total Fat; 3 g Carbohydrate; 188 mg Sodium

Pictured on page 131.

Pork Tenderloin

Sauce adds a spicy flavor. Grab the tenderloins when they go on sale and have them, seasoned, ready in the freezer. ⊕ Only three minutes to prepare and less than one hour to cook.

Seasoning salt	2 tsp.	10 mL
Curry powder	1/4 tsp.	1 mL
Chili powder	1/4 tsp.	1 mL
Pepper	1/4 tsp.	1 mL
Pork tenderloin (2 large)	3 lbs.	1.4 kg
Peach Sauce:		
Water	2 tbsp.	30 mL
Canned peach pie filling, chopped	19 oz.	540 mL
White vinegar	2 tbsp.	30 mL
Ground nutmeg	1/8 tsp.	0.5 mL
Ground cloves, scant measure	1/8 tsp.	0.5 mL

Combine first 4 ingredients in bowl.

Coat pork with spice mixture. Place in small roaster. Cover. Bake in 325°F (160 °C) oven for 50 to 60 minutes until no pink remains. Meat thermometer should reach 160°F (70°C).

Peach Sauce: Pour water into roaster after removing tenderloin. Stir to loosen all bits of pork and drippings. Pour into saucepan.

Add pie filling, vinegar, nutmeg and cloves. Heat, stirring often, until hot. Makes 2 cups (500 mL) sauce. Cut pork into slices. Serve with sauce. Serves 8.

1 serving with 2 tbsp. (30 mL) sauce: 235 Calories; 37 g Protein; 4.4 g Total Fat; 10 g Carbohydrate; 426 mg Sodium

Pictured on page 125.

Sweet And Sour Pork

Great served over rice. Glossy coating. ⊕ Have all ingredients measured ahead of time.

Pork leg, cut into strips, 2 inches (5 cm) long, 1/2 inch (12 mm) thick	1 1/2 lbs.	680 g
Cooking oil	1 tbsp.	15 mL
Chopped onion	1 1/2 cups	375 mL
Canned pineapple chunks, with juice	19 oz.	540 mL
White vinegar	2 tbsp.	30 mL
Lemon juice	2 tbsp.	30 mL
Soy sauce	2 tbsp.	30 mL
Green peppers, slivered	2	2
Brown sugar, packed	1/2 cup	125 mL
Cornstarch	2 tbsp.	30 mL

Stir-fry pork in cooking oil in frying pan until no pink remains.

Add next 5 ingredients. Cover. Simmer for 45 minutes.

Add green pepper. Cover. Simmer for 15 minutes until pork is tender and green pepper is tender-crisp.

Combine brown sugar and cornstarch in small cup. Add to pork mixture. Heat until boiling and thickened. Serves 6.

1 serving: 341 Calories; 25 g Protein; 8.2 g Total Fat; 43 g Carbohydrate; 431 mg Sodium

Pictured on page 125.

Bottom Left: Jumpin' Jambalaya, page 132
Top Left: Beef Brisket, page 124
Bottom Right: Baked Ham Slices, page 125
Top Right: Sauced Pork Balls, page 125

Snappy Crustless Quiche

Ham And Pasta Bake

An attractive meal-in-one dish. ☺ *This is a casserole that can be baked one day and reheated and served the next, or even frozen. Flavor is even better when reheated.*

Elbow macaroni	2 cups	500 mL
Boiling water	3 qts.	3 L
Cooking oil (optional)	1 tbsp.	15 mL
Salt	2 tsp.	10 mL
All-purpose flour	¼ cup	60 mL
Salt	1 tsp.	5 mL
Pepper	⅛ tsp.	0.5 mL
Dry mustard	½ tsp.	2 mL
Onion flakes	1 tbsp.	15 mL
Milk	2½ cups	625 mL
Frozen chopped broccoli	10 oz.	300 g
Boiling water, to cover		
Diced or cubed cooked ham (about ¾ lb., 340 g)	2 cups	500 mL
Grated medium or sharp Cheddar cheese	¾ cup	175 mL
Topping:		
Hard margarine (or butter)	2 tbsp.	30 mL
Fine dry bread crumbs	½ cup	125 mL

Cook macaroni in first amount of boiling water, cooking oil and salt in large, uncovered, saucepan for 5 to 7 minutes until tender but firm. Drain.

Combine flour, salt, pepper, dry mustard and onion flakes in medium saucepan. Gradually mix in milk so no lumps remain. Heat and stir until boiling and thickened.

Cook broccoli in second amount of boiling water until tender-crisp. Drain. Add to sauce. Stir in macaroni.

Add ham and cheese. Stir. Turn into ungreased 2 quart (2 L) casserole dish.

Topping: Melt margarine in saucepan. Stir in bread crumbs. Sprinkle over all. Bake in 350°F (175°C) oven for about 30 minutes until browned. Serves 6.

1 serving: 428 Calories; 27 g Protein; 14 g Total Fat; 49 g Carbohydrate; 1540 mg Sodium

Pictured on page 126.

Snappy Crustless Quiche

Just enough spices for a mid-morning brunch. ☺ *To prepare in the morning, or even the night before, the first seven ingredients can be placed in baking dish. Combine remaining dry ingredients into another bowl, adding eggs and milk just before baking.*

Finely chopped onion	¼ cup	60 mL
Finely chopped green pepper	¼ cup	60 mL
Chopped chives	1 tbsp.	15 mL
Canned sliced mushrooms, drained	10 oz.	284 mL
Chopped cooked ham (about 5 slices)	1 cup	250 mL
Grated mozzarella cheese	¾ cup	175 mL
Grated sharp Cheddar cheese	¼ cup	60 mL
Large eggs	3	3
Salt	⅛ tsp.	0.5 mL
Pepper	1/16 tsp.	0.5 mL
Dried sweet basil	1/16 tsp.	0.5 mL
Dried whole oregano	1/16 tsp.	0.5 mL
Paprika	1/16 tsp.	0.5 mL
Garlic powder	1/16 tsp.	0.5 mL
Biscuit mix	¾ cup	175 mL
Milk	1¼ cups	300 mL

Sprinkle first 7 ingredients in order given, in layers, in greased 10 inch (25 cm) casserole or quiche dish.

Beat eggs in bowl. Add next 6 ingredients. Beat.

Add biscuit mix and milk. Beat well. Pour over layers in casserole. Bake in 400°F (205°C) oven for about 30 minutes until knife inserted in center comes out clean. Let stand for 3 minutes before serving. Serves 6.

1 serving: 263 Calories; 16 g Protein; 13.8 g Total Fat; 18 g Carbohydrate; 919 mg Sodium

Pictured above.

Sausage Strata

Very attractive. Lots of sausage and cheese. Mustard gives an added zip to the taste. ☺ The casserole can be prepared the day before up to the baking stage. Cover, refrigerate and bake the next day.

Bread slices, crusts removed	5-6	5-6
Sausage meat	1 lb.	454 g
Chopped onion	1 cup	250 mL
Diced green pepper	1 cup	250 mL
Grated sharp Cheddar cheese	1 cup	250 mL
Large eggs	4	4
Skim evaporated milk	13½ oz.	385 mL
Prepared mustard	1 tbsp.	15 mL
Seasoning salt	½ tsp.	2 mL
Pepper	1/16 tsp.	0.5 mL
Bread slices, crusts removed	5-6	5-6
Crushed flakes of corn cereal	½ cup	125 mL
Hard margarine (or butter), melted	1 tbsp.	15 mL

Cover bottom of greased 9 x 9 inch (22 x 22 cm) pan with first amount of bread slices.

Scramble-fry sausage in frying pan for 3 minutes. Add onion and green pepper. Scramble-fry for 2 minutes until sausage is no longer pink and onion is soft. Drain. Sprinkle over bread layer in pan.

Sprinkle with cheese.

Combine next 5 ingredients in small bowl. Soak the second amount of bread slices in the milk mixture. Place over cheese. Pour remaining milk mixture very carefully over top. Pan will be very full.

Combine crushed cereal and margarine in small bowl. Sprinkle over top. Bake, uncovered, in 350°F (175°C) oven for 40 minutes until set. Serves 6.

1 serving: 503 Calories; 24 g Protein; 26.3 g Total Fat; 42 g Carbohydrate; 993 mg Sodium

Pictured below.

Sausage Strata

Mixed Grill

Although spicy-hot barbecue sauce is used, it is toned down by the condensed lemonade. ☺ This makes enough for a crowd, or freeze in two batches in the marinade for a quick stand-by barbecue.

Pork spareribs, cut into 3 rib sections	6 lbs.	2.7 kg
Garlic powder	½ tsp.	2 mL
Chicken parts, skin removed	12	12
Garlic powder	½ tsp.	2 mL
Bay leaves	2	2
Water	3 cups	750 mL
Frozen concentrated lemonade, thawed	12½ oz.	355 mL
Spicy-hot barbecue sauce	1⅔ cups	400 mL

Place ribs in roaster. Sprinkle with first amount of garlic powder. Arrange chicken parts over top. Sprinkle with second amount of garlic powder. Drop bay leaves along edge. Pour water over top. Cover. Bake in 325°F (160°C) oven for about 1½ hours, turning chicken at half-time. Drain off liquid and discard or save for soup stock. Remove ribs and chicken to large bowl or sealable plastic bag. Discard bay leaves.

Stir concentrated lemonade with barbecue sauce in small bowl. Pour over combined chicken and ribs or divide the chicken and ribs into 2 separate bowls or sealable freezer bags. Cover or seal. At this point the chicken and ribs can be marinated in the refrigerator for 6 to 8 hours, overnight or frozen.

To Barbecue: Remove ribs and chicken to heated barbecue. Cook over low heat for 20 to 30 minutes, turning and basting often with marinade.

To Oven Cook: Line baking sheet with foil. Grease foil. Arrange ribs and chicken in single layer on foil. Pour marinade over top. Bake in 325°F (160°C) oven for 30 minutes until tender, turning at half-time and basting with marinade. Serves 12.

1 serving: 470 Calories; 38 g Protein; 24.5 g Total Fat; 22 g Carbohydrate; 430 mg Sodium

Pictured on page 125.

Pork Meatballs, page 127   Easy Chutney, below

Special Curry

Curry can be increased to suit your taste. Great served over rice. ☉ To save time, prepare the vegetables while the meat is boiling.

Lamb (or beef) stew meat, cut bite size	2 lbs.	900 g
Chopped onion	1½ cups	375 mL
Water	3 cups	750 mL
Beef bouillon powder	1 tbsp.	15 mL
Medium carrots, diced	2	2
Large apples, peeled and cubed	2	2
Crushed pineapple, with juice	1 cup	250 mL
Chopped celery	½ cup	125 mL
Raisins	⅓ cup	75 mL
Plum jam	2 tbsp.	30 mL
Chutney	2 tbsp.	30 mL
Granulated sugar	4 tsp.	20 mL
Curry powder	2 tsp.	10 mL
Salt	2 tsp.	10 mL
Pepper	1 tsp.	5 mL
Cornstarch	¼ cup	60 mL
Water	¼ cup	60 mL

Place first 4 ingredients in saucepan. Bring to a boil. Boil slowly for 1 hour.

Add next 11 ingredients. Stir. Bring to a boil. Boil slowly for about 30 minutes until lamb is very tender.

Mix cornstarch and water in cup. Stir into boiling mixture until it returns to a boil and thickens. Makes about 9 cups (2.25 L) curry.

1½ cups (375 mL) curry: 375 Calories; 32 g Protein; 8.5 g Total Fat; 43 g Carbohydrate; 1322 mg Sodium; good source of Dietary Fiber

Pictured below.

Easy Chutney

An eye-catching go-with. Especially nice with pork. ☉ You can make this almost any time of the year. Make ahead and refrigerate for several months.

Canned tomatoes, with juice, chopped	2 × 28 oz.	2 × 796 mL
Pears, peeled and chopped	3	3
Peaches, peeled and chopped	3	3
Yellow pepper, chopped	1	1
Red pepper, chopped	1	1
Granulated sugar	2 cups	500 mL
White vinegar	2 cups	500 mL
Mixed pickling spice, tied in double layer of cheesecloth	2 tbsp.	30 mL
Garlic cloves, minced	2	2

Combine all 9 ingredients in large Dutch oven. Heat, stirring often, as it comes to a boil. Boil rapidly, uncovered, for 10 minutes. Lower heat. Simmer for 45 minutes. Check consistency. Continue to boil, for about 45 minutes, until mixture thickens. Pour into hot sterilized jars to within ¼ inch (6 mm) of top. Place sterilized metal lids on jars and screw metal bands on securely. For added assurance against spoilage, you may choose to process in a boiling water bath for 10 minutes. Makes 8 cups (2 L) chutney.

⅓ cup (75 mL) chutney: 96 Calories; 1 g Protein; 0.2 g Total Fat; 25 g Carbohydrate; 337 mg Sodium

Pictured above.

Special Curry

Chicken Capers

Tangy taste. ⊙ Marinate overnight. When ready to cook, dip into crumbs, drizzle with melted butter and bake.

Light sour cream	2 cups	500 mL
Lemon juice	¼ cup	60 mL
Worcestershire sauce	1 tbsp.	15 mL
Seasoning salt	1 tbsp.	15 mL
Paprika	1 tsp.	5 mL
Pepper	½ tsp.	2 mL
Boneless, skinless chicken breast halves	10	10
Soda cracker crumbs (see Note)	2 cups	500 mL
Hard margarine (or butter), melted	3 tbsp.	50 mL

Place first 6 ingredients in bowl. Stir together well.

Add chicken. Spoon sour cream mixture over every piece. Cover. Refrigerate overnight.

Place cracker crumbs in pie plate. Coat each piece of chicken with crumbs. Discard leftover sour cream mixture. Line baking sheet with foil for easy cleanup. Spray with no-stick cooking spray. Arrange chicken on foil.

Drizzle 1 tsp. (5 mL) melted butter over each piece. Bake in 325°F (160°C) oven for 1¼ to 1½ hours until tender. Serves 10.

1 serving: 284 Calories; 30 g Protein; 11.2 g Total Fat; 15 g Carbohydrate; 688 mg Sodium

Note: Various crackers can be used, such as Breton, Ritz or graham. Different tastes but each is good.

Pictured on page 133.

Jumpin' Jambalaya

Lots of texture, with a zippy taste. ⊙ Make ahead and freeze. Reheat when needed.

Sausage meat (or spicy Italian sausage with casing removed)	1 lb.	454 g
Finely chopped onion	¾ cup	175 mL
Canned stewed tomatoes	2 × 14 oz.	2 × 398 mL
Condensed chicken broth	10 oz.	284 mL
Water	1 cup	250 mL
Uncooked instant white rice	3 cups	750 mL
Salt	1 tsp.	5 mL
Chili powder	1 tsp.	5 mL
Ground thyme	½ tsp.	2 mL
Cayenne pepper	⅛ tsp.	0.5 mL
Finely chopped green pepper	1 cup	250 mL
Frozen cooked medium shrimp, thawed	12 oz.	340 g

Scramble-fry sausage and onion in large Dutch oven leaving some large chunks.

Add next 8 ingredients. Bring to a boil, stirring often. Cover. Boil slowly for 10 minutes, stirring occasionally.

Add green pepper and shrimp. Stir. Turn off heat. Allow pot to stand on warm burner for about 10 minutes until liquid is absorbed. Makes about 10 cups (2.5 L) jambalaya.

1 cup (250 mL) jambalaya: 378 Calories; 17 g Protein; 19.3 g Total Fat; 33 g Carbohydrate; 1062 mg Sodium

Pictured on page 128.

Party Chicken

Excellent served with rice or mashed potatoes. ⊙ Removing the skin takes the most time so do that in the morning. Cover drumsticks with plastic wrap to prevent drying out. Refrigerate until ready to bake.

Chicken drumsticks, skin removed (about 3 lbs., 1.4 kg)	14	14
Apricot jam	¾ cup	175 mL
Thousand Island dressing	⅓ cup	75 mL
Envelope dry onion soup mix, stirred before dividing	½ × 1½ oz.	½ × 42 g

Arrange chicken in small roaster or ungreased baking pan in single layer. Stir jam, dressing and soup mix together in bowl. Spoon over chicken, being sure to get some on every piece. Cover. Bake in 350°F (175°C) oven for 1½ to 2 hours. Makes 14 drumsticks and about 1½ cups (375 mL) sauce. Serves 6.

1 serving: 348 Calories; 31 g Protein; 10.3 g Total Fat; 32 g Carbohydrate; 548 mg Sodium

Pictured below.

Chicken Breasts Royal

Elegant look. Subtle mushroom and wine flavor.
⊕ This can be assembled in the morning and refrigerated until ready to bake.

Boneless, skinless chicken breast halves	8	8
Condensed cream of mushroom soup	10 oz.	284 mL
Non-fat sour cream	1 cup	250 mL
All-purpose flour	¼ cup	60 mL
Green onions, chopped	6	6
White (or alcohol-free) wine	¼ cup	60 mL
Seasoning salt	½ tsp.	2 mL
Paprika	¼ tsp.	1 mL
Liquid gravy browner	½ tsp.	2 mL

Arrange chicken in single layer in greased 9 x 13 inch (22 x 33 cm) pan or small roaster.

Place soup, sour cream, flour and onion in bowl. Stir well.

Add wine, seasoning salt, paprika and gravy browner. Stir. Spoon over chicken. Bake, uncovered, in 350°F (175°C) oven for 1¼ hours until tender (or up to 2 hours, if frozen breasts are used). Serves 8.

1 serving: 199 Calories; 29 g Protein; 4.4 g Total Fat; 8 g Carbohydrate; 492 mg Sodium

Pictured below.

Top Left: Curried Turkey Noodles, this page
Bottom Left: Party Chicken, page 132
Top Right: Chicken Capers, page 132
Bottom Right: Chicken Breasts Royal, above

Curried Turkey Noodles

Serve with a salad or vegetable. ⊕ Only 30 minutes from start to finish. Cook noodles while sauce is simmering.

Cooking oil	2 tsp.	10 mL
Boneless, skinless turkey breasts or cutlets, cut bite size	2 lbs.	900 g
Condensed cream of mushroom soup	10 oz.	284 mL
Milk, soup can full	10 oz.	284 mL
Finely chopped onion	½ cup	125 mL
Curry powder	½-1 tsp.	2-5 mL
Salt	1 tsp.	5 mL
Pepper	¼ tsp.	1 mL
Medium noodles	12 oz.	340 g
Boiling water	3 qts.	3 L
Cooking oil (optional)	1 tbsp.	15 mL
Salt	2 tsp.	10 mL

Heat cooking oil in non-stick frying pan. Add turkey. Brown both sides well. Transfer to plate.

Add next 6 ingredients to frying pan. Cover. Simmer for 15 minutes until onion is soft. Add turkey. Cover to keep warm.

Cook noodles in boiling water, cooking oil and salt in large uncovered Dutch oven for 5 to 7 minutes until tender but firm. Drain. Arrange on warmed platter. Top with turkey mixture. Serves 8.

1 serving: 352 Calories; 35 g Protein; 5.8 g Total Fat; 37 g Carbohydrate; 721 mg Sodium

Pictured on page 132.

Top Left: Chicken Julienne, below   Bottom Left: Festive Chicken, below   Center Right: Turkey Birds, page 135

Chicken Julienne

Tasty served over noodles or over split buns.
🕐 *Make up to two days ahead. Reheats*
well when ready to serve.

Hard margarine (butter browns too fast)	2 tsp.	10 mL
Boneless, skinless chicken breasts, cut into julienne strips	1½ lbs.	680 g
Chopped green onion	¼ cup	60 mL
Sliced fresh mushrooms	2 cups	500 mL
Evaporated milk	¾ cup	175 mL
White (or alcohol-free) wine	½ cup	125 mL
Parsley flakes	1 tsp.	5 mL
Salt	⅛ tsp.	0.5 mL
Pepper	¹⁄₁₆ tsp.	0.5 mL

Heat margarine in non-stick frying pan. Add chicken, onion and mushrooms. Stir-fry until no pink remains in chicken. Remove to bowl.

Pour evaporated milk and wine into frying pan. Boil until liquid is reduced to half and is about the thickness of evaporated milk. Add chicken mixture. Stir.

Add parsley, salt and pepper. Heat, stirring often, until close to boiling. Makes 3½ cups (875 mL) stir-fry.

¾ cup (175 mL) stir-fry: 238 Calories; 38 g Protein; 3.7 g Total Fat; 7 g Carbohydrate; 245 mg Sodium

Pictured above.

Festive Chicken

Deep red sauce. 🕐 *This recipe whips up in no time.*
Keep these ingredients on hand for last minute entertaining.

Boneless, skinless chicken breast halves (or skinless chicken thighs)	6	6
Envelope dry tomato vegetable soup mix	1 × 2½ oz.	1 × 71 g
Apple juice	1 cup	250 mL
Paprika	¼ tsp.	1 mL
Worcestershire sauce	½ tsp.	2 mL

Arrange chicken in greased casserole dish large enough to hold in single layer.

Stir soup mix, apple juice, paprika and Worcestershire sauce together in saucepan. Heat on medium until hot and soup is well mixed in. Pour over chicken. Cover. Bake in 350°F (175°C) oven for 1 to 1½ hours until tender. Serves 6.

1 serving: 189 Calories; 29 g Protein; 2.1 g Total Fat; 12 g Carbohydrate; 878 mg Sodium

Pictured above.

Turkey Birds

This only takes 30 minutes to prepare—but your guests will think it took longer! ☺ Make the stuffing the night before, then prepare the "birds" in the morning. Keep refrigerated until ready to bake.

Bacon slices, diced	2	2
Finely chopped onion	¾ cup	175 mL
Finely chopped celery	½ cup	125 mL
Finely chopped mushrooms	1 cup	250 mL
Large egg	1	1
Chicken bouillon powder	1 tsp.	5 mL
Fine dry bread crumbs	1½ cups	375 mL
Poultry seasoning	½ tsp.	2 mL
Salt	¼ tsp.	1 mL
Pepper	⅛ tsp.	0.5 mL
Turkey scallopini, cut into 8 equal pieces	1 lb.	454 g
Hard margarine (butter browns too fast)	1 tbsp.	15 mL
All-purpose flour	¼ cup	60 mL
Chicken bouillon powder	½ tbsp.	7 mL
Boiling water	1½ cups	375 mL
Gravy:		
All-purpose flour	¼ cup	60 mL
Water	⅓ cup	75 mL
Salt, just a pinch		
Pepper, just a pinch		
Liquid gravy browner, optional	1-2 tsp.	5-10 mL

Sauté bacon in frying pan for 1 minute.

Add onion, celery and mushrooms. Sauté until all vegetables are soft. Drain.

Beat egg in medium bowl. Stir in next 5 ingredients. Mix well. Add bacon mixture. Stir.

Pound each scallopini to ⅛ inch (3 mm) thickness. Divide stuffing and place mound in center of each scallopini. Roll up snugly, folding in sides as you go. Use wooden pick to skewer closed or tie with butchers' string.

Melt margarine in non-stick frying pan. Coat rolls with flour. Brown well. Arrange rolls in 4 quart (4 L) casserole dish just large enough to hold in single layer.

Combine second amount of bouillon powder and boiling water in small bowl. Pour over rolls. Cover. Bake in 350°F (175°C) oven for 45 minutes until tender. Remove rolls to platter. Cover to keep warm.

Gravy: Mix flour, water, salt and pepper in small bowl until smooth. Pour liquid from casserole into small saucepan. Heat until boiling. Whisk in flour mixture until boiling and thickened.

Stir in gravy browner. Serves 8.

1 serving: 244 Calories; 18 g Protein; 7.6 g Total Fat; 25 g Carbohydrate; 556 mg Sodium

Pictured on page 134.

Turkey Loaf

Nice compact texture. Easy one-bowl method. ☺ Freezes well.

Non-fat sour cream	¾ cup	175 mL
Large eggs	2	2
Finely chopped onion	½ cup	125 mL
Finely chopped celery	½ cup	125 mL
Frozen peas, thawed	1 cup	250 mL
Salt	1 tsp.	5 mL
Pepper	¼ tsp.	1 mL
Poultry seasoning, just a pinch		
Fine dry bread crumbs	¾ cup	175 mL
Ground turkey	2 lbs.	900 g

Mix first 9 ingredients in bowl.

Add ground turkey. Mix well. Pack into greased 9 x 5 x 3 inch (22 x 12.5 x 7.5 cm) loaf pan. Bake in 350°F (175°C) oven for 1¼ hours. Cuts into 10 slices.

1 slice: 169 Calories; 24 g Protein; 2.9 g Total Fat; 10 g Carbohydrate; 433 mg Sodium

Pictured below.

Chicken Loaf

Use ground chicken instead of ground turkey.

Turkey Loaf

Turkey Hash   Handy Dandy Chicken

Turkey Hash

Serve with rice or noodles. Easy to double.
⏲ Have cabbage chopped and the rest of ingredients
assembled. Prepare when ready.

Coarsely chopped cabbage	4 cups	1 L
Boiling water		
Ground turkey	½ lb.	225 g
Canned tomatoes, with juice, broken up	14 oz.	398 mL
Dried whole oregano	¾ tsp.	4 mL
Onion powder	¼ tsp.	1 mL
Salt	¾ tsp.	4 mL
Pepper	¼ tsp.	1 mL

Cook cabbage in boiling water until tender. Drain.

Scramble-fry ground turkey in non-stick frying pan until no pink remains.

Add tomatoes, oregano, onion powder, salt and pepper. Add cabbage. Heat and stir until mixture is hot. Makes 4 cups (1 L) hash.

1 cup (250 mL) hash: 102 Calories; 14 g Protein; 1.3 g Total Fat; 9 g Carbohydrate; 721 mg Sodium

Pictured on this page.

Chicken Hash

Use ground chicken instead of ground turkey.

Turkey Scallopini

Try this low-fat tasty combination over fettuccine noodles.
Quick and easy to prepare. ⏲ Save some time by pounding
cutlets in the morning. Cover and refrigerate.

Cooking oil	1 tsp.	5 mL
Turkey cutlets, pounded flat	1¼ lbs.	560 g
All-purpose flour	¼ cup	60 mL
Medium tomato, diced	1	1
Green onion, chopped	1-2	1-2
Dried whole oregano	½ tsp.	2 mL
Dried sweet basil	¼ tsp.	1 mL
Garlic powder	⅛ tsp.	0.5 mL
Salt, sprinkle		
Pepper, sprinkle		

Heat cooking oil in non-stick frying pan. Coat turkey with flour. Add to pan. Brown both sides until well cooked. Remove to platter. Cover to keep warm.

Add remaining 7 ingredients to pan. Stir-fry for about 2 minutes. Serve over scallopini. Serves 4.

1 serving: 202 Calories; 32 g Protein; 3.6 g Total Fat; 8 g Carbohydrate; 89 mg Sodium

Pictured on page 137.

Handy Dandy Chicken

Just add a salad. Only 15 minutes to prepare.
⏲ Removing the skin takes the most time, so do that in
the morning, then cover with plastic wrap to prevent
drying out. Refrigerate until ready to bake.

Uncooked instant white rice	2 cups	500 mL
Canned mushroom stems and pieces, drained	10 oz.	284 mL
Apple juice	¾ cup	175 mL
Condensed cream of mushroom soup	10 oz.	284 mL
Condensed cream of chicken soup	10 oz.	284 mL
Chicken parts, skin removed	3 lbs.	1.4 kg
Envelope dry vegetable soup mix	1 × 1½ oz.	1 × 42 g

Combine first 5 ingredients in bowl. Stir well. Turn into ungreased 9 × 13 inch (22 × 33 cm) pan.

Arrange chicken over top in single layer, meaty side up. Sprinkle with soup mix. Cover. Bake in 350°F (175°C) oven for 1½ to 2 hours until chicken is tender. Turn chicken twice during baking so dry soup gets distributed a bit. Finish with attractive meaty side up. Serves 6.

1 serving: 408 Calories; 30 g Protein; 11.8 g Total Fat; 44 g Carbohydrate; 1324 mg Sodium

Pictured above.

Turkey Breast Roast

You may want to tie this with butchers' string just before putting in the roaster. ☺ Pound the turkey pieces and make first part of stuffing in the morning. Finish stuffing and assemble just before baking.

Herb Stuffing:		
Fine dry bread crumbs	2 cups	500 mL
Ground thyme	⅛ tsp.	0.5 mL
Ground rosemary	⅛ tsp.	0.5 mL
Garlic powder	⅛ tsp.	0.5 mL
Large egg, fork-beaten	1	1
Hard margarine (or butter), melted	1 tbsp.	15 mL
Water	1 tbsp.	15 mL
Boneless, skinless turkey breasts (1½ lbs., 680 g, each)	2	2
Gravy, see Turkey Roast, on this page		

Herb Stuffing: Stir first 4 ingredients together in bowl.

Add egg, margarine and water. Mix well.

Pound turkey to flatten somewhat. Spread stuffing on 1 piece. Cover with second piece. Press edges together. Carefully lift and place in greased roaster. Cover. Bake in 325°F (160°C) oven for about 1½ hours until tender. Meat thermometer should read 185°F (85°C).

Make gravy. Keep warm. Makes 3 cups (750 mL) gravy. Slice turkey to serve 8.

1 serving: 346 Calories; 47 g Protein; 4.6 g Total Fat; 26 g Carbohydrate; 370 mg Sodium

Pictured on this page.

Turkey Roast

Serve sliced for an attractive presentation. Very quick to prepare—less than five minutes. ☺ Or make ahead and freeze the roast and gravy separately.

Boneless, skinless turkey roast	4 lbs.	1.8 kg
Lemon-lime soft drink	1 cup	250 mL
Poultry seasoning	¼ tsp.	1 mL
Salt	½ tsp.	2 mL
Pepper	⅛ tsp.	0.5 mL
Gravy:		
Drippings, plus water to make	2½ cups	625 mL
Water	⅔ cup	150 mL
All-purpose flour	6 tbsp.	100 mL
Salt	⅛ tsp.	0.5 mL
Pepper	⅛ tsp.	0.5 mL
Liquid gravy browner	¼ tsp.	1 mL

Place turkey roast in small roaster.

Mix soft drink with poultry seasoning, salt and pepper in cup. Pour over turkey. Cover. Roast in 325°F (160°C) oven for 2¼ to 2½ hours until tender. Meat thermometer should read 185°F (85°C). Serves 10.

Gravy: Measure drippings and add first amount of water. Return to roaster. Heat until boiling.

Whisk second amount of water gradually into flour in bowl until no lumps remain. Stir into drippings until boiling and thickened.

Add second amount of salt, second amount of pepper and gravy browner. Stir. Makes 3 cups (750 mL) gravy. Serves 10.

1 serving: 226 Calories; 41 g Protein; 2.9 g Total Fat; 6 g Carbohydrate; 288 mg Sodium

Pictured below.

Top: Turkey Roast, this page
Center: Turkey Breast Roast, this page
Bottom: Turkey Scallopini, page 136

Pies

Dinner is done, and now it's time to offer your
guests dessert. A piece of homemade pie is always
enjoyed and received with a smile. Don't forget to enhance
your presentation with a slice of cheese or piece of decorative
fruit on the side. Try using a simple fluted edge around
your pie to make it look special. Remember, little extras
can transform the ordinary, into the extraordinary.

One convenience to preparing pie is that
you can make your pastry dough six to eight weeks
in advance and freeze it. When it's time to make dessert,
thaw the dough in your refrigerator, roll it out, and voilà, you
have a simple and luscious dessert presentation. Who would
have imagined making a pie could be so easy?

Chocolate Chiffon Pie

An unbaked pie that is thick and light.
🕐 *Use a ready-made pie shell to save time.*

Envelope unflavored gelatin	1 x ¼ oz.	1 x 7 g
Water	½ cup	125 mL
Milk	1 cup	250 mL
Granulated sugar	⅓ cup	75 mL
Cocoa	½ cup	125 mL
All-purpose flour	2 tbsp.	30 mL
Salt	¼ tsp.	1 mL
Egg yolks (large)	4	4
Vanilla	1 tsp.	5 mL
Egg whites (large), room temperature	4	4
Cream of tartar	½ tsp.	2 mL
Granulated sugar	⅔ cup	150 mL
Baked 9 inch (22 cm) pie shell	1	1

Sprinkle gelatin over water in medium saucepan. Let stand for 1 minute.

Add milk. Heat, stirring often, on medium until gelatin is dissolved and mixture starts to boil.

Mix next 6 ingredients in small bowl. Add a little hot milk mixture and stir until smooth. Pour back into saucepan. Stir until boiling and thickened. Chill until mixture mounds nicely when spooned.

Beat egg whites and cream of tartar together in medium bowl until soft peaks form. Gradually add second amount of sugar, as you continue beating, until mixture is stiff.

Make sure chilled filling will pile nicely before adding egg whites. Fold egg white mixture into chilled filling. Turn into baked pie shell. Chill for at least 4 hours before cutting. Cuts into 8 thick wedges.

1 wedge: 288 Calories; 8 g Protein; 10.9 g Total Fat; 43 g Carbohydrate; 294 mg Sodium; good source of Dietary Fiber

Pictured on page 139.

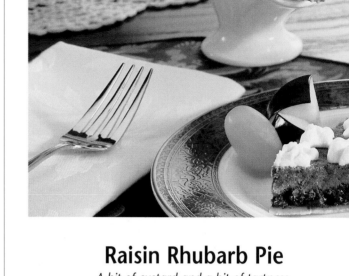

Raisin Rhubarb Pie

A bit of custard and a bit of tartness.
🕐 *This can be made ahead and frozen.*

Raisins	2 cups	500 mL
Water	¾ cup	175 mL
Brown sugar, packed	1 cup	250 mL
Granulated sugar	½ cup	125 mL
All-purpose flour	⅓ cup	75 mL
Salt	¼ tsp.	1 mL
Lemon juice	1 tsp.	5 mL
Rhubarb, fresh or frozen, cut into 1 inch (2.5 cm) lengths	1½ cups	375 mL
Pastry for 2 crust pie, your own or a mix		
Granulated sugar, sprinkle	¼-½ tsp.	1-2 mL

Combine raisins and water in saucepan. Bring to a boil. Cover. Simmer slowly for 5 minutes.

Measure next 4 ingredients into small bowl. Stir well. Stir into simmering raisins until it returns to a boil and thickens. Remove from heat.

Add lemon juice. Stir in rhubarb. Let stand until cool. To hasten this process, stir while resting pan in cold water in sink.

Roll pastry and line ungreased 9 inch (22 cm) pie plate. Pour filling into shell. Dampen edge. Roll 1 more crust and put over top. Trim and crimp to seal. Cut slits in top to vent.

Sprinkle with second amount of sugar. Bake on bottom shelf in 375°F (190°C) oven for about 40 minutes until rhubarb is cooked and crust is browned. Cuts into 8 wedges.

1 wedge: 525 Calories; 5 g Protein; 15.3 g Total Fat; 97 g Carbohydrate; 375 mg Sodium

Pictured on page 138.

Two-Layer Pumpkin Pie, below

Two-Layer Pumpkin Pie

A great combination of pumpkin and mincemeat.
☺ Make ahead and freeze without the whipped topping.

Mincemeat pie filling	¾ cup	175 mL
Applesauce	½ cup	125 mL
Minute tapioca	2 tsp.	10 mL
Unbaked 9 inch (22 cm) pie shell	1	1
Large egg	1	1
Granulated sugar	⅓ cup	75 mL
Ground cinnamon	½ tsp.	2 mL
Ground nutmeg	¼ tsp.	1 mL
Ground ginger	¼ tsp.	1 mL
Canned pumpkin, without spices	1 cup	250 mL
Frozen whipped topping (in a tub), thawed	1½ cups	375 mL

Stir pie filling, applesauce and tapioca together in bowl.

Turn into pie shell. Smooth out evenly.

Beat egg in bowl. Add sugar, cinnamon, nutmeg, ginger and pumpkin. Beat to mix. Spoon over mincemeat layer. Bake on bottom shelf in 400°F (205°C) oven for 10 minutes. Reduce heat to 325°F (160°C). Continue to bake for 45 minutes until knife inserted close to center comes out clean.

Garnish with whipped topping. Cuts into 8 wedges.

1 wedge: 277 Calories; 3 g Protein; 12.6 g Total Fat; 40 g Carbohydrate; 204 mg Sodium

Pictured above.

Jam Pie

Not your usual shape for a pie—but just
as good! ☺ Freezes well.

Hard margarine (or butter), softened	1 cup	250 mL
Granulated sugar	½ cup	125 mL
Large egg	1	1
Brandy or whiskey (or water plus 2 tsp., 10 mL, brandy flavoring)	¼ cup	60 mL
All-purpose flour	3 cups	750 mL
Thick jam (any flavor)	1½ cups	375 mL

Cream margarine and sugar together well in bowl. Beat in egg and brandy.

Add flour. Mix well. Pinch off ⅔ of the dough into small pieces. Flatten in ungreased 9 x 13 inch (22 x 33 cm) pan, covering bottom and about ½ inch (12 mm) up sides. Pat out evenly since dough isn't rolled.

Spread with jam. Roll out remaining ⅓ of dough on lightly floured working surface. Cut into strips about ½ inch (12 mm) wide and as long as needed to make a criss-cross lattice crust on top. Bake in 350°F (175°C) oven for about 35 minutes until golden brown. Cuts into 15 pieces.

1 piece: 346 Calories; 3 g Protein; 13.7 g Total Fat; 51 g Carbohydrate; 162 mg Sodium

Pictured below.

Jam Pie

Chocolate Angel Pie

Chocolate Angel Pie

It's a good thing that angels share their treats.
☺ The meringue can be made several days before.
Store airtight. Make the filling the morning of and
refrigerate until needed.

Meringue Crust:		
Egg whites (large), room temperature	3	3
Baking powder	1 tsp.	5 mL
Cream of tartar	¼ tsp.	1 mL
Vanilla	1 tsp.	5 mL
Granulated sugar	1 cup	250 mL
Cracker crumbs (not soda)	1 cup	250 mL
Chopped walnuts	1 cup	250 mL
Filling:		
Semisweet chocolate chips	1½ cups	375 mL
Cream cheese, softened	4 oz.	125 g
Granulated sugar	¼ cup	60 mL
Milk	2 tbsp.	30 mL
Vanilla	1 tsp.	5 mL
Frozen whipped topping (in a tub), thawed	1 cup	250 mL

Meringue Crust: Beat egg whites in medium bowl until soft peaks form. Add baking powder, cream of tartar and vanilla. Gradually add sugar, as you continue beating, until mixture is stiff.

Fold in cracker crumbs and walnuts. Press evenly in greased 9 inch (22 cm) pie plate, pressing egg white mixture up sides of plate. Bake in 325°F (160°C) oven for 25 to 30 minutes. Cool thoroughly on rack.

Filling: Melt chocolate chips in saucepan on lowest heat, stirring often. Remove from heat.

Using same beaters, beat cream cheese, sugar, milk and vanilla in bowl until smooth and fluffy. Beat in melted chocolate.

Fold in whipped topping. Pour onto meringue. Spread evenly. Chill for 2 to 3 hours. Cuts into 8 wedges.

1 wedge: 520 Calories; 7 g Protein; 30 g Total Fat; 62 g Carbohydrate; 206 mg Sodium

Pictured on this page.

Strawberry Custard Pie

This is a soft pie. Be sure it is well chilled.
☺ Can be made the day before, especially the pie shell.

Toasted sliced almonds	½ cup	125 mL
Baked 9 inch (22 cm) pie shell (or Graham Crust, page 144)	1	1
Instant vanilla pudding powders, 4 serving size each	2	2
Milk	2 cups	500 mL
Frozen whipped topping (in a tub), thawed	1 cup	250 mL
Sliced fresh strawberries	1½ cups	375 mL
Glaze:		
Water	½ cup	125 mL
Cornstarch	1 tbsp.	15 mL
Granulated sugar	¼ cup	60 mL
Mashed (or puréed) strawberries	½ cup	125 mL

Scatter almonds in pie shell.

Beat pudding powder and milk together in bowl until smooth.

Fold in whipped topping. Pour over almonds. Chill for 1 hour.

Spoon sliced strawberries over top of chilled pie.

Glaze: Stir all 4 ingredients together in saucepan. Heat and stir until boiling and thickened. Cool. Spoon over strawberries. Chill several hours or overnight. Cuts into 8 wedges.

1 wedge: 347 Calories; 5 g Protein; 14.1 g Total Fat; 52 g Carbohydrate; 249 mg Sodium

Pictured on page 138/139.

Fresh Strawberry Pie

What a showpiece! Check around for the reddest, freshest strawberries. ⏱ Bake the pie shell the day before.

Whole hulled strawberries	5 cups	1.25 L
Baked 9 inch (22 cm) pie shell, your own or a mix	1	1
Water	1²/₃ cups	400 mL
Granulated sugar	1 cup	250 mL
Drops of red food coloring	6	6
Cornstarch	3 tbsp.	50 mL
Water	¹/₃ cup	75 mL
Package strawberry-flavored gelatin (jelly powder)	1 × 3 oz.	1 × 85 g
Topping:		
Frozen whipped topping (in a tub), thawed	1 cup	250 mL
Sliced fresh strawberries, for garnish		

Pile strawberries, pointed ends up, into pie shell.

Pour first amount of water and sugar into saucepan. Add food coloring to make a strawberry color. Heat, stirring often, until boiling.

Stir cornstarch into second amount water. Stir into boiling red mixture, until it returns to a boil and thickens. Remove from heat.

Add strawberry gelatin. Stir to dissolve. Cool. Carefully pour or spoon mixture over berries. Use a pastry brush to dab places that don't cover. Chill.

Topping: Pipe whipped topping around outer edge of strawberries. Garnish with sliced strawberries. Cuts into 8 wedges.

1 wedge: 355 Calories; 3 g Protein; 12.9 g Total Fat; 59 g Carbohydrate; 174 mg Sodium

Pictured on page 144.

Nutty Mousse Pie

Creamy rich flavor. ⏱ May be prepared the day before.

Chocolate Crust:		
Hard margarine (or butter)	¹/₃ cup	75 mL
Chocolate wafer crumbs	1¹/₄ cups	300 mL
Filling:		
Large marshmallows	30	30
Milk	¹/₂ cup	125 mL
Semisweet chocolate chips	1 cup	250 mL
Brown sugar, packed	¹/₃ cup	75 mL
Frozen whipped topping (in a tub), thawed	2 cups	500 mL
Topping:		
Frozen whipped topping (in a tub), thawed	2 cups	500 mL
Chopped pecans	¹/₃ cup	75 mL

Chocolate Crust: Melt margarine in saucepan. Stir in wafer crumbs. Press into ungreased 9 inch (22 cm) pie plate. Bake in 350°F (175°C) oven for 10 minutes. Cool.

Filling: Combine first 4 ingredients in large saucepan. Heat on medium-low, stirring often, until melted and smooth. Chill, stirring and scraping down sides of bowl often, until a thick paste. It should pile and hold its shape awhile before becoming smooth.

Fold in whipped topping. Turn into pie shell.

Topping: Spread whipped topping over top. Sprinkle with pecans. Cuts into 8 wedges.

1 wedge: 533 Calories; 4 g Protein; 30.9 g Total Fat; 65 g Carbohydrate; 163 mg Sodium

Pictured below.

Nutty Mousse Pie

Banana Cream Pie, below   Fresh Strawberry Pie, page 143   Frosty Peanut Butter Pie, below

Banana Cream Pie

Garnish with more banana slices if desired.
☉ This can be made the day before and refrigerated.

Graham Crust:		
Hard margarine (or butter)	⅓ cup	75 mL
Graham cracker crumbs	1¼ cups	300 mL
Granulated sugar	3 tbsp.	50 mL
Filling:		
Banana, thinly sliced	1	1
Light cream cheese, softened	4 oz.	125 g
Granulated sugar	½ cup	125 mL
Envelope dessert topping, prepared according to package directions	1	1
Banana, thinly sliced	1	1

Graham Crust: Melt margarine in saucepan. Stir in graham crumbs and sugar. Press in bottom and up sides of ungreased 9 inch (22 cm) pie plate. Bake in 350°F (175°C) oven for 10 minutes. Cool.

Filling: Lay first amount of banana slices in bottom of crust.

Beat cream cheese and sugar together in separate bowl until light. Fold in dessert topping. Spread ½ of cheese mixture over banana layer. Cover with second amount of banana slices, then with remaining cheese mixture. Chill. Cuts into 8 wedges.

1 wedge: 300 Calories; 4 g Protein; 14.7 g Total Fat; 41 g Carbohydrate; 372 mg Sodium

Pictured above.

Frosty Peanut Butter Pie

Very rich and smooth. Smaller pieces will be appreciated by your guests. ☉ A perfect make-ahead-and-freeze pie.

Graham Crust, see Banana Cream Pie, on this page	1	1
Chocolate Layer:		
Chocolate sundae topping	⅔ cup	150 mL
Powdered coffee whitener	1 tbsp.	15 mL
Filling:		
Light cream cheese, softened	4 oz.	125 g
Icing (confectioner's) sugar	1 cup	250 mL
Smooth peanut butter	⅓ cup	75 mL
Milk	½ cup	125 mL
Envelope dessert topping, prepared according to package directions	1	1
Finely chopped peanuts	2 tbsp.	30 mL

Prepare crust. Cool.

Chocolate Layer: Stir sundae topping and coffee whitener together in small bowl until blended. Spread in bottom of cooled crust.

Filling: Beat cream cheese, icing sugar, peanut butter and first amount of milk together in medium bowl until smooth.

Fold dessert topping into cream cheese mixture. Pour over chocolate layer. Freeze.

Sprinkle with peanuts. Serve immediately. Cuts into 12 wedges.

1 wedge: 311 Calories; 6 g Protein; 17 g Total Fat; 37 g Carbohydrate; 311 mg Sodium

Pictured above.

Salads

Even a simple green salad can be made impressive with a little consideration to its presentation. Arranging the salad on individual plates can be very colorful and attractive. A quick garnish with slices of fresh fruit turns a plain salad into a spectacular side dish.

Salads are usually served either before or during a main course, but they can also be offered to guests after the main course, cleansing the palate before dessert.

Shrimpy Rice Salad

This is a beautiful platter presentation for a buffet.
🕐 *Cook the rice the day before. Prepare and add vegetables and shrimp to rice in the morning. Cover and refrigerate. Prepare lettuce, tomatoes and dressing in the morning. Cover and refrigerate each separately. Assemble salad just before serving.*

Long grain white rice	1 cup	250 mL
Boiling water	2 cups	500 mL
Sliced pimiento-stuffed olives	½ cup	125 mL
Chopped celery	⅓ cup	75 mL
Slivered or chopped green pepper	¼ cup	60 mL
Chopped pimiento	¼ cup	60 mL
Finely chopped red onion	¼ cup	60 mL
Cooked shrimp (or crabmeat), canned, fresh or frozen, thawed	1 cup	250 mL
Low-fat salad dressing (or mayonnaise)	3 tbsp.	50 mL
Milk	1 tbsp.	15 mL
Lemon juice	1 tsp.	5 mL
Salt	½ tsp.	2 mL
Pepper	½ tsp.	2 mL
Shredded iceberg lettuce	4 cups	1 L
Medium tomatoes, each cut into 8 wedges	2	2
French dressing	½ cup	125 mL

Cook rice in boiling water for about 15 minutes until tender and liquid is absorbed. Turn into bowl. Cool.

Add next 6 ingredients. Stir.

Mix salad dressing, milk, lemon juice, salt and pepper in small bowl. Add to rice mixture. Stir well.

Spread lettuce on platter. Spoon salad mixture in center almost to edge. Arrange tomato wedges around outside edge. Drizzle French dressing over just before serving. Makes 8½ cups (2.1 L) salad.

1 cup (250 mL) salad: 207 Calories; 6 g Protein; 9.4 g Total Fat; 25 g Carbohydrate; 707 mg Sodium

Pictured below.

Shrimpy Rice Salad

Buffet Salad

Lovely contrast of colors and textures. Start this two days in advance for first marinating. ☺ Leftover salad can be kept in its marinade in refrigerator for up to one week.

Marinade:

Condensed tomato soup	10 oz.	284 mL
Granulated sugar	¾ cup	175 mL
White vinegar	¾ cup	175 mL
Cooking oil	2 tbsp.	30 mL
Medium red onion, thinly sliced	1	1
Slivered green pepper	¾ cup	175 mL
Slivered red or yellow pepper	¾ cup	175 mL
Sliced carrot (a crinkle slicer makes carrots attractive)	4 cups	1 L
Boiling water		
Cauliflower florets	3½ cups	875 mL
Boiling water		
Canned sliced water chestnuts, drained	8 oz.	227 mL
Grated medium Cheddar (or mozzarella) cheese, optional	1 cup	250 mL

Marinade: Stir first 7 ingredients together in saucepan. Bring to a boil. Boil for 2 minutes.

Cook carrot in boiling water until tender-crisp. Drain.

Cook cauliflower in boiling water until tender-crisp. Drain.

Place water chestnuts in 2 quart (2 L) heat-proof container. Add carrot and cauliflower. Pour hot marinade over all. Cool slightly. Cover. Marinate in refrigerator for 1 to 2 days before serving. Scoop out with slotted spoon to serve, reserving marinade. Sprinkle with cheese. Return leftovers to marinade and store, covered, in refrigerator. Makes 6½ cups (1.6 L) salad.

½ cup (125 mL) salad: 89 Calories; 2 g Protein; 1.4 g Total Fat; 19 g Carbohydrate; 118 mg Sodium

Pictured below.

Mixed Green Salad

This also works well using just spinach leaves. ☺ Make dressing two or three days in advance. Cook and crumble bacon, and do eggs the day before. Drizzle dressing over salad just before serving.

Tangy Dressing:

Water	⅓ cup	75 mL
Cornstarch	1 tsp.	5 mL
Granulated sugar	⅓ cup	75 mL
Ketchup	⅓ cup	75 mL
White vinegar	¼ cup	60 mL
Cooking oil	1 tbsp.	15 mL
Steak sauce	1 tsp.	5 mL
Salt	1 tsp.	5 mL
Pepper	⅛ tsp.	0.5 mL

Salad:

Bacon slices, cooked crisp and crumbled	4	4
Sliced fresh mushrooms	1 cup	250 mL
Sliced pimiento-stuffed olives	¼ cup	60 mL
Hard-boiled eggs, chopped	2	2
Bean sprouts	1½ cups	375 mL
Assortment of lettuce greens, lightly packed	8 cups	2 L

Tangy Dressing: Stir water and cornstarch together in small saucepan over medium until boiling and thickened.

Stir in sugar to dissolve. Add next 6 ingredients. Remove from heat. Makes 1¼ cups (300 mL) dressing.

Salad: Toss all 6 ingredients together in bowl. Divide among salad plates. Drizzle ½ cup (125 mL) dressing over top and serve remainder on the side. Serves 8.

1 serving: 126 Calories; 5 g Protein; 5.5 g Total Fat; 16 g Carbohydrate; 682 mg Sodium

Pictured on front cover.

Buffet Salad

Rice Artichoke Salad

Peach Melba Salad

Rice Artichoke Salad

Creamy salad. Flecks of color throughout. ☺ Make rice two or three days in advance. Keep chilled. Cut up vegetables night before serving. Make dressing and assemble salad in morning.

Long grain white rice	1 cup	250 mL
Water	2 cups	500 mL
Chicken bouillon powder	1 tbsp.	15 mL
Small green pepper, chopped	1	1
Sliced green onion	¼ cup	60 mL
Sliced radish	¼ cup	60 mL
Jars marinated artichoke hearts, drained	2 × 6 oz.	2 × 170 mL
Dressing:		
Low-fat salad dressing (or mayonnaise)	⅓ cup	75 mL
Milk	1 tbsp.	15 mL
Curry powder (or more to taste)	1/4 tsp.	1 mL

Cook rice slowly in water and bouillon powder in small saucepan for about 15 minutes until rice is tender and liquid is absorbed. Cool.

Add next 4 ingredients. Stir together.

Dressing: Mix salad dressing with milk and curry powder in bowl. Add to rice mixture. Stir. Makes 6 cups (1.5 L) salad.

¾ cup (175 mL) salad: 141 Calories; 3 g Protein; 3.1 g Total Fat; 25 g Carbohydrate; 415 mg Sodium

Pictured above.

Peach Melba Salad

Pretty enough—and sweet enough—for salad or dessert! Serve on shredded lettuce for salad. ☺ Make first thing in morning. Keep refrigerated until serving time.

Packages raspberry-flavored gelatin (jelly powder)	2 × 3 oz.	2 × 85 g
Boiling water	1 cup	250 mL
Canned peach pie filling	19 oz.	540 mL
Frozen whole raspberries	10 oz.	300 g
Lemon juice	1 tsp.	5 mL
Topping:		
Non-fat peach yogurt	1 cup	250 mL
Envelope dessert topping (not prepared)	1	1
Milk	⅓ cup	75 mL

Stir gelatin into boiling water in bowl until dissolved.

Stir in pie filling, raspberries and lemon juice. Pour into greased 9 × 9 inch (22 × 22 cm) pan. Chill until firm.

Topping: Stir yogurt vigorously in bowl until smooth. Prepare topping with milk. Add to yogurt. Stir together well. Spread over jellied salad. Chill for 30 minutes. Cuts into 12 medium pieces.

1 piece: 151 Calories; 3 g Protein; 1.7 g Total Fat; 33 g Carbohydrate; 63 mg Sodium

Pictured above.

Cucumber Mousse

A bit of crunch from cucumber. A mild hint of pickle
adds to flavor. ⊕ A good make-the-day-before salad.

Finely chopped English cucumber, with peel, well drained	2 cups	500 mL
Packages lemon-flavored gelatin (jelly powder)	2 × 3 oz.	2 × 85 g
Salt	2 tsp.	10 mL
Boiling water	1⅔ cups	400 mL
White vinegar	3 tbsp.	50 mL
Onion powder	½ tsp.	2 mL
Sour cream	1 cup	250 mL
Salad dressing (or mayonnaise)	½ cup	125 mL

Prepare cucumber first so it will have plenty of time to drain.

Combine gelatin, salt and boiling water in bowl. Stir until gelatin is dissolved.

Add vinegar and onion powder. Stir. Chill, stirring and scraping down sides of bowl often, until it shows signs of thickening.

Add sour cream and salad dressing. Stir together to blend. Fold in cucumber. Turn into 4 cup (1 L) mold. Chill. Makes 4 cups (1 L) mousse.

½ cup (125 mL) mousse: 207 Calories; 3 g Protein; 11.9 g Total Fat; 23 g Carbohydrate; 850 mg Sodium

Pictured below.

Spinach Apple Toss

Makes a large salad; cuts in half easily. ⊕ Fry, drain, cool
and crumble bacon whenever you have a few minutes. Put
into small plastic bag and freeze until ready to use.

Bacon slices	8	8
Red eating apples (such as Delicious), with peel, coarsely chopped	2	2
Bags fresh spinach, leaves torn bite size (about 12 cups, 3 L, firmly packed)	2 × 10 oz.	2 × 283 g
Tangy Orange Dressing:		
Low-fat salad dressing (or mayonnaise)	⅔ cup	150 mL
Frozen concentrated orange juice, thawed	⅓ cup	75 mL

Fry bacon until crisp. Drain on paper towel. Crumble or dice.

Combine apple and spinach in large bowl. Add bacon.

Tangy Orange Dressing: Stir salad dressing and concentrated orange juice together in small bowl. Pour over spinach mixture. Toss to coat. Serves 12.

1 serving: 101 Calories; 3 g Protein; 5.9 g Total Fat; 10 g Carbohydrate; 212 mg Sodium

Pictured on page 125.

Coleslaw

Bright and colorful with creamy white dressing.
⊕ Grate this in morning, or even the day before.
Add dressing shortly before serving.

Shredded green cabbage, packed	6 cups	1.5 L
Shredded red cabbage (for color)	½ cup	125 mL
Medium carrots, grated	2	2
Chopped green onion	⅓ cup	75 mL
Dressing:		
Light sour cream	1 cup	250 mL
Low-fat salad dressing (or mayonnaise)	2 tbsp.	30 mL
White vinegar	1½ tbsp.	25 mL
Celery seed	⅛ tsp.	0.5 mL
Salt	½ tsp.	2 mL
Pepper	¼ tsp.	1 mL

Combine first 4 ingredients in large bowl. Stir.

Dressing: Mix all 6 ingredients in small bowl. Stir well. Makes 1⅓ cups (325 mL) dressing. Pour over cabbage mixture. Toss thoroughly. Makes 8 cups (2 L) coleslaw.

½ cup (125 mL) coleslaw: 30 Calories; 1 g Protein; 1.6 g Total Fat; 3 g Carbohydrate; 113 mg Sodium

Pictured on this page.

Coleslaw   Cucumber Mousse

Pretzel Salad

Serve with parkerhouse or other rolls. Can also be served as a dessert. ☺ The perfect make-ahead answer to a bridal shower lunch, or for a ladies' meeting.

Bottom Layer:

Hard margarine (or butter)	¾ cup	175 mL
Pretzel crumbs (about 6 oz., 170 g)	2 cups	500 mL
Granulated sugar	3 tbsp.	50 mL

Filling:

Envelopes unflavored gelatin	2 × ¼ oz.	2 × 7 g
Water	1 cup	250 mL
Light cream cheese, softened	8 oz.	250 g
Granulated sugar	1 cup	250 mL
Envelopes dessert topping, prepared according to package directions	2	2

Topping:

Packages strawberry-flavored gelatin (jelly powder)	2 × 3 oz.	2 × 85 g
Boiling water	2 cups	500 mL
Frozen sliced strawberries, in syrup	15 oz.	425 g
Shredded lettuce, lightly packed	3 cups	750 mL

Bottom Layer: Melt margarine in saucepan. Stir in pretzel crumbs and sugar. Press in ungreased 9 × 13 inch (22 × 33 cm) pan. Bake, uncovered, in 350°F (175°C) oven for about 10 minutes. Cool.

Filling: Sprinkle gelatin over water in saucepan. Let stand for 1 minute. Heat, stirring until gelatin is dissolved. Refrigerate, stirring and scraping down sides often, until thickened.

Beat cream cheese and sugar together in separate bowl until smooth. Add gelatin mixture. Beat.

Fold in dessert topping. Spread over bottom layer, smoothing top. Chill.

Topping: Stir strawberry gelatin and boiling water together in bowl until dissolved. Add strawberries and syrup. Let stand until strawberries can be broken up a bit. Stir often until strawberries are thawed and mixture is thickened. Spoon over filling. Chill. Cuts into 15 pieces.

Divide lettuce among 15 plates. Place salad piece over top of each. Serves 15.

1 serving: 319 Calories; 5 g Protein; 14 g Total Fat; 46 g Carbohydrate; 427 mg Sodium

Pictured on this page.

Top: Raspberry Salad Bottom: Pretzel Salad

Raspberry Salad

Serve as a first course at your next dinner party. ☺ Make dressing at least two days ahead, or whenever time permits. Once it has cooled completely, store in airtight container on shelf. Use as needed. Double recipe if you wish.

Raspberry Dressing:

Whole raspberries, fresh or frozen	3 cups	750 mL
White vinegar	1 cup	250 mL
Granulated sugar, approximately	1½ cups	375 mL

Salad:

Mixed torn greens, lightly packed	6 cups	1.5 L
Green onions, sliced	1-2	1-2
Fresh mushrooms, sliced	12	12
Toasted sliced almonds	2 tbsp.	30 mL

Raspberry Dressing: Place raspberries and vinegar in bowl. Stir. Cover. Let stand on counter for 48 hours. Drain. Measure juice.

Add an equal amount of sugar to juice in saucepan. Stir often as you bring to a boil. Boil gently for 15 minutes. Cool. Makes 2 cups (500 mL) raspberry dressing.

Salad: Place greens, onion, mushrooms and almonds in bowl. Pour ⅓ cup (75 mL) raspberry dressing over top. Store remaining dressing in covered container in refrigerator. Toss well. Serves 6.

1 serving: 74 Calories; 2 g Protein; 1.8 g Total Fat; 14 g Carbohydrate; 18 mg Sodium

Pictured above.

Quickie Clam Chowder

Clam Chowder

Thick, almost stew-like. For an extra special occasion add shrimp, scallops, lobster or any other seafood.
🕐 Can be made ahead and frozen.

Large potatoes, cubed	3	3
Large carrots, cubed	3	3
Boiling water, to cover		
Bacon slices, diced	10-12	10-12
Large green pepper, diced	1	1
Chopped celery	1½ cups	375 mL
Chopped onion	1½ cups	375 mL
Reserved clam liquid		
Condensed cream of potato soup	2 × 10 oz.	2 × 284 mL
Lemon pepper	¼ tsp.	1 mL
Salt	1 tsp.	5 mL
Pepper	⅛ tsp.	0.5 mL
Canned baby clams, drained, liquid reserved	2 × 10 oz.	2 × 284 mL
Canned stewed tomatoes	14 oz.	398 mL
Milk	1½ cups	375 mL

Cook potato and carrot in boiling water in large saucepan until tender. Do not drain.

Fry bacon until crisp. Remove to dish. Discard fat except for 1 tbsp. (15 mL).

Add green pepper, celery and onion to frying pan. Sauté until soft. Add to potato mixture along with bits from pan. Add bacon.

Add liquid from clams, potato soup, lemon pepper, salt and pepper. Stir. Boil gently for 10 to 15 minutes.

Add clams, tomatoes and milk. Heat through, without boiling, to prevent curdling. Makes 20 cups (5 L) chowder.

1 cup (250 mL) chowder: 130 Calories; 10 g Protein; 3.7 g Total Fat; 14 g Carbohydrate; 607 mg Sodium

Pictured on page 153.

Quickie Clam Chowder

Green pepper adds a flavorful twist. Only 15 minutes preparation time. 🕐 Using commercial scalloped potatoes is a real time-saver!

Box scalloped potatoes with sauce packet	1 × 5½ oz.	1 × 155 g
Milk and water, according to package directions		
Finely chopped green pepper	¼ cup	60 mL
Grated carrot	¼ cup	60 mL
Finely chopped onion	¼ cup	60 mL
Milk	2 cups	500 mL
Milk	½ cup	125 mL
All-purpose flour	2 tbsp.	30 mL
Canned baby clams, with liquid	1 × 10 oz.	1 × 284 mL

Empty potatoes and sauce packet into large heavy saucepan. Stir in first amount of milk and water as package directs, green pepper, carrot and onion. Heat and stir until boiling. Reduce heat. Cover. Simmer for about 30 minutes, stirring occasionally, until potatoes are softened and breaking up.

Stir in second amount of milk. Heat to just boiling.

Mix third amount of milk gradually into flour in cup until smooth. Stir into boiling liquid until boiling again and thickened.

Add clams with liquid. Heat through. Makes 8 cups (2 L) chowder.

1 cup (250 mL) chowder: 195 Calories; 14 g Protein; 6 g Total Fat; 21 g Carbohydrate; 514 mg Sodium

Pictured above.

Green Chili Soup

Very light green in color and a mild chili flavor.
Easy to double. ☺ Make the day before and
reheat just before serving.

Water	1 cup	250 mL
Finely chopped onion	¼ cup	60 mL
Light cream cheese, softened, cut up	4 oz.	125 g
Non-fat sour cream	½ cup	125 mL
Canned diced green chilies, with liquid	4 oz.	114 mL
Garlic powder	⅛ tsp.	0.5 mL
Chicken bouillon powder	1 tsp.	5 mL
Milk	1 cup	250 mL
Skim evaporated milk	½ cup	125 mL
Salt	⅛ tsp.	0.5 mL
Pepper, sprinkle		

Place water and onion in saucepan. Cook until onion is soft. Cool. Turn water and onion into blender.

Add cream cheese, sour cream, chilies with liquid, garlic powder and bouillon powder to blender. Process until smooth. Turn into saucepan.

Add both milks, salt and pepper. Heat through. Makes 4 cups (1 L) soup.

1 cup (250 mL) soup: 137 Calories; 9 g Protein; 6.1 g Total Fat; 12 g Carbohydrate; 825 mg Sodium

Pictured on this page.

Turkey Soup

An old-fashioned thick, full-bodied soup. For chunkier
soup, vegetables can be diced. ☺ Make ahead and freeze,
or store, covered, in refrigerator for up to three days.

Turkey wings, skin removed	2	2
Chopped onion	1 cup	250 mL
Chopped celery	⅓ cup	75 mL
Grated carrot	1 cup	250 mL
Grated potato	1 cup	250 mL
Thinly sliced cabbage	1 cup	250 mL
Water	6 cups	1.5 L
Chicken bouillon powder	1 tbsp.	15 mL
Salt	1 tsp.	5 mL
Pepper	¼ tsp.	1 mL

Place all 10 ingredients in Dutch oven. Bring to a boil, stirring occasionally. Cover. Boil slowly for 30 minutes. Remove wings. Cut off turkey and discard bones. Chop turkey and return to soup. Makes 6 cups (1.5 L) soup.

1 cup (250 mL) soup: 81 Calories; 8 g Protein; 0.7 g Total Fat; 10 g Carbohydrate; 815 mg Sodium

Pictured on this page.

Turkey Soup   Green Chili Soup

Black Bean Soup

For a heartier texture, mash first seven ingredients
instead of puréeing. ☺ Make up to three days
in advance, or freeze and reheat.

Canned black beans, drained and rinsed	19 oz.	540 mL
Condensed beef bouillon	10 oz.	284 mL
Onion flakes	1 tbsp.	15 mL
Water	1 cup	250 mL
Sherry (or alcohol-free sherry)	2 tbsp.	30 mL
Garlic powder	¼ tsp.	1 mL
Dried crushed chilies	¼ tsp.	1 mL
Cornstarch	2 tsp.	10 mL
Water	1 tbsp.	15 mL
Canned black beans, drained and rinsed	19 oz.	540 mL
Sour cream, for garnish (optional)		
Chopped parsley, for garnish	1 tsp.	5 mL

Purée first 7 ingredients in blender. Pour into saucepan. Heat, stirring often, until soup is boiling.

Stir cornstarch into second amount of water in small cup. Stir into boiling soup to boil and thicken.

Stir in second amount of black beans. Heat through.

Top each bowl with dollop of sour cream. Swirl lightly. Sprinkle with parsley. Makes 4 cups (1 L) soup.

1 cup (250 mL) soup: 166 Calories; 11 g Protein; 0.9 g Total Fat; 28 g Carbohydrate; 721 mg Sodium; good source of Dietary Fiber

Pictured on page 153.

Squares

One of the simplest things to have on

hand when unexpected company arrives is a plateful of

assorted squares. Easy and convenient, they can be made

and frozen months in advance. Serve with coffee or tea

for a sweet, satisfying afternoon or evening snack.

Your guests will feel as though you have been

hard at work making these squares just

for their visit...shhh!

Marble Squares

Small chunks of chocolate throughout.
Only 15 minutes preparation time. ⏱ Keep a container
of chopped walnuts in the freezer for use in a variety
of recipes. Freeze before or after cutting.

Hard margarine (or butter), softened	¹⁄₂ cup	125 mL
Brown sugar, packed	¹⁄₂ cup	125 mL
Granulated sugar	¹⁄₄ cup	60 mL
Large egg	1	1
Vanilla	³⁄₄ tsp.	4 mL
All-purpose flour	1 cup	250 mL
Salt	¹⁄₂ tsp.	2 mL
Chopped walnuts (optional)	¹⁄₂ cup	125 mL
Semisweet chocolate chips	1 cup	250 mL

Cream margarine and both sugars together in bowl. Beat in egg and vanilla.

Add flour, salt and walnuts. Stir to moisten. Turn into greased 9 x 9 inch (22 x 22 cm) pan.

Sprinkle chocolate chips over top. Place in 350°F (175°C) oven for about 3 minutes until chips are soft. Run knife back and forth to marble. Return to oven. Bake for about 20 minutes until wooden pick inserted in center comes out clean. Cool. Cuts into 36 squares.

1 square: 83 Calories; 1 g Protein; 4.7 g Total Fat; 10 g Carbohydrate; 73 mg Sodium

Pictured on page 159.

Candy Bars

Tastes like a chocolate-covered granola bar. Only
15 minutes preparation time. ⏱ Make up
to two days ahead, or freeze.

Hard margarine (or butter), softened	1 cup	250 mL
Brown sugar, packed	1 cup	250 mL
Quick-cooking rolled oats (not instant)	3 cups	750 mL
Corn syrup	¹⁄₂ cup	125 mL
All-purpose flour	1 cup	250 mL
Icing:		
Semisweet chocolate chips	1¹⁄₂ cups	375 mL
Smooth peanut butter	1 cup	250 mL
Finely chopped peanuts (optional)	2-3 tbsp.	30-50 mL

Melt margarine in saucepan. Mix in brown sugar, rolled oats, corn syrup and flour. Spread in greased 9 x 13 inch (22 x 33 cm) pan. Bake in 350°F (175°C) oven for 15 to 18 minutes. Cool to lukewarm.

Icing: Combine chocolate chips and peanut butter in saucepan. Heat on low, stirring often, until chips are melted. Spread over squares in pan.

Sprinkle with peanuts if desired. Cool. Cuts into 54 bars.

1 bar: 140 Calories; 2 g Protein; 8.2 g Total Fat; 16 g Carbohydrate; 71 mg Sodium

Pictured below.

Candy Bars

Fudge Squares

Like a chocolate oatmeal cookie, but with more pizazz.
🕑 Freeze before or after cutting.

Hard margarine (or butter), softened	½ cup	125 mL
Brown sugar, packed	1 cup	250 mL
Large egg	1	1
Vanilla	1 tsp.	5 mL
All-purpose flour	1¼ cups	300 mL
Quick-cooking rolled oats (not instant)	1¼ cups	300 mL
Baking soda	1 tsp.	5 mL
Salt	½ tsp.	2 mL
Filling:		
Sweetened condensed milk	½ cup	125 mL
Semisweet chocolate chips	1 cup	250 mL
Vanilla	½ tsp.	2 mL
Salt	¼ tsp.	1 mL
Chopped walnuts (or pecans)	½ cup	125 mL

Cream butter and brown sugar together in bowl. Beat in egg and vanilla.

Add flour, rolled oats, baking soda and salt. Stir together. Pack about ⅔ in greased 9 x 9 inch (22 x 22 cm) pan.

Filling: Combine condensed milk, chocolate chips, vanilla and salt in saucepan. Heat and stir until chips are melted.

Stir in walnuts. Spoon over mixture in pan. Crumble remaining oat mixture over top as best you can. Press lightly. Bake in 350°F (175°C) oven for 25 to 30 minutes until browned. Cool. Cuts into 36 squares.

1 square: 130 Calories; 2 g Protein; 6.4 g Total Fat; 17 g Carbohydrate; 137 mg Sodium

Pictured below.

Outer: Easy Fudge
Inner: Fudge Squares

Easy Fudge

A cinch for the non-cook. Easy, rich and oh so smooth.
🕑 Make ahead and keep refrigerated until just ready to serve. Can be left at room temperature, once served, for up to 30 minutes.

Icing (confectioner's) sugar	3 cups	750 mL
Cocoa	½ cup	125 mL
Evaporated milk	¼ cup	60 mL
Hard margarine (or butter), cut into small chunks	1 cup	250 mL
Vanilla	2 tsp.	10 mL
Pecan halves (optional)	¾ cup	175 mL

Measure icing sugar and cocoa into ungreased 2 quart (2 L) casserole dish. Do not stir.

Add evaporated milk and margarine Do not stir. Cook, uncovered, on high (100%) in microwave for about 3½ minutes until butter is just melted. Add vanilla. Beat with an electric mixer until smooth. Turn into foil-lined 8 x 8 inch (20 x 20 cm) pan. Place in freezer for 40 minutes to set quickly, then refrigerate. Cuts into 64 squares.

Top each square with pecan half.

1 square: 52 Calories; trace Protein; 3.1 g Total Fat; 6 g Carbohydrate; 37 mg Sodium

Pictured on this page.

Graham Brownies

Golden brown, chewy and moist. 🕑 Keep these four ingredients on hand for last minute entertaining. Very quick to prepare. If freezing, cut first.

Graham cracker crumbs	1 cup	250 mL
Semisweet chocolate chips	1 cup	250 mL
Chopped walnuts (or pecans)	½ cup	125 mL
Sweetened condensed milk (see Note)	11 oz.	300 mL

Mix all 4 ingredients well in bowl. Spread in greased 8 x 8 inch (20 x 20 cm) pan. Bake in 350°F (175°C) oven for about 35 minutes. Cut while warm. Cuts into 25 squares.

1 square: 142 Calories; 3 g Protein; 6.5 g Total Fat; 21 g Carbohydrate; 89 mg Sodium

Note: If using 14 oz. (398 mL) sweetened condensed milk, use 1⅓ cups (325 mL) graham cracker crumbs.

Pictured on page 159.

Center Left: Almond Cheese Squares, below   Top Right: Sour Cream Squares, below   Bottom Right: Turtle Squares, page 158

Almond Cheese Squares

Light, puffy texture. This can also work as a dessert—just cut larger pieces and serve with a fork.
🕐 *Freeze whole so you have a choice.*

Bottom Layer:

White cake mix (1 layer size)	1	1
Large eggs	2	2
Almond flavoring	1 tsp.	5 mL

Top Layer:

Cream cheese, softened	8 oz.	250 g
Icing (confectioner's) sugar	3 cups	750 mL
Large eggs	2	2
Almond flavoring	1 tsp.	5 mL
Sliced almonds	¼ cup	60 mL

Bottom Layer: Combine all 3 ingredients in bowl. Mix well. Spread in greased 9 x 13 inch (22 x 33 cm) pan.

Top Layer: Beat cream cheese in bowl. Beat in icing sugar. Add second amount of eggs and flavoring. Beat together well. Pour over cake layer.

Sprinkle with almonds. Press almonds lightly with back of spoon. Bake in 350°F (175°C) oven for about 35 minutes. Cool. Cuts into 54 squares.

1 square: 73 Calories; 1 g Protein; 2.8 g Total Fat; 11 g Carbohydrate; 37 mg Sodium

Pictured above.

Sour Cream Squares

If you enjoy raisin pie, this will be a favorite.
🕐 *Freezes well.*

Bottom Layer:

Hard margarine (or butter), softened	1 cup	250 mL
Brown sugar, packed	1 cup	250 mL
All-purpose flour	1¼ cups	300 mL
Baking soda	1 tsp.	5 mL
Salt	½ tsp.	2 mL
Quick-cooking rolled oats (not instant)	1½ cups	375 mL

Filling:

Granulated sugar	¾ cup	175 mL
Cornstarch	1½ tbsp.	25 mL
Sour cream	1½ cups	375 mL
Raisins	2 cups	500 mL
Vanilla	1 tsp.	5 mL

Bottom Layer: Mix all 6 ingredients in bowl until crumbly. Press ½ crumbs (about 2 cups, 500 mL) into greased 9 x 13 inch (22 x 33 cm) pan. Bake in 350°F (175°C) oven for 7 minutes until golden brown.

Filling: Stir all 5 ingredients together in saucepan. Heat and stir until boiling and thickened. Pour over bottom layer. Crumble remaining crumbs over top. Bake for about 30 minutes. Cool. Cuts into 54 squares.

1 square: 108 Calories; 1 g Protein; 4.8 g Total Fat; 16 g Carbohydrate; 98 mg Sodium

Pictured above.

Crispy Butterscotch Squares

If you spread the topping carefully, you can create a "tiger" look of chocolate and orange swirls.
⊙ This freezes best left whole; cut when partially thawed.

Sweetened condensed milk	½ cup	125 mL
Corn syrup	2 tbsp.	30 mL
Brown sugar, packed	½ cup	125 mL
Hard margarine (or butter)	¼ cup	60 mL
Crisp rice cereal	5 cups	1.25 L
Chopped walnuts (or pecans), optional	1 cup	250 mL
Topping:		
Semisweet chocolate chips	1 cup	250 mL
Butterscotch chips	1 cup	250 mL

Place first 4 ingredients in large saucepan. Bring to a boil, stirring often, over medium-low heat. Boil for 5 minutes, stirring constantly. Remove from heat. Beat slowly with spoon until mixture slightly thickens.

Add rice cereal and walnuts. Stir together well to coat. Pack in greased 9 x 13 inch (22 x 33 cm) pan.

Topping: Sprinkle chocolate chips and butterscotch chips on top. Heat in 200°F (95°C) oven for 4 to 5 minutes until softened. Spread with knife, making swirls. Cool completely before cutting. Cuts into 54 squares.

1 square: 72 Calories; 1 g Protein; 2.5 g Total Fat; 13 g Carbohydrate; 46 mg Sodium

Pictured on page 159.

Nutty Fudge

Nice balance of sweet and nutty flavors. ⊙ Keep a supply of chopped nuts in the freezer. This fudge can be frozen whole or pre-cut into squares.

Granulated sugar	2 cups	500 mL
White corn syrup	½ cup	125 mL
Water	½ cup	125 mL
Hard margarine (or butter)	1 tbsp.	15 mL
Salt, just a pinch		
Chopped walnuts (or pecans)	2 cups	500 mL

Stir first 5 ingredients in saucepan on medium-low until boiling.

Add walnuts. Boil, without stirring, for 15 to 20 minutes until soft ball stage on candy thermometer or until a small spoonful forms a soft ball in cold water. Remove from heat. Let stand for 15 minutes. Beat with spoon for about 10 minutes until lighter in color and starting to thicken. Pour into greased 8 x 8 inch (20 x 20 cm) pan. Cool. Cuts into 64 squares.

1 square: 61 Calories; 1 g Protein; 2.7 g Total Fat; 9 g Carbohydrate; 4 mg Sodium

Pictured on page 159.

Turtle Squares

This has a chewy base and a toffee layer.
⊙ Freezes well.

Bottom Layer:		
Hard margarine (or butter)	1 cup	250 mL
Quick-cooking rolled oats (not instant)	1¾ cups	425 mL
Brown sugar, packed	1 cup	250 mL
All-purpose flour	¾ cup	175 mL
Cocoa	¼ cup	60 mL
Baking soda	½ tsp.	2 mL
Chopped pecans (or walnuts)	½ cup	125 mL
Filling:		
Sweetened condensed milk	½ cup	125 mL
Brown sugar, packed	½ cup	125 mL
Hard margarine (or butter)	½ cup	125 mL
Corn syrup	2 tbsp.	30 mL
Topping:		
Semisweet chocolate chips	⅔ cup	150 mL
Hard margarine (or butter)	2 tbsp.	30 mL

Bottom Layer: Melt margarine in medium saucepan. Add next 6 ingredients. Stir together well. Press in greased 9 x 13 inch (22 x 33 cm) pan. Bake in 350°F (175°C) oven for about 15 minutes.

Filling: Measure all 4 ingredients into heavy medium saucepan over medium heat. Stir. Bring to a boil. Boil slowly, stirring continually, for 5 minutes. This burns easily on the bottom. Remove from heat. Beat slowly with spoon for about 2 minutes, until mixture shows signs of thickening a bit. Do not overbeat or it will be too hard upon cooling. Spread over bottom layer. Cool.

Topping: Melt chocolate chips and margarine in small saucepan on lowest heat, stirring often. Spread over cooled filling. Cuts into 54 squares.

1 square: 125 Calories; 1 g Protein; 7.9 g Total Fat; 14 g Carbohydrate; 88 mg Sodium

Pictured on page 157.

1. **Crispy Butterscotch Squares,** page 158
2. **Graham Brownies,** page 156
3. **Nutty Fudge,** page 158
4. **Marble Squares,** page 155

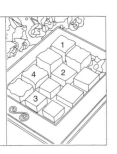

Vegetables

Don't take vegetables for granted—they are

versatile, colorful, snappy, delicious and incredibly

easy to make into spectacular side dishes! With these

recipes you have a wonderful opportunity to offer

a change from the ordinary to your friends and family.

Create a unique and memorable dining experience

with this exceptional selection of recipes.

Pattypan Squash

Buy this unique squash when in season for a more reasonable price. ☺ Only ten minutes from start to finish.

Pattypan squash, about 24 (small have best flavor)	1½ lbs.	680 g
Boiling water		
Garlic Butter:		
Hard margarine (or butter), softened	2 tbsp.	30 mL
Garlic salt	⅛ tsp.	0.5 mL

Cook squash in boiling water in saucepan for 3 to 6 minutes until tender. Drain.

Garlic Butter: Cream margarine and garlic salt together with spoon. Add to squash. Toss. Serves 6.

1 serving: 58 Calories; 1 g Protein; 4.2 g Total Fat; 5 g Carbohydrate; 75 mg Sodium

Pictured on this page.

Special Carrots

Easy to double if serving a larger crowd.
☺ Have this assembled, waiting in the refrigerator until ready to bake and serve.

Thinly sliced carrot	5 cups	1.25 L
Coarsely chopped onion	1 cup	250 mL
Boiling water		
Light salad dressing (or mayonnaise)	¼ cup	60 mL
Light sour cream	¼ cup	60 mL
Salt	½ tsp.	2 mL
Pepper	¹⁄₁₆ tsp.	0.5 mL
Topping:		
Hard margarine (or butter)	1 tbsp.	15 mL
Fine dry bread crumbs	¼ cup	60 mL

Cook carrot and onion in boiling water in saucepan until tender. Drain and mash. Turn into greased 1½ quart (1.5 L) casserole dish.

Mix salad dressing, sour cream, salt and pepper in small bowl. Spread over carrot mixture.

Topping: Melt margarine in small saucepan. Add bread crumbs. Stir. Sprinkle over top. Bake, uncovered, in 375°F (190°C) oven for 25 to 25 minutes until browned. Makes 4½ cups (1.1 L) carrots.

½ cup (125 mL) carrots: 75 Calories; 1 g Protein; 3.8 g Total Fat; 9 g Carbohydrate; 271 mg Sodium

Pictured on page 168/169.

Pattypan Squash

Nutty Glazed Carrots

Pecans add a nice crunch. ☺ Cut carrots ahead of time and keep in cold water. Very quick to prepare.

Carrots, cut bite size	2 lbs.	900 g
Boiling water		
Salt	1 tsp.	5 mL
Hard margarine (or butter)	2 tbsp.	30 mL
All-purpose flour	1 tbsp.	15 mL
Brown sugar, packed	¼ cup	60 mL
Water	½ cup	125 mL
Toasted chopped pecans (or walnuts), optional	3 tbsp.	50 mL

Cook carrot in boiling water and salt until tender. Drain.

Melt margarine in small saucepan. Mix in flour and brown sugar. Add water, stirring until boiling and thickened. Pour over carrot. Toss.

Sprinkle with pecans. Serves 8.

1 serving: 108 Calories; 1 g Protein; 3.2 g Total Fat; 20 g Carbohydrate; 111 mg Sodium; good source of Dietary Fiber

Pictured on page 163.

Broccoli Casserole

Nice combination of flavors. ☺ Assemble in the morning and refrigerate until ready to bake.

Chopped broccoli (stems, chopped, and florets, cut bite size)	5 cups	1.25 L
Boiling water		
Sour cream	1 cup	250 mL
Grated Edam (or medium Cheddar) cheese	1 cup	250 mL
Celery seed	⅛ tsp.	0.5 mL
Garlic powder	⅛ tsp.	0.5 mL
Salt	½ tsp.	2 mL
Pepper, sprinkle		
Toasted chopped pecans (or almonds)	¼ cup	60 mL

Cook broccoli in boiling water until tender-crisp. Drain very well.

Mix next 6 ingredients in bowl. Spread ½ of broccoli in greased 1½ quart (1.5 L) casserole dish. Cover with ½ of sour cream mixture. Repeat layers.

Sprinkle with pecans. Bake, uncovered, in 325°F (160°C) oven for about 30 minutes until bubbly hot. Serves 6.

1 serving: 207 Calories; 11 g Protein; 15.3 g Total Fat; 10 g Carbohydrate; 472 mg Sodium; good source of Dietary Fiber

Pictured on this page.

Top Left: Mashed Turnip Mallow, below
Center Right: Herb And Garlic Potatoes, page 167
Bottom Left: Broccoli Casserole, this page

Mashed Turnip Mallow

A real favorite! Excellent color and texture. ☺ Can be made ahead and frozen without the marshmallow topping. Add marshmallows when reheating.

Yellow turnip, peeled and diced	2¼ lbs.	1 kg
Boiling water	2 cups	500 mL
Salt	½ tsp.	2 mL
Granulated sugar	½ tsp.	2 mL
Hard margarine (or butter)	3 tbsp.	50 mL
Salt (optional)	½ tsp.	2 mL
Pepper	⅛ tsp.	0.5 mL
Instant potato flakes (optional), approximately	½ cup	125 mL
Miniature marshmallows (or large, cut in half), approximately	1⅓ cups	325 mL

Cook turnip in boiling water, first amount of salt and sugar in saucepan until very tender. Drain and mash. A food processor works well.

Add margarine, second amount of salt and pepper. If turnip is watery, add potato flakes. Mash. A bit more or less can be added according to texture. Turn into ungreased 2 quart (2 L) casserole dish. Bake in 350°F (175°C) oven for about 20 minutes until heated through.

Cover with marshmallows. Bake for about 7 minutes until golden brown. Serves 8.

1 serving: 88 Calories; 1 g Protein; 4.5 g Total Fat; 13 g Carbohydrate; 121 mg Sodium

Pictured above.

Eggplant Parmigiana,
page 163

Italian Vegetable Bowl

*Lots of bright colors. Herbs and garlic come through nicely.
☺ To save time, have vegetables cut and measured
ahead of time. Simply cook when ready.*

Olive (or cooking) oil	1 tsp.	5 mL
Garlic clove, minced	1	1
Coin-size sliced carrot	2 cups	500 mL
Water	2 tbsp.	30 mL
Broccoli florets	1 cup	250 mL
Cauliflower florets	1 cup	250 mL
Baby zucchini (about 3 inches, 7.5 cm, long), left whole (or 3 cups, 750 mL, sliced)	1 lb.	454 g
Dried sweet basil	1 tsp.	5 mL
Dried whole oregano	½ tsp.	2 mL
Water	3 tbsp.	50 mL
Canned diced tomatoes, drained	14 oz.	398 mL
Granulated sugar	½ tsp.	2 mL
Salt	¼ tsp.	1 mL
Pepper	⅛ tsp.	0.5 mL

Heat cooking oil in frying pan. Add garlic. Heat, stirring
constantly until softened.

Add carrot and water. Cover. Cook for 3 minutes on
medium-high.

Add next 6 ingredients. Cover. Cook for about 5 minutes
until vegetables are tender-crisp. Do not overcook.

Add tomatoes, sugar, salt and pepper. Stir gently. Cover for
about 1 minute until heated through. Makes 8 cups (2 L)
vegetables.

½ cup (125 mL) vegetables: 22 Calories; 1 g Protein; 0.5 g Total Fat; 4 g Carbohydrate;
    92 mg Sodium

Pictured on front cover and on page 166.

Braised Vegetables

*The aroma of this Chinese-style dish will tantalize your
guests. ☺ Have all vegetables cut and measured ahead
of time. Takes only about ten minutes to stir-fry.*

Cooking oil	2 tsp.	10 mL
Chopped onion	1 cup	250 mL
Medium carrots, cut julienne	2	2
Grated gingerroot	1 tbsp.	15 mL
Garlic clove, minced (or ¼ tsp., 1 mL, garlic powder)	1	1
Water	¼ cup	60 mL
Bok choy, white ends, cut into large pieces	4½ cups	1.1 L
Broccoli florets	2 cups	500 mL
Bok choy, green ends, cut into large pieces	5 cups	1.25 L
Pea pods, fresh or frozen	2 cups	500 mL
Canned miniature cobs of corn, drained	14 oz.	398 mL
Salt, sprinkle		
Pepper, sprinkle		
Cornstarch	1 tbsp.	15 mL
Water	1 tbsp.	15 mL
Soy (or oyster) sauce	2 tbsp.	30 mL
Granulated sugar	½ tsp.	2 mL

Heat cooking oil in wok or frying pan. Add onion, carrot,
ginger and garlic. Stir-fry for 2 minutes.

Add first amount of water, bok choy white pieces and
broccoli. Stir. Cover. Cook for 3 to 4 minutes.

Add bok choy green pieces, pea pods and corn cobs.
Sprinkle with salt and pepper. Stir-fry for 2 minutes.

Stir cornstarch, second amount of water, soy sauce and
sugar together in small bowl. Push vegetables to side of
pan. Pour cornstarch mixture into pan. Stir to thicken,
gradually stirring vegetables back in. Makes 11 cups (2.75 L)
vegetables.

1 cup (250 mL) vegetables: 71 Calories; 4 g Protein; 1.2 g Total Fat; 14 g Carbohydrate;
    244 mg Sodium

Pictured on page 171.

Golden Eggplant Casserole

A great accompaniment to any meal. ☺ *Assemble the day before and refrigerate until ready to bake.*

Large eggplant, peeled and cubed (about 2½ cups, 625 mL)	1	1
Boiling water		
Salt	1 tsp.	5 mL
Soda crackers, crumbled	18	18
Grated medium or sharp Cheddar cheese	½ cup	125 mL
Chopped celery	¼ cup	60 mL
Chopped pimiento	2 tbsp.	30 mL
Hard margarine (or butter), melted	1 tbsp.	15 mL
Salt	½ tsp.	2 mL
Pepper	⅛ tsp.	0.5 mL
Skim evaporated milk (or light cream)	1 cup	250 mL

Cook eggplant in boiling water and first amount of salt for 5 to 10 minutes. It should still be firm. Drain.

Add remaining 8 ingredients. Stir. Spoon into greased 1½ quart (1.5 L) casserole dish. Bake, uncovered, in 350°F (175°C) oven for about 45 minutes. Serves 6.

1 serving: 139 Calories; 7 g Protein; 6.4 g Total Fat; 13 g Carbohydrate; 469 mg Sodium

Pictured on page 165.

Eggplant Parmigiana

Golden cheese layer on top. ☺ *Assemble to the baking stage the day before or the morning of. Bake when needed.*

Medium eggplants (about 2 lbs., 900 g), peeled and sliced	2	2
Boiling water		
Salt	½ tsp.	2 mL
All-purpose flour	½ cup	125 mL
Dried whole oregano	½ tsp.	2 mL
Dried sweet basil	½ tsp.	2 mL
Salt	½ tsp.	2 mL
Pepper	⅛ tsp.	0.5 mL
Cooking oil (or hard margarine)	2 tbsp.	30 mL
Tomato sauce	14 oz.	398 mL
Process mozzarella cheese slices	8	8
Grated Parmesan cheese	½ cup	125 mL

Cook eggplant in boiling water and first amount of salt for 5 to 10 minutes. It should still be firm. Drain. Cool slightly.

Combine flour and seasonings.

Dip eggplant slices into flour mixture. Brown in cooking oil in frying pan.

Pour tomato sauce into 2 quart (2 L) casserole dish to depth of ¼ inch (6 mm). Layer ⅓ of eggplant slices, ⅓ of remaining tomato sauce, ⅓ of mozzarella cheese and ⅓ of Parmesan cheese. Repeat to use all ingredients. Cover. Bake in 400°F (205°C) oven for 20 minutes. Remove cover. Bake for 10 minutes. Serves 8.

1 serving: 218 Calories; 12 g Protein; 13.5 g Total Fat; 13 g Carbohydrate; 1034 mg Sodium

Pictured on page 162.

Quick Potato Casserole, page 169

Nutty Glazed Carrots, page 161

Rice Elegant, page 170   Onion Casserole, below

Onion Casserole

A nice accompaniment for a roast. ☺ This can be assembled the day before, adding the crumb topping just before baking.

Sliced onion	6 cups	1.5 L
Boiling water		
Salt	⅛ tsp.	0.5 mL
Pepper	¼ tsp.	1 mL
Grated Monterey Jack (or Swiss) cheese	1 cup	250 mL
Condensed cream of chicken soup	10 oz.	284 mL
Milk	½ cup	125 mL
Soy sauce	1 tsp.	5 mL
Topping:		
Hard margarine (or butter)	1½ tbsp.	25 mL
Fine dry bread crumbs	6 tbsp.	100 mL
Imitation bacon bits (optional)	1 tsp.	5 mL

Cook onion in boiling water until tender. Drain. Turn into ungreased 2 quart (2 L) casserole dish.

Sprinkle with salt and pepper. Scatter cheese over top.

Stir soup, milk and soy sauce together in bowl. Pour over all. Stir.

Topping: Melt margarine in saucepan. Stir in bread crumbs and bacon bits. Sprinkle over onion. Bake, uncovered, in 350°F (175°C) oven for about 30 minutes until hot and browned. Makes 5½ cups (1.4 L).

½ cup (125 mL): 127 Calories; 5 g Protein; 7.1 g Total Fat; 11 g Carbohydrate; 394 mg Sodium

Pictured above.

Company Bean Bake

Bright and colorful. Serve with buttered hot biscuits. ☺ Can be made ahead and frozen.

Bacon slices (about ½ lb., 227 g), diced	8	8
Chopped onion	3 cups	750 mL
Brown sugar, packed	1 cup	250 mL
White vinegar	¼ cup	60 mL
Canned kidney beans, drained	14 oz.	398 mL
Canned pork and beans	14 oz.	398 mL
Frozen lima beans	1⅓ cups	325 mL
Canned sliced mushrooms, drained	10 oz.	284 mL

Sauté bacon until almost cooked. Drain fat. Add onion to frying pan. Sauté until bacon is cooked and onion is soft. Drain fat.

Add brown sugar and vinegar. Stir. Bring to a boil. Boil for 10 minutes.

Put next 4 ingredients into ungreased 2 quart (2 L) casserole dish. Add bacon mixture. Stir well. Bake, uncovered, in 350°F (175°C) oven for about 1 hour. Makes about 6 cups (1.5 L) beans.

1 cup (250 mL) beans: 413 Calories; 15 g Protein; 5.5 g Total Fat; 81 g Carbohydrate; 873 mg Sodium; excellent source of Dietary Fiber

Pictured on page 165.

Baked Beans

So good you will want to double—or even triple—this recipe. An easy one-dish recipe. ☺ Only five minutes preparation time!

Canned beans in tomato sauce	4 × 14 oz.	4 × 398 mL
Canned chick peas (garbanzo beans), drained	19 oz.	540 mL
Canned kidney beans, with liquid	14 oz.	398 mL
Mild, medium or hot salsa	1½ cups	375 mL
Brown sugar, packed	½ cup	125 mL
Onion flakes	¼ cup	60 mL

Combine all 6 ingredients in roaster. Bake, uncovered, in 350°F (175°C) oven for 50 to 60 minutes until bubbly hot and browning around edge. Makes about 10 cups (2.5 L) beans.

1 cup (250 mL) beans: 332 Calories; 14 g Protein; 1.5 g Total Fat; 72 g Carbohydrate; 1580 mg Sodium; excellent source of Dietary Fiber

Pictured on page 168.

Creamed Mushrooms

Can't think of a second vegetable? Try this easy one.
🕐 *Make in the morning and gently reheat before serving.*

Hard margarine (or butter)	2 tbsp.	30 mL
All-purpose flour	2 tbsp.	30 mL
Salt	½ tsp.	2 mL
Pepper	⅛ tsp.	0.5 mL
Chicken bouillon powder	¼-½ tsp.	1-2 mL
Parsley flakes	½ tsp.	2 mL
Milk	1 cup	250 mL
Canned whole mushrooms, drained	2 × 10 oz.	2 × 284 mL

Melt margarine in saucepan. Mix in flour, salt, pepper, bouillon powder and parsley.

Stir in milk until mixture is boiling and thickened.

Add mushrooms. Stir. Heat through. Makes 2 cups (500 mL).

⅓ cup (75 mL) mushrooms (with sauce): 63 Calories; 2 g Protein; 4.2 g Total Fat; 6 g Carbohydrate; 624 mg Sodium

Pictured below.

Potato And Turnip Crunch

Good with meat and gravy. 🕐 *Potato and turnip can be prepared up to two days ahead or even use leftovers from another meal.*

Diced cooked potato	4 cups	1 L
Diced cooked yellow turnip	2 cups	500 mL
Salt, sprinkle		
Pepper, sprinkle		
Hard margarine (or butter)	2 tbsp.	30 mL
Finely diced onion	¼ cup	60 mL
Crushed flakes of corn cereal	1 cup	250 mL

Combine potato and turnip in greased 2 quart (2 L) casserole dish. Sprinkle with salt and pepper.

Melt margarine in frying pan. Add onion. Sauté until soft. Remove from heat. Stir in cereal. Sprinkle over vegetables. Bake, uncovered, in a 350°F (175°C) oven for 25 to 30 minutes until heated through and topping is browned. Serves 6.

1 serving: 200 Calories; 4 g Protein; 4.1 g Total Fat; 39 g Carbohydrate; 241 mg Sodium; good source of Dietary Fiber

Pictured below.

Top Left:
Creamed Mushrooms, above

Bottom Left:
Potato And Turnip Crunch, this page

Top Right:
Company Bean Bake, page 164

Bottom Right:
Golden Eggplant Casserole, page 163

Potato Patties

Potato Casserole

A nice luncheon addition. ☺ *Using frozen hash brown potatoes saves time. Only 15 minutes preparation time.*

Hard margarine (or butter)	¼ cup	60 mL
Frozen shredded hash brown potatoes	5 cups	1.25 L
Large eggs	4	4
Hot milk	1 cup	250 mL
Finely chopped onion	⅓ cup	75 mL
Onion salt	1 tsp.	5 mL
Paprika	½ tsp.	2 mL
Salt	¼ tsp.	1 mL
Pepper	¼ tsp.	1 mL
Grated sharp Cheddar cheese	1 cup	250 mL

Melt margarine in large saucepan. Add potato. Stir well.

Beat eggs in bowl. Add milk, onion, onion salt, paprika, salt and pepper. Mix. Add to potato mixture. Stir. Turn into greased 3 quart (3 L) casserole dish. Bake, uncovered, in 350°F (175°C) oven for about 50 minutes.

Sprinkle with cheese. Bake for 5 minutes until cheese is melted. Serves 6.

1 serving: 378 Calories; 15 g Protein; 19.8 g Total Fat; 37 g Carbohydrate; 664 mg Sodium; good source of Dietary Fiber

Pictured below.

Potato Patties

Great to have with bacon and eggs or with lunch. ☺ *Use leftover mashed potato to save time.*

Warm mashed cooked potato	2 cups	500 mL
Seasoning salt	½ tsp.	2 mL
Salt	⅛ tsp.	0.5 mL
Garlic salt	⅛ tsp.	0.5 mL
Parsley flakes	1 tsp.	5 mL
Hard margarine (or butter)	½ tbsp.	7 mL

Mix potato, seasoning salt, salt, garlic salt and parsley together in bowl. Using ⅓ cup (75 mL) each, shape into patties. If potato is quite dry, add a bit more water or milk.

Heat margarine in non-stick frying pan. Add patties. Brown both sides. Makes 6 patties.

1 patty: 86 Calories; 2 g Protein; 1 g Total Fat; 18 g Carbohydrate; 213 mg Sodium

Variation: Add 1 tsp. (5 mL) chopped chives to potatoes.

Pictured above.

Potato Casserole, above   Italian Vegetable Bowl, page 162

Spicy Baked Potatoes And Onions

*The spices really do come through. ☺ Bake this
ahead and reheat when ready to serve.*

Large baking potatoes, cut into 2 inch (5 cm) chunks	5	5
Medium onions, cut into 8 pieces each	2	2
Hard margarine (or butter)	2 tbsp.	30 mL
Seasoning salt	1 tsp.	5 mL
Cayenne pepper	1/8 tsp.	0.5 mL
Dried sweet basil	1 tsp.	5 mL
Garlic powder	1/8 tsp.	0.5 mL

Place potato and onion in large bowl.

Combine remaining 5 ingredients in small cup. Microwave
on full (100%) power for 30 seconds to melt butter. Stir.
Pour over vegetables. Toss well to coat. Turn into ungreased
9 x 13 inch (22 x 33 cm) pan. Cover with foil. Bake in 425°F
(220°C) oven for 30 minutes. Shake pan without removing
foil. Bake for 30 minutes. Test for doneness and cook longer
if necessary. Serves 8.

1 serving: 107 Calories; 2 g Protein; 3.1 g Total Fat; 18 g Carbohydrate; 211 mg Sodium

Pictured on this page.

Herb And Garlic Potatoes

*Very easy to increase to feed a crowd.
☺ Allow extra oven time when casserole has been
refrigerated, frozen or increased in volume.*

Hot mashed potato	3 cups	750 mL
Non-fat herb and garlic-flavored spreadable cream cheese	1/2 cup	125 mL
Non-fat (or light) sour cream	1/2 cup	125 mL
Green onion, thinly sliced	1	1
Salt	1/2 tsp.	2 mL
Pepper	1/8 tsp.	0.5 mL
Grated sharp Cheddar cheese	1/2 cup	125 mL

Mash first 6 ingredients together in saucepan or bowl. Turn
into greased 1 1/2 quart (1.5 L) casserole dish. Cover. At this
point it may be refrigerated or frozen. Bake in 350°F
(175°C) oven for about 30 minutes until heated through.

Sprinkle with cheese. Bake, uncovered, for about 5 minutes
until cheese is melted. Serves 6.

1 serving: 181 Calories; 7 g Protein; 3.5 g Total Fat; 31 g Carbohydrate; 302 mg Sodium

Pictured on page 161.

Top Left: Spicy Baked Potatoes And Onions, this page
Bottom Left: Chinese Chicken Rice, page 170
Center Right: Stuffing Patties, below

Stuffing Patties

*Great with meat and gravy. An easy way to do stuffing.
☺ Prepare patties in the morning and either refrigerate and
bake when ready, or bake ahead and reheat just before serving.*

Hard margarine (or butter)	1/4 cup	60 mL
Chopped onion	1 1/2 cups	375 mL
Chopped celery	1 1/2 cups	375 mL
Ground sage	1 tsp.	5 mL
Ground thyme	1/2 tsp.	2 mL
Chicken bouillon powder	2 tsp.	10 mL
Salt	1 tsp.	5 mL
Pepper	1/4 tsp.	1 mL
Bread slices, cubed	16	16
Water	1/2 cup	125 mL

Heat margarine in frying pan. Add onion and celery. Sauté
until soft.

Mix in next 5 ingredients. Turn into bowl, using rubber
spatula to add all margarine in pan.

Add bread cubes and water. Stir well. Shape into 9 patties,
using about 1 cup (250 mL) for each. Arrange on greased
baking sheet. For moister patties, cover with foil before
baking. For firmer patties, bake uncovered. Bake in 400°F
(205°C) oven for about 10 minutes. Makes 9 patties.

1 patty: 200 Calories; 5 g Protein; 7.3 g Total Fat; 29 g Carbohydrate; 782 mg Sodium

Pictured above.

Baked Beans, page 164   Mashed Potatoes, below   Special Carrots, page 160

Home Fries

Great for entertaining for brunch.
🕐 *Use leftover potatoes to save on time.*

Medium potatoes, cooked and cooled	6	6
Cooking oil	1 tbsp.	15 mL
Chopped or sliced onion	1 cup	250 mL
Chopped red pepper	½ cup	125 mL
Chopped green pepper	½ cup	125 mL
Salt, sprinkle		
Pepper, sprinkle		

Cut potatoes into bite-size pieces.

Heat cooking oil in frying pan. Add onion and peppers. Sauté until onion is golden and peppers are soft. Add potato. Sprinkle with salt and pepper. Fry until heated through. Serves 8.

1 serving: 124 Calories; 3 g Protein; 1.9 g Total Fat; 25 g Carbohydrate; 6.5 mg Sodium

Variation: Add minced ham or minced corned beef when frying potato.

Pictured on page 171.

Mashed Potatoes

Takes ordinary potatoes up a notch or two.
🕐 *This can be made ahead of time and reheated when needed. Freezes well.*

Medium potatoes, peeled and quartered	10	10
Boiling water		
Hard margarine (or butter), softened	¼ cup	60 mL
Sour cream	½ cup	125 mL
Milk	½ cup	125 mL
Onion salt	2 tsp.	10 mL
Salt	½ tsp.	2 mL
Pepper	⅛ tsp.	0.5 mL
Parmesan cheese, sprinkle		

Cook potatoes in boiling water until tender. Drain. Mash.

Add next 6 ingredients. Mash together well.

Sprinkle with Parmesan cheese. Serves 8.

1 serving: 234 Calories; 4 g Protein; 8.6 g Total Fat; 36 g Carbohydrate; 602 mg Sodium

Pictured above.

Shrimp Fried Rice, this page

Shrimp Fried Rice

Lots of pink shrimp in the browned rice. ☺ Cook rice ahead of time and have it waiting in the refrigerator. Separate cooked rice with wet hands.

Long grain white rice (or 4³/₄ cups,1.25 L, cooked)	1¹/₄ cups	300 mL
Boiling water	2¹/₂ cups	625 mL
Cooking oil	1 tbsp.	15 mL
Thinly sliced onion	¹/₂ cup	125 mL
Chopped fresh mushrooms	1 cup	250 mL
Sliced green onion	¹/₃ cup	75 mL
Soy sauce	2 tbsp.	30 mL
Ground ginger	¹/₄ tsp.	1 mL
Salt	¹/₂ tsp.	2 mL
Pepper, just a pinch		
Cooked baby shrimp, thawed if frozen	¹/₂ lb.	225 g
Large eggs	2	2
Water	1¹/₂ tbsp.	25 mL

Combine rice and boiling water in saucepan. Boil gently for about 15 minutes until tender and water is absorbed. Cool completely. To hasten cooling, spread rice on baking sheets.

Heat cooking oil in frying pan. Add onion. Sauté until soft.

Add mushrooms and green onion. Sauté until slightly softened.

Stir in soy sauce, ginger, salt and pepper. Add rice. Heat, stirring often until steaming hot.

Stir in shrimp to heat through.

Beat eggs with water. Pour over all. Stir until eggs begin to set. Serve hot. Makes 6 cups (1.5 L).

¹/₂ cup (125 mL) fried rice: 113 Calories; 6 g Protein; 2.2 g Total Fat; 16 g Carbohydrate; 315 mg Sodium

Pictured on this page.

Chicken Fried Rice

Omit shrimp. Add about 1¹/₂ cups (375 mL) chopped cooked chicken.

Quick Potato Casserole

Place onion soup mix in a sealable plastic bag and crush with a rolling pin. ☺ Make casserole in the morning and reheat when ready.

Medium potatoes, peeled, quartered lengthwise and sliced into 1 inch (2.5 cm) chunks	5 lbs.	2.3 kg
Hard margarine (or butter), melted	¹/₄ cup	60 mL
Envelope dry onion soup mix, crushed	1 × 1¹/₂ oz.	1 × 42 g
Sour cream, for garnish		

Layer ¹/₂ of potato chunks in greased 3 quart (3 L) casserole dish.

Dip pastry brush into melted margarine. Dab onto potato.

Sprinkle with ¹/₂ of soup mix. Cover with second ¹/₂ of potatoes. Dab with margarine. Sprinkle with remaining soup mix. Cover. Bake in 350°F (175°C) oven for about 1¹/₄ hours until tender. Garnish with sour cream. Makes about 11 cups (2.75 L).

1 cup (250 mL) casserole: 175 Calories; 4 g Protein; 4.9 g Total Fat; 30 g Carbohydrate; 404 mg Sodium

Pictured on page 163.

Chinese Chicken Rice

Almost a luncheon meal in itself. ☺ Instead of running to the grocery store, use up the vegetables you have on hand in your refrigerator.

Long grain white rice	1 cup	250 mL
Water	2 cups	500 mL
Chicken bouillon powder	1 tbsp.	15 mL
Cooking oil	1 tbsp.	15 mL
Boneless, skinless chicken breast half, diced	1	1
Chopped vegetables (bok choy, green or red pepper, bean sprouts, pea pods or other)	2 cups	500 mL
Water	½ cup	125 mL
Boiling water	1 cup	250 mL
Chicken bouillon powder	2 tsp.	10 mL
Large eggs, fork-beaten	5	5

Cook rice in first amount of water and bouillon powder in saucepan for about 15 minutes until rice is tender and liquid is absorbed.

Heat cooking oil in frying pan. Add chicken and vegetables. Stir-fry for 2 to 3 minutes.

Add second amount of water. Cover. Cook for 8 to 10 minutes until vegetables are tender and water is evaporated.

Add cooked rice, boiling water and second amount of bouillon powder. Heat and stir.

Add eggs. Stir as eggs cook. Makes 6 cups (1.5 L).

½ cup (125 mL) rice: 121 Calories; 7 g Protein; 3.7 g Total Fat; 15 g Carbohydrate; 307 mg Sodium

Pictured on page 167.

Rice Elegant

An oniony flavor that goes so well with beef. ☺ Make ahead and reheat when ready to serve.

Uncooked long grain white rice	1 cup	250 mL
Water	2½ cups	625 mL
Envelope dry onion soup mix	1 × 1½ oz.	1 × 42 g
Sliced fresh mushrooms	2 cups	500 mL

Combine all 4 ingredients in saucepan. Simmer slowly for 15 to 20 minutes until rice is tender and liquid is absorbed. Makes 4 cups (1 L).

½ cup (125 mL) rice: 109 Calories; 3 g Protein; 0.6 g Total Fat; 23 g Carbohydrate; 472 mg Sodium

Pictured on page 164.

Special Rice Bake

Complementary flavors, especially the dill and Parmesan with brown rice. ☺ Make the rice in the morning and reheat just before adding remaining ingredients.

Long grain brown rice	¾ cup	175 mL
Boiling water	1½ cups	375 mL
Salt	¾ tsp.	4 mL
Creamed cottage cheese, run through blender	1½ cups	375 mL
Chopped green onion	¼ cup	60 mL
Parsley flakes	½ tsp.	2 mL
Dill weed	1 tsp.	5 mL
Onion powder	¼ tsp.	1 mL
Grated fresh Parmesan cheese	2 tbsp.	30 mL

Cook rice in boiling water and salt slowly for about 45 minutes until tender and liquid is absorbed.

Add next 5 ingredients to rice. Stir. Turn into greased 1 quart (1 L) casserole dish.

Sprinkle with Parmesan cheese. Cover. Bake in 350°F (175°C) oven for 30 to 35 minutes until bubbly hot. Makes 3 cups (750 mL).

½ cup (125 mL) rice: 145 Calories; 10 g Protein; 1.9 g Total Fat; 21 g Carbohydrate; 623 mg Sodium

Pictured on page 171.

Onion Rice

Very flavorful. ☺ Keep these ingredients in the cupboard for spur-of-the moment dinner guests. Or bake and freeze, ready to thaw and reheat at the last minute.

Uncooked long grain white rice	1 cup	250 mL
Condensed onion soup	10 oz.	284 mL
Condensed chicken broth	10 oz.	284 mL

Stir all 3 ingredients together in ungreased 2 quart (2 L) casserole dish. Cover. Bake in 350°F (175°C) oven for about 1 hour until rice is tender and liquid is absorbed. Stir. Makes 3½ cups (875 mL).

½ cup (125 mL) rice: 135 Calories; 5 g Protein; 1.2 g Total Fat; 25 g Carbohydrate; 634 mg Sodium

Pictured on page 171.

Stress-Free Entertaining

From the moment the invitation is made to the final farewell

as you bid your last guest good night, there are details, details, details.

You can't ignore the details and hope for a successful party.

So how can you take care of every little thing and still relax

and enjoy your company? Stop worrying—here are a few guidelines,

tips and ideas to help keep the "easy" in "entertaining."

Remember the three most important rules of entertaining

1. Always leave time for yourself to relax and get ready without being rushed! It may be the last hour or so before guests arrive, or it may be for an hour or so in the morning—just do it!

2. Delegate whatever you can, or when the offer is made!

3. Never apologize for something you might have forgotten, or didn't get done from your "list"—no one else knows what was on that list except you. Smile and forget it!

Plan Ahead

This section is full of ideas on how to make

the planning portion of your event less harried,

more enjoyable and, ultimately, very successful.

It highlights the key points in planning ahead,

provides tips on how to keep things simple,

suggests how much food and beverage to serve,

shows you how to handle unexpected guests

and finally, how to run your event

without extra effort on your part.

1. Questions to Ask

- Is there a specific occasion (birthday, homecoming) or theme (seafood, ethnic)?

- Is this a formal or more informal event?

- How many people are coming and how well do they know each other?

- What is your budget for this event?

- When is the best day for purchasing the freshest produce on your grocery list?

- When do you need your guests to RSVP?

- Will you be serving appetizers before dinner?

- Will you be serving a sit-down dinner or would a buffet work better?

- What kind of beverages will be served?

- Do you want decorations?

- Will you need to borrow extra dishes, or purchase paper plates and napkins?

- Does furniture have to be moved?

- Any special cleaning required?

2. Lists to Make

Make separate lists for the following:

- ❏ Invited guests and their RSVP. (Don't forget to include yourself and other household members.)

- ❏ Recipes to be made and their page numbers. Note anything that can be made in advance and frozen, made several days before, and other preparations that can be done the night before or morning of.

- ❏ Groceries needed (divide list into fresh and non-perishable.)

- ❏ Other items to be purchased—cocktail napkins? Candles?

- ❏ Custom orders—a special cut or size of roast? Flowers?

3. Create a Timetable

- When is the best day to purchase the fresh produce on your grocery list?

- When should you shop for all non-perishables (groceries and other items)? Shop well in advance and keep together in an out-of-the-way place until needed.

- What food can be made ahead and frozen? Made ahead and refrigerated? Made the night before or morning of?

- What cleaning needs to be done ahead of time? The day of? Just before guests arrive?

- When should items be ordered that you had noted earlier?

> How much food to make depends on the length of your event. Use page 175 as a guide.

4. Final Preparations

These final steps can help to ensure that your event runs smoothly:

- ❏ Check glasses and silver; clean or polish if necessary.

- ❏ Set the table the night before. It's a great timesaver and it looks like you have everything under control (whether you do or not!).

- ❏ Place your serving dishes, trays, bowls and serving utensils out on the counter. Tape a piece of paper to each dish with the name of the recipe or item that it will hold so that you aren't trying to remember at the last minute.

- ❏ Choose background music and arrange in the order you would like it to play.

- ❏ Pre-chop whatever you can. Store in sealed bags or containers in the refrigerator.

- ❏ Make punch base the day before and store in containers in the refrigerator. Add the soft drink and ice cubes just before serving. Make a fruit-filled ice ring well in advance and freeze until just before serving.

Entertaining Tips

• Go light on appetizers if you are also serving dinner. If guests are offered too many, they may become too full to enjoy their meal. Alternately, guests may hardly touch the appetizers in anticipation of dinner and all your effort will be wasted.

• Serve larger trays of cold appetizers and smaller trays of hot ones. Keep remaining hot appetizers in the oven or ready to be heated in the microwave. Use to refill the first tray or have a second tray ready to fill and replace the first one.

• Time spent on a fancy dessert is not always necessary, particularly for guests who may prefer a lighter dessert. Serve smaller portions, or plan a frozen dessert that can be sliced off for those who would like a piece, and then returned to the freezer for another occasion. A variety of squares or a tray of fruit and cheese with a dip would also satisfy a sweet tooth.

• Clean only those rooms that guests will be using.

• Wash, dry and put away any preparation dishes that you can. Keep the dishwasher empty for loading during or after the party.

• Make room in your refrigerator for leftovers to help keep cleanup quick.

• Have two or three clean dish cloths ready in case of spills or splashes.

Menu Planning

When choosing your recipes, provide a balance of the following:

• hot and cold

• sweet and savory

• rich and light

• light and dark colors

• homemade and store-bought

• fresh and frozen

• meat and meatless

• variety from the food groups

• alcoholic and non-alcoholic beverages

Finally, for those times when planning ahead and making lists are impossible, keep the following items on hand for unexpected and last-minute company:

In the cupboard:

• An assortment of crackers and chips
• Salad dressing or mayonnaise
• Cans of tuna, salmon, shrimp and crabmeat
• Dried herbs and spices such as basil, dill and cinnamon, as well as garlic powder
• Envelopes of dessert topping
• Chocolate chips and chocolate baking squares
• Variety of flavored gelatin (jelly) powders
• Pie crust mix
• Ready-made graham crumb crusts or chocolate crumb crusts

In the refrigerator: *

• Variety of hard cheeses
• Grated Parmesan cheese
• Large eggs
• Italian dressing

In the freezer: *

• Deli meats
• Packages of frozen chopped spinach
• Garlic butter (Soften one block of hard margarine, mix in 1 tbsp., 15 mL, garlic salt or garlic powder and put in small plastic container.)
• Pre-made crêpes
• Tortillas, pita breads
• Packages of frozen strawberries and raspberries in syrup
• Frozen whipped topping (in a tub)
• Frozen baked angel food cake
• Frozen undecorated cheesecake

* Some items will have a "best before" date or limited freezer life so don't overstock.

Keep a Record of Everything for the Next Time

This way you will know what you served, how much you served and to whom. You will be able to judge what worked, what didn't and if you had enough.

How much to make?

The length of your event, the ages of your guests, the time of day and the type of event will all affect the quantity of food you will need. The amounts listed below are approximate only, so judge accordingly.

Appetizers

Allow four to five "bites" per guest if serving a meal,
10 to 12 "bites" per guest if no other courses.

Beverages

Allow about three to five 6 oz. (175 mL) non-alcoholic drinks, about two to four 1½ oz. (45 mL) alcoholic drinks (plus mix), or about two to three 6 oz. (175 mL) glasses of wine per guest. Allow about two to three cups of coffee per guest. And don't forget to stock up on ice cubes!

Cheese

Allow 1 to 2 oz. (28 to 56 g) of cheese per guest if there are other appetizers, and a meal is being served. Allow 5 to 6 oz. (140 to 170 g) of cheese if there are other appetizers and a meal is not being served.

Dessert

Allow approximately one 3 inch (7.5 cm) square piece of fancy pan dessert per guest or ⅛ of a 9 inch (22 cm) pie per guest.

Meat

Allow an average of 3 to 5 oz. (85 to 140 g) of cooked meat per guest, especially if appetizers are being served.

Pasta

Allow about 3 oz. (85 g) of uncooked pasta per guest if it is the main course, about 1½ to 2 oz. (42 g to 56 g) if a side dish.

Salads

Allow about ¾ cup (175 mL) per guest.

Squares

Allow about three 1 inch (2.5 cm) pieces per guest.

Vegetables

Allow about ½ cup (125 mL) per guest of each vegetable if only two vegetables are being served. If more than two vegetables are being served, allow ¼ cup (60 mL) of each vegetable per guest.

Table Settings & Decorations

Setting a table is fun, simply because there are

so many ways to do it. Add a few special touches

such as a colorful centerpiece you made yourself,

and the results can be stunning.

A beautifully set table is certain to draw instant attention

and should be considered a key part of your decorations.

Your guests will think, "With the table looking this

fabulous, I can hardly wait to taste the food!"

From the tablecloth to the napkins, from

the centerpiece to the place settings, all

serve to set off the food you have prepared

and add to its presentation. In this section, we feature

the different styles of buffet and sit-down dinner table

settings, offer you suggestions on the use of tablecloths

and napkins, and show you some quick

centerpiece and place card ideas.

Paying attention to these final details

will add to your personal satisfaction and

to the ambiance you create for your guests.

The Table

Whether serving a dinner, a buffet spread or a selection of appetizers, the table you set will become a focus of your entertaining. There are several basics to consider when planning how you will decorate the table.

First, you must decide how people will approach the table and where you want it located. Do you need extra floor space to allow your guests to meander back and forth, pouring drinks or nibbling at appetizers? If so, then consider the Against-The-Wall Buffet, page 177. Will you be inviting your guests to sit at the table for a cheery breakfast or a candlelight dinner? Check out the various place settings for a Sit-Down Dinner, page 177. Is there a large crowd that you will need to direct in order to feed everyone? Then your answer is the One or Two-Line Buffet, page 177.

Once you have decided the location and purpose of using your table, then the next consideration is how you will decorate it. Think about overall color, keeping in mind the color and pattern of the dishes you will be using. Do you want to have a monochromatic theme, sticking to the same basic color but varying the shades? What about using complementary colors? Or how about a dramatic contrast of colors? Would a solid or a pattern work best? And most important, what do you have on hand that could be used?

Napkins and a centerpiece are the last considerations to complete your picture-perfect tabletop. Now is also the time to decide if you want place cards. Keep these final touches simple so that they don't overpower or overshadow your food. You don't want the table to look overcrowded, either.

Setting The Table

Sit-Down Dinner

Neat and orderly settings will make any table look inviting. Plates and cutlery should be 1 inch (2.5 cm) in from the edge of the table. Cutlery should be placed close together but should not touch, and should be aligned with the bottom of the plate. Set only the cutlery needed. Too much cutlery on a table can be overwhelming and look cluttered.

1. Dinner Fork
2. Dinner Knife
3. Teaspoon
4. Dessert Fork

5. Salad Fork
6. Soup Spoon
7. Juice Glass
8. Water Glass

9. Wine Glass
10. Butter Knife

This is a basic table setting. This works if the salad is served with the main course. The teaspoon can be used for a spoon-eaten dessert, or dessert forks can be brought in on dessert plates.

Setting for main course and dessert. This works if salad is served with the main course. A separate salad fork is not needed.

Setting for salad course and main course. The teaspoon can be used for a spoon-eaten dessert or dessert forks can be brought in on dessert plates.

Setting for soup, salad, main course and dessert. To serve salad after the main course, move the salad fork to the right of the dinner fork.

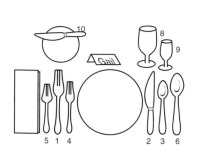

Buffet Dinner

Guests should be able to move easily around the buffet table and serve themselves in a logical order. Traffic should flow toward the seating area.

1. Plates
2. Meat
3. Vegetable
4. Gravy
5. Salad (Tossed)

6. Salad (Jellied)
7. Salt, Pepper
8. Condiments
9. Butter
10. Dinner Rolls

11. Water, Milk
12. Glasses
13. Napkins, Cutlery
14. Coffee/Tea
15. Dessert

16. Spoons
17. Mints
18. Centerpiece
19. Cups, Saucers
20. Cream, Sugar

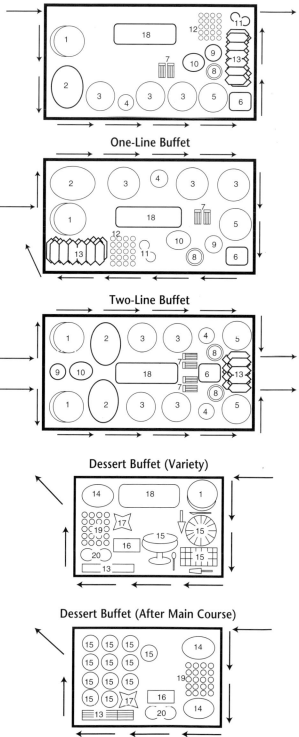

Tablecloths

Your table presentation begins with its covering. The color or mix of colors, the simplicity or complexity, the drama or frivolity you choose will direct what you do with the rest of the table decorations.

Naturally, the simplest covering is no covering at all. The richness of mahogany or cherrywood, the warmth of oak or walnut, the drama of a burled walnut or a glass tabletop, or the country air of pine, can provide the look you want, as well as highlight your presentation of dishes and food. This works best for buffets, but care should be taken to use trivets or hot pads under hot dishes.

You might want to consider the added visual of an 18 inch (45 cm) wide runner down the center length of the table.

If you would like to have your guests sit at the table and yet still show off the wood grain, place mats provide protection and cut down on the noisy movement of cutlery and glasses. The addition of a matching or complementary runner further protects the wood and can eliminate the need for trivets.

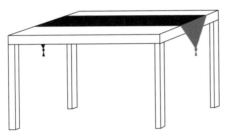

If you choose to use a tablecloth, there are several options: A single tablecloth, solid or patterned, is simple and elegant. A smaller square tablecloth, in an accent color, laid diamond-fashion over top, adds a sense of frivolity.

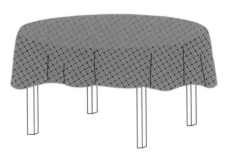

For more drama, choose a colorful solid tablecloth (or table liner) and lay a full-size lace cloth (in ivory or white) over top.

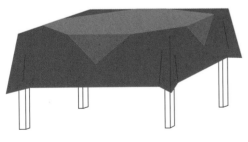

Try using a rectangular tablecloth on an oval table; the extended pointed corners make a more visually emphatic statement. It's even acceptable to have place mats on a tablecloth to create a layered effect.

Fabric stores carry a beautiful selection of 60 inch (150 cm) wide fabrics that make lovely tablecloths and/or napkins. You can purchase the exact length that works best for your table, allowing about 6 inches (15 cm) finished overhang at each end. Turn under and stitch the edges or serge with a complementary, or even a contrasting, color.

Napkins

There are no set rules to how you select your napkins—they can match the tablecloth, be a darker or lighter shade of the tablecloth, bring in a pretty pattern for a subtle accent, or provide the complementary or contrasting color accent.

An easy finishing touch is to tie your napkins with a tassel, gift ribbon or raffia, as shown in these samples.

1. Buffet Pocket, page 30
2. Buffet Wrap, page 30
3. Fireworks, page 31
4. Bouquet, page 31
5. Standing Fan, page 31
6. Buffet Envelope, page 30
7. Fancy Fan, page 31

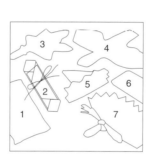

You may want to go the extra step and try a simple napkin fold. We have shown, on pages 30 and 31, the steps to create three simple buffet folds (incorporating the silverware), and four easy single but pretty napkin folds. The completed napkins are shown on pages 30 and 31, and on this page at the left.

When planning the layout for your buffet table, be creative with the napkins. It is handiest for your guests if the napkins also contain the silverware. But don't just plunk them on the table—design a pattern or contain them in a basket, as shown here.

Glossary of Glasses

The glasses in which you serve your drinks are every bit
as important as the ingredients, the taste and the garnishes.
With such a variety it is essential to know which drink
should be served in which glass. In some cases there are reasons
for the choice of glass. A Martini glass is held by its stem
so the hand does not warm the glass. A brandy snifter is
rested in the palm to warm the drink and release its aroma.
The narrowness of a champagne flute is a design to
preserve the bubbles. Pictured on the next two pages is a
selection of glasses to help in choosing the most suitable glass.

1. **Collins Glass:** A tall, straight-sided glass. Holds 1¼ to 2 cups (300 to 500 mL). Excellent for drinks like Tom Collins.

2. **Large Goblet:** Varies greatly in shape and size. Used for serving water or wine spritzers or any exotic drink. Holds 1 to 2 cups (250 to 500 mL).

3. **Brandy Balloon Snifter:** For straight brandy or brandy-based drinks. Holds ¾ to 3 cups (175 to 750 mL).

4. **Red Wine Glass:** Slightly larger than the white wine glass. Holds 1 to 1¼ cups (250 to 300 mL).

5. **Martini (Cocktail) Glass:** A stemmed, triangular-shaped, wide-rimmed glass used for martinis or other cocktails. Holds ½ to ¾ cup (125 to 175 mL).

6. **Champagne Flute:** A tall, stemmed glass used for champagne and sparkling wine drinks. Holds ¾ to 1 cup (175 to 250 mL).

7. **Highball Glass:** A smaller glass than the Collins. General type of glass and can be used for many types of drinks. Holds 1 to 1¼ cups (250 to 300 mL).

8. **Double Cocktail Glass or Champagne Saucer:** A large, rounded cocktail glass used for serving cream-based or slushy drinks such as a Daiquiri. Holds ¾ to 1¼ cups (175 to 300 mL).

9. **Liqueur Glass:** Used for serving short, straight drinks. Holds 1 to 2 oz. (30 to 60 mL).

10. **White Wine Glass:** A bit smaller than the red wine glass. Holds ¾ to 1 cup (175 to 250 mL).

11. **Old Fashioned Glass:** A short, straight-sided tumbler. Holds ½ to 1 cup (125 to 250 mL).

The Final Touches
Centerpieces and Place Cards

Centerpiece—the name says it all! It is the center of attention, the focal point
of the table. Whether dramatic or subtle, the choice is yours.

The Garden Path

When flowers that have strong stems and large heads (such as gerbera daisies or tulips) are in the stores or in your garden, create this subtle arrangement. Use empty film canisters filled ¾ with water to hold single flower heads. Place the containers in a meandering fashion on your buffet table. At your dining table, either cluster them in the center, or spread them apart slightly and intersperse with short pillar candles. Using individual flowers allows you the versatility to stay with a single color or multiple colors, as shown here.

Herbal Halo

This absolutely stunning centerpiece is inexpensive, takes less than an hour to make, and can be made up to three days in advance! It is subtly aromatic and best suited for a luncheon or breakfast table. But it is also a show-stopper as a dip holder on a buffet table, as shown on page 27. It is also gorgeous as the focal point on your coffee table, again with a dip.

The inexpensive ring oasis can be purchased at a florist, but you may have to special order it, so give yourself lots of time. Find out which day your local grocer gets in fresh herbs. You only need a small quantity (about four to five good stocks of each) of the herbs we used as filler (sage, rosemary, and thyme). We used a larger amount (about 15 to 20 stocks) of mint. Have lots of nice crisp parsley on hand (which is the cheapest of the herbs) and you're all set. Soak the ring in water until it is quite wet. (The oasis should come with its own little tray.) Starting at the bottom outside and

inside edges, insert parsley stems to nicely cover in the sides. Then insert the sage stocks in four spots about equidistant from each other on the top. Add about four mint stocks in each of the four sections and then add the rosemary and thyme to complete the halo. Check for empty spots and fill in with whatever you want. If you are making it in advance, place in a large plastic bag, seal and refrigerate. Every 24 hours, remove from bag and let sit in one inch (2.5 cm) of water for about one minute.

Floral Halo: Use the oasis ring and single flower heads (pansies would be gorgeous) with about 1 inch (2.5 cm) stems to make a floral halo. Set a pillar candle in the center.

Holly Halo: Use the oasis ring and small stocks of fresh holly to make a Christmas wreath. Set a red or white pillar candle in the center or a dish of holiday candies.

The simplest centerpiece can sometimes be the most eye-catching.

This orange pepper flower holder has a simplicity that shows off the natural beauty of both the carnations and the pepper. To make, cut flowers to about 1½ times the height of the pepper. Wash and "polish" the pepper. Turn the pepper upside down and "dig" small holes with the tip of a paring knife into each knobby end. Hold under the tap to fill with water, wipe off, then insert your flowers. Also see photo on page 48.

Variation: Use several different colors of peppers, all about the same size and cluster in the center of the table. The colors are perfect for a Mexican theme, while red and green peppers show off beautifully at Christmas.

Our exquisite lemon flower holder will capture everyone's attention. To make, carefully select really yellow lemons that have a nice shape. Gerbera daisies have a nice thick stem and large flower so cut them about 2½ times the height of the lemon. Wash and "polish" the lemon. Lay it on its side and let it come to a natural balance. Using the tip of a tiny paring knife, cut a hole into the center of the top slightly larger than the width of the stem. Dig down into the lemon as far as you can without widening the hole. Because the lemon is acidic, line the inside of the hole with plastic wrap and fill with a bit of water. Insert the flowers. Cut two leaves from shiny green foil or paper. Tape or glue onto ends of wooden picks. Insert both "leaves" into the hole in lemon.

Variation: Use small lemons and place only one flower and leaf in each. Assemble as above. Using a permanent marker, print your guests' names on the side of each lemon. Voilà—place cards!

Other simple place card ideas include purchasing tiny gift bags that are so popular nowadays. Fill with after-dinner mints or chocolates and a bit of colored tissue paper. Using a gold writing pen or permanent marker, write your guests' names on the front, being careful not to smear the ink before it dries. An even simpler and more versatile place card is to purchase a package of the plain white ones (check card shops or wedding supply stores).

You now have a number of options: You can color them, draw on them, or find sheets of small stickers that pick up on your theme or colors. There are hundreds of different stickers to choose from, including shapes, animals, specific holidays, words, nature scenes, and many more.

Place cards ensure that dinner guests aren't necessarily seated with their spouse or partner. They allow you to seat left-handed people on the outside left corners to prevent "collisions" of elbows. Place cards guide your elderly aunt into a suitably comfortable chair. There are all kinds of reasons to use place cards when you have more than six people sitting down for dinner.

Purchase several bunches of tiny wired silk flowers at a craft store or department store. Pull the stems apart. Wrap single flowers around napkins and stems of wine glasses, two or three together around candlesticks and basket handles. Set bunches in small vases, pitchers or other containers. The flowers are subtle but provide common spots of color around your table. Find other places in the living room and guest bathroom to twist them. You've now created a decorating theme that threads its way wherever your guests go. This is especially pretty for a wedding or baby shower.

Your guests are due to arrive in a few hours, and it's time to survey your lists one last time to make certain everything has been done. Turn the music on low and indulge in a few quiet, relaxing moments. Now— wasn't that easy!

Measurement Tables

Throughout this book measurements

are given in Conventional and Metric measure.

To compensate for differences between the two

measurements due to rounding, a full metric measure

is not always used. The cup used is the standard

8 fluid ounce. Temperature is given in degrees

Fahrenheit and Celsius. Baking pan measurements

are in inches and centimetres as well as quarts

and litres. An exact metric conversion is

given below as well as the working

equivalent (Standard Measure).

Oven temperatures

Fahrenheit (°F)	Celsius (°C)
175°	80°
200°	95°
225°	110°
250°	120°
275°	140°
300°	150°
325°	160°
350°	175°
375°	190°
400°	205°
425°	220°
450°	230°
475°	240°
500°	260°

Pans

Conventional Inches	Metric Centimetres
8x8 inch	20x20 cm
9x9 inch	22x22 cm
9x13 inch	22x33 cm
10x15 inch	25x38 cm
11x17 inch	28x43 cm
8x2 inch round	20x5 cm
9x2 inch round	22x5 cm
10x4¹/₂ inch tube	25x11 cm
8x4x3 inch loaf	20x10x7.5 cm
9x5x3 inch loaf	22x12.5x7.5 cm

Spoons

Conventional Measure	Metric Exact Conversion Millilitre (mL)	Metric Standard Measure Millilitre (mL)
¹/₈ teaspoon (tsp.)	0.6 mL	0.5 mL
¹/₄ teaspoon (tsp.)	1.2 mL	1 mL
¹/₂ teaspoon (tsp.)	2.4 mL	2 mL
1 teaspoon (tsp.)	4.7 mL	5 mL
2 teaspoons (tsp.)	9.4 mL	10 mL
1 tablespoon (tbsp.)	14.2 mL	15 mL

Cups

¹/₄ cup (4 tbsp.)	56.8 mL	60 mL
¹/₃ cup (5¹/₃ tbsp.)	75.6 mL	75 mL
¹/₂ cup (8 tbsp.)	113.7 mL	125 mL
²/₃ cup (10²/₃ tbsp.)	151.2 mL	150 mL
³/₄ cup (12 tbsp.)	170.5 mL	175 mL
1 cup (16 tbsp.)	227.3 mL	250 mL
4¹/₂ cups	1022.9 mL	1000 mL (1 L)

Dry measurements

Conventional Measure Ounces (oz.)	Metric Exact Conversion Grams (g)	Metric Standard Measure Grams (g)
1 oz.	28.3 g	28 g
2 oz.	56.7 g	56 g
3 oz.	85.0 g	85 g
4 oz.	113.4 g	125 g
5 oz.	141.7 g	140 g
6 oz.	170.1 g	170 g
7 oz.	198.4 g	200 g
8 oz.	226.8 g	250 g
16 oz.	453.6 g	500 g
32 oz.	907.2 g	1000 g (1 kg)

Casseroles (Canada & Britain)

Standard Size Casserole	Exact Metric Measure
1 qt. (5 cups)	1.13 L
1¹/₂ qts. (7¹/₂ cups)	1.69 L
2 qts. (10 cups)	2.25 L
2¹/₂ qts. (12¹/₂ cups)	2.81 L
3 qts. (15 cups)	3.38 L
4 qts. (20 cups)	4.5 L
5 qts. (25 cups)	5.63 L

Casseroles (United States)

Standard Size Casserole	Exact Metric Measure
1 qt. (4 cups)	900 mL
1¹/₂ qts. (6 cups)	1.35 L
2 qts. (8 cups)	1.8 L
2¹/₂ qts. (10 cups)	2.25 L
3 qts. (12 cups)	2.7 L
4 qts. (16 cups)	3.6 L
5 qts. (20 cups)	4.5 L

Index

C